THE LOSS OF THE
WAGER

THE NARRATIVES OF JOHN BULKELEY
AND THE HON. JOHN BYRON

with an introduction by
Alan Gurney

THE BOYDELL PRESS

New edition 2004
The Boydell Press, Woodbridge

A Voyage to the South Seas in the Years 1740–1 by John
Bulkeley and John Cummins was first published in 1743,
and *The Narrative of the Honourable John Byron* in 1768.
In this edition Bulkeley's account is reprinted from the
first edition and Byron's from an edition published in 1785

ISSN 1743–4769
ISBN 1 84383 096 5

first person singular

The Boydell Press is an imprint of Boydell & Brewer Ltd
PO Box 9, Woodbridge, Suffolk IP12 3DF, UK
and of Boydell & Brewer Inc.
668 Mt. Hope Avenue, Rochester, NY 14620, USA
website: www.boydellandbrewer.com

A catalogue record of this publication is available
from the British Library

Library of Congress Cataloging-in-Publication Data
applied for

This publication is printed on acid-free paper

Printed in Great Britain by
Antony Rowe Ltd, Chippenham, Wiltshire

Contents

Introduction   vii

A VOYAGE TO THE SOUTH SEAS IN THE YEARS 1740-1

Dedication   xix

Preface   xxiii

A Voyage to the South Seas   1

THE NARRATIVE OF THE HONOURABLE JOHN BYRON

Preface   125

The Narrative   129

Epilogue   235

Bibliography   239

Introduction

The Admiralty *Pilots*, published by the Hydrographic Office, are the seafarer's Baedekers. Totalling seventy-seven volumes they cover the world's coastlines, oceans and seas. Inside their sober navy-blue cloth covers they contain sage advice on dangers, safe anchorages, reefs, and currents; and when paraded on a chart-room bookshelf, their gilt-lettered spines on show, they make for an impressive display of hard won nautical information.

The *South American Pilot* has this to say regarding a small island on the Chilean coast some 500 nautical miles north of Cape Horn:

> Isla Wager lies close E of Isla Byron; it can be identified by Monte Anson, which is conical and 438m (1,436 ft) high, on the N side of the island . . . also by Monte Wager, with a flat summit of 652m (2,139 ft) situated in the middle of the island.

A few lines later the *Pilot* also mentions that a cove, Bahia Speedwell, is 'difficult to approach' and that Canal Cheap 'is deep throughout.' A few miles north of Wager Island the *Pilot* details the Islas Marinas (Marine Islands) comprising Crosslet, Hereford, Smith, and Hales Islands. Such English sounding names in a Spanish speaking country pose a question, and perhaps to the curious they also hint at a story. The curious would be right.

The story is an eighteenth-century melodrama set in a ferociously inhospitable climate and along one of the world's more remote and dangerous coastlines. *The South American Pilot* is brutally explicit on the climate: 'The area covered by this volume is exposed to an almost unbroken series of depressions which move E across or to the S of it. Except in regions sheltered from the prevailing W winds, the weather in all seasons is predominantly cold and stormy with much cloud and rain.' As to the location, a glance at any map or chart of South America's dangling, scorpion-like tail, shows a deadly, fractured coastline of reefs, islands and channels. 'One sight of such a coast,' wrote Charles Darwin, having sailed in the *Beagle* between reefs known as the Furies and looked out on a sea so covered with breakers that it was known as the Milky Way, 'is enough to make a landsman dream for a week about shipwrecks, peril, and death.' Add disease, starvation, treachery, murder, insanity and mutiny (all lubricated by brandy and wine) to Darwin's nightmare, and one holds the essence of the story that followed upon the *Wager*'s shipwreck on 14 May 1741 in the Golfo de Peñas – which can be translated as the Gulf of Sorrows – and the trials, tribulations and horrors which fell upon her men and their struggle for survival and escape: all told in *A Voyage to the South Seas* by John Bulkeley and John Cummins, and *The Narrative of the Honourable John Byron* by John Byron.

The *Wager*, 599 tons and 24 guns, sailed from England on 18 September 1740 as one of eight ships under the command of Commodore George Anson: six men-of-war, the *Centurion, Gloucester, Severn, Pearl, Wager, Tryal,* and two merchant ships, the *Anna* and the *Industry,* carrying supplies. Great Britain and Spain had been at war for a year, and the squadron's destination was the Pacific where Anson had been ordered to 'annoy and distress the Spaniards . . . by taking, sinking, burning, or otherwise destroying all their ships and vessels that you shall meet with . . . to seize, surprise, or take any of the towns or places belonging to the Spaniards on the coast.'

The *Wager*, an East Indiaman bought into the Royal Navy, carried artillery and military stores for the land forces, merchandise goods to win over the native population, wine and brandy for the squadron. Overloaded with these stores, she also carried twice her number of usual human cargo: the seamen being outnumbered by marines (most of them raw and young recruits who had never loaded a musket) and old decrepit soldiers (most of them over 60 years old and some over 70), out-pensioners from the Chelsea Hospital known as 'invalids.' These were the land forces that were going to wreak havoc amongst the Spanish colonies and possessions.

'No man will be a sailor who has contrivance enough to get himself into jail; for being in a ship is being in a jail, with the chance of being drowned. A man in jail has more room, better food, and commonly better company.' So runs Dr Samuel Johnson's acid opinion on life at sea. Most of the *Wager*'s complement would have agreed. Many of the crew had been press-ganged, some had come from jail. And the regulation 14 inches allowed between hammocks had been reduced to cram in the land forces. Such crowded and fetid conditions, plus a diet of salt meat and weevil infested biscuit, made every ship of the squadron an ideal breeding ground for various diseases.

Disease, particularly the disease known as scurvy, killed more men of the Georgian navy than cannon ball, musket shot, drowning and shipwreck combined. Pascoe Thomas of the *Centurion* described in clinical detail his own sufferings from scurvy: 'Several hard nodes now began to rise in my legs, thighs, and arms, and not only many more black spots appeared in the skin, but these spread till almost my legs and thighs were as black as a Negro; and this accompanied with such an excessive pains in the joints of the knees, ankles and toes, as I thought before I experienced them, that human nature could never have supported. It next advanced to the mouth; all my teeth were presently loose, and my gums, overcharged with extravagated blood, fell down almost quite over my teeth. This occasioned my breath to stink much, yet without affecting my lungs; but I believe, one week more at sea would have ended me, and less than a month more, all the rest.'

Scurvy, a deficiency disease, is brought on by lack of Vitamin

C. Sir Richard Hawkins, the Elizabethan seaman, called scurvy 'the plague of the sea' and recommended fresh lemons and oranges as a cure. The East India Company had been issuing lemon juice aboard its fleet for over a century before the sailing of Anson's squadron. The Dutchmen Wilhelm Schouten and Jacob le Maire bought twenty thousand lemons at Sierra Leone before their historic 1616 rounding of Cape Horn. Captain John Smith – the founder of Virginia – in his 1627 *Seaman's Grammar* recommended that ships carry 'the juice of the lemons for the scurvy. Some it may be will say I would have men feast than fight, but I say the want of these necessaries occasions the loss of more men than in any English fleet hath been slain since eighty-eight.'*

The Admiralty, aware of the ravages caused by scurvy, placed its faith in elixir of vitriol (sulphuric acid) mixed with alcohol, sugar and spices. The crowded conditions aboard warships also led to deaths from another disease, typhus. Also known as ship or jail fever, typhus is spread by lice. The purser of the *Tryal*, the smallest warship of the squadron, recorded that during the weeks spent in rounding Cape Horn – a time of constant gales, freezing temperatures, mountainous seas, and with men dying daily – that the living were 'almost devoured by vermin' and that he had seen 'above a peck [two gallons] of lice on a man even after he was dead.' The sea conditions off Cape Horn meant no galley fires; and aboard the *Tryal* the men lived on water and ship's biscuit toasted over burning brandy: 'to kill the numerous insects it abounded with.' Captain Dandy Kidd of the *Pearl*, who was buried at sea in the South Atlantic, predicted on his deathbed that the whole enterprise would end in 'poverty, vermin, famine, death and destruction.' Which was either a remarkable instance of second sight, or written into the narrative stories after all the facts were known.

* Eighty-eight refers to 1588, the year of the Spanish Armada.

The delay in sailing from England – recruiting and victualling problems, and constant westerly winds – led to the fleet attempting the rounding of Cape Horn at the worst possible time: the southern autumn. The squadron's battle started on 7 March 1741 after an easy and quick passage through the Le Maire Strait separating Staten Island from Tierra del Fuego. 'We passed those memorable streights,' runs the official narrative, 'ignorant of the dreadful calamities which were then impending, and just ready to break upon us; ignorant that the time drew near when the squadron would be separated never to unite again, and that this day of our passage was the last cheerful day that the greatest part of us would ever live to enjoy.'

Certain vignettes remain vivid in the mind after a reading of the various accounts of the two month battle to clear Cape Horn. Of mountainous seas, endless storms, snow and sleet; of men with frostbitten fingers grappling with frozen sails and ice covered rigging; of dead bodies, some in rolled-up hammocks acting as a burial shroud, rolling across sea-washed decks, their living companions too weak to pitch them overboard; of masts and yards going by the board; of streaming rigging and strips of sail thrashing in the wind; of the *Centurion*, unable to set any sails in one storm, setting her men in the rigging and along the yards to provide windage so that the ship could wear and steer down wind; of men being pitched overboard and drowning; of seas sweeping across decks and ripping of hatches and scuttles; of hulls and decks working in the tormented seas so that every seam poured water, and not a dry place below; of one ship, its pumps broken, with the men bailing with buckets; of one veteran soldier, wounded fifty years previously at the Battle of the Boyne, and now dying of scurvy, whose wounds opened up as if fresh, and with a broken limb, long since healed, fractured again as if newly broken; of the terrible time when they thought themselves clear of Tierra del Fuego only to find themselves two miles off its coast: the east setting current and the violent westerly winds having set them some three hundred miles east of their estimated position. That fearful day was 13 April. It was to take them another three weeks before they knew that they had last won free and had rounded Cape Horn.

When the *Wager*, a virtual wreck, drove ashore to her last resting place, her complement of men – 243 when leaving England and with 45 soldiers transferred to the *Centurion* and the *Severn* before the rounding of Cape Horn – numbered 152: scurvy, typhus, and dysentery making the grim accounting of the missing.

Such then is the background to the narratives of John Bulkeley and John Byron. A ship's company demoralized and debilitated by ten weeks of battling against the elements, disease and death: a struggle which had left only a dozen men capable of working the ship before her piling ashore. The shore no welcoming palm-tree girted island, but a grim, rain-sodden and gale lashed one, covered with bog and a dense scrub forest of southern beech.

The first thing that strikes one when reading the narratives is the complete and utter breakdown of authority aboard the *Wager*. Suddenly, at a stroke, the strict hierarchical discipline of the Royal Navy tumbles into total anarchy. The scenes aboard the grounded vessel, her masts cut down and her hull pounded by waves, are ones straight out of the *Grand Guignol*. Men break into the weapon chests and arm themselves with swords, muskets and pistols. Brandy and wine barrels are broached and drunks reel around the deck, some to fall down hatches and then drown in the flooded bilges. Some men sing Psalms, others fight. One man is murdered, strangled to death. This bacchanalia becomes Surrealist when men break open the merchandise chests containing clothing, and then parade the deck wearing velvet coats, laces and ribbons over their soiled canvas trousers and shirts.

Out of this anarchy emerges the gunner, John Bulkeley, a Daniel Defoe character who carries a copy of Thomas á Kempis's *The Imitation of Christ*, and, like Robinson Crusoe, keeps a daily journal. *A Voyage to the South Seas*, based on this journal, is the extraordinary story of the anarchic and starving weeks spent on the island, followed by the equally harrowing voyage in the *Speedwell*, the *Wager*'s longboat, lengthened and decked by John Cummins the ship's carpenter, to Brazil. By January 1743 both men were home in England, reunited with their families in Portsmouth. A few months later *A Voyage to the South Seas* was published, and avidly read by a public hungry for accounts of voyages, travels and adventures: preferably ones laced with descriptions of pagan natives and their strange ways. *A Voyage to the South Seas* did not disappoint.

The Honourable John Byron sailed aboard the *Wager* as a seventeen-year-old midshipman. But his escape from Wager Island, to the north and into the hands of the Spanish, rather than the southern route through the Strait of Magellan taken by the *Speedwell*, meant that he was not reunited with his family – in a manner which might have been penned by Henry Fielding for an incident in *Tom Jones* – until 1746. Byron's *Narrative* did not appear until 1768.

The two accounts, describing different travels, carry the same theme: the demoralizing effect of starvation and deprivation on humans. On the voyage in the *Speedwell*, when men were reduced to gnawing on sealskin which had been used as a hatchway cover, Bulkeley noted that: 'Hunger is void of all compassion; every person was so intent on the preservation of his own life, that he was regardless of another's, and the bowels of commiseration were shut up.' Byron wrote in similar vein on the pleadings for food of a dying seaman: 'But we were become so hardened against the impression of others suffering by our own; so familiarised to scenes of this and every other kind of misery, that the poor man's dying intreaties were vain.'

Byron travelled north with a party led by the *Wager*'s commander, Captain David Cheap. But it is doubtful if any of the party could have survived without the help of the coast's nomadic natives, the canoe-borne Alacaluf. These were a far remove from the 'noble savage' popularised by Rousseau and the accounts of the Pacific voyages of James Cook and Louis Bougainville. The Alacaluf men realized at once that Cheap was the leader of these strange folk who had appeared on their shores. Leaders were to be treated with respect, and those under them with cuffs and kicks: which was the treatment received by Byron, the second son of a peer, in a classic case of master-servant inversion.

Bulkeley's imperative in publishing his account was twofold: to make money (he and his family had received no wages since the wreck of the *Wager*), and to place on record the complicated events which had led to the leaving of Cheap and a handful of people on Wager Island: an act which could have been construed as mutiny, the penalty being death. Also, being an orderly man, his comment in the Preface to the *Voyage* shows his attempt to create some order out of the anarchy into which the survivors had fallen: 'There was a necessity for action, and a great deal of it too; and had we been as indolent and regardless for the preservation of the people, as others who were superior in command, there would not have been a single man, who was shipwreck'd in the *Wager*, now in England to give any relation of the matter.' In the event the inevitable court martial, delayed until the return of Captain Cheap, and held at Spithead on 15 April 1746, only looked into the causes leading to the *Wager*'s loss.

A few weeks after the court martial John Bulkeley was offered the command of the ten-gun *Royal George*, a 70-ton cutter carrying a crew of sixty. But having cast his experienced eye over her, he refused the command claiming that she was 'too small to bear the sea.' He was proved right. On her next voyage she sank in the Bay of Biscay with the loss of all hands. Bulkeley soon removed himself to Pennsylvania where, in 1757, a second edition of the *Voyage* was published.

Byron returned to Patagonia. In 1764 he sailed from England

commanding an expedition of two vessels, the frigate *Dolphin* and the sloop *Tamar*. It took seven weeks to sail through the Strait of Magellan before entering into the Pacific. Byron spent no time investigating Wager Island. In fact his circumnavigation is memorable for its speed, its paucity of new discoveries, its ignoring of his Admiralty instructions, its criticism by the Royal Society for the lack of scientific results, and the derisory laughter from the general public on the tales of Patagonian giants. John Charnock, the naval biographer, thought Byron 'a brave and excellent officer, but, a man extremely unfortunate.' To the seamen who served under him he was known as 'Foul-weather Jack' for his unique ability to attracting storms. As a father he sired a handsome, profligate, dissolute son in a Guards Regiment: Captain 'Mad Jack' Byron, who in turn fathered the poet Lord Byron. The scene in *Don Juan*, claimed Byron, was based on 'those related in my grand-dad's *Narrative*.'

But the wreck of the *Wager* gave birth to more than books written by survivors and a small footnote in English literature. Admiralty law, at the time of the *Wager*'s wreck, held that a seaman's wages ceased when a ship was wrecked and lost. Why then should a seaman, receiving no wages, be still liable to naval discipline? This was a loophole which mutineers could slither. In 1747 an Act was passed which extended both wages and naval discipline after shipwreck or capture.

Another result, not so much concerning the *Wager* but the whole of Anson's expedition, was an epochal study into scurvy. The appalling losses to scurvy prompted a twenty-eight-year-old Royal Navy surgeon, Dr James Lind, to investigate the causes and a cure. In the world's first controlled dietary experiment, he found that the juice of oranges and lemons was a certain cure. It took the Admiralty decades before it ordered that lemon juice be served to its seamen. But even then it made a qualification: the men had to spend six weeks on salt rations before the issue of the lemon juice.

And what of Crosslet, Hereford, Smith and Hales, the young marines who have a group of islands named after them? The young men mentioned in this Introduction. Read on and find their fate in Byron's *Narrative*.

A Voyage to the South Seas
in the Years 1740–1

Dedication

To the Honourable
EDWARD VERNON, Esq,
Vice-Admiral of the Blue, &c.

Sir,

We have presum'd to put the following sheets under your protection, tho' we have not the honour of being personally known to you, nor have applied to you for the liberty of using your celebrated name on this occasion.

As this book is a faithful extract from the journals of two British seamen, late officers in his majesty's navy, we thought we could not more properly dedicate it than to a British admiral.

We know your detestation of flattery; and you know, from long experience, that a British seaman hath a spirit too brave to stoop to so degenerate a practice.

The following pages we hope will recommend themselves to you, because they are written in a plain maritime stile, and void of partiality and prejudice.

The distresses mention'd in this book have perhaps not been equal'd in our age; and we question whether any navigators living have, for so long a continuance, suffer'd such variety of hardships, as the unfortunate people of the *Wager*.

After surviving the loss of the ship, and combating with famine and innumerable difficulties, a remnant of us are return'd to our native country; but even here we are still unfortunate, destitute of employment, almost without support, or any prospect of being restor'd to our stations, till some important questions are decided, which cannot be cleared up till the arrival of our late captain, or at least the commodore.

We, sir, who present you with this book, have been several years in the navy, and thought ourselves well acquainted with its laws and discipline, and have many certificates to produce, that we have always acted in obedience to command ; but the proceedings of the officers and people, since the loss of the ship, are reckon'd so dark and intricate, that we know not what to expect, nor what will be the result of our superiors' determination.

The only consolation, we have in our present anxiety, is placed in a confidence of the unbiass'd integrity, justice, and humanity of the right honourable persons who will one day determine for or against us.

When you read our account of the affair, you'll find the facts impartially related, the whole narrative written without the least shadow of prejudice or malice, and no more in favour of ourselves, than of the other officers concern'd : we stand or fall by the truth; if truth will not support us, nothing can.

In our voyage from the Brazil to Lisbon, we were oblig'd to you for the generous treatment we met with from an enemy, a subject of Spain, a person of distinction, and a passenger in the same ship: your virtues have procur'd you the esteem even of your enemies.

Your zeal for the national service deserves the love of every honest Briton : to leave an abundant fortune, your family, and your country, to hazard your life in the most perilous expeditions, with no other motive than to retrieve the honour of the nation, shows the spirit of a true British hero, and deserves the highest commendations.

That you, sir, may never deviate from your integrity, but continue a terror to the enemies of Britain, an honour to his majesty's service, and an ornament to your country, are the sincere wishes of,

Honourable Sir,
your most dutiful,
and most obedient
humble servants,

JOHN BULKELEY
JOHN CUMMINS

Preface

As an introduction, we think proper to acquaint the reader with our reasons for causing the following sheets to be made publick to the world. The chief motive, which induced us to this task, was to clear our characters, which have been exceedingly blemish'd by persons who (next to Heaven) owe the preservation of their lives to our skill, and indefatigable care; and who having an opportunity of arriving before us in England, have endeavour'd to raise their reputation on the ruin of our's.

It will appear to the reader, on perusal of the following pages, that this journal was attempted to be taken from us by violence at Rio Janeiro; that we have preserved it, at the hazard of our lives; that there was no journal kept after the loss of the ship, by any officers but ourselves; and if we had not been careful in making remarks on each day's transactions, persons must have continued in the dark, in relation to all the subsequent proceedings.

It is a very usual thing to publish voyages, especially when the navigators have met with any extraordinary events. We believe, our expedition, though it was not a secret, is allowed to be an extraordinary one, and consequently attended with extraordinary events: indeed while the commodore was with us, every thing went well, but when the squadron separated, things began to have a new face; after the loss of the *Wager*, there was a general disorder and confusion among the people, who were now no longer implicitly obedient. There were two seamen particularly, who propagated this confusion, they said they had suffer'd ship-wreck in his majesty's ship the *Biddeford*, and received no wages from the day that the ship was lost; that when they were out of pay, they look'd upon themselves as their own masters, and no longer subjected to command. The people however were not altogether infected, but still continued to pay a dutiful respect to their commander; but when the captain had rashly shot Mr Cozens (whose fate the reader will find particularly related) they then grew very turbulent and unruly, the captain daily lost the love of the men, who with their affection lost their duty.

Our confining the captain is reckoned an audacious and unprecedented action, and our not bringing him home with us, is reckon'd worse; but the reader will find that necessity absolutely compell'd us to act as we did, and that we had sufficient reasons for leaving him behind.

Our attempt for liberty in sailing to the southward through the Streights of Magellan with such a number of people, stow'd in a long-boat, has been censur'd as a mad undertaking. Desperate diseases require desperate remedies; had we gone to the northward, there appear'd no probability of escaping the Spaniards, and when we had fallen into their hands, 'tis not unlikely but they might have employed us as drudges in their mines for life, therefore we rather chose to encounter all difficulties than to become slaves to a merciless enemy.

Some persons have objected against our capacity for keeping a journal of this nature; but several judges of maritime affairs, allow this work to be exact and regular. We think, persons with a common share of understanding are capable of committing to paper daily remarks of matters worthy their observation, especially of facts in which they themselves had so large a share. We only relate such things as could not possibly escape our knowledge, and what we actually know to be true. We don't set up for naturalists and men of great learning, therefore have avoided meddling with things above our capacity.

We are also condemn'd by many for being too busy and active for persons in our stations. There was a necessity for action, and a great deal of it too; and had we been as indolent and regardless for the preservation of the people, as others who were superior in command, there would not have been a single man, who was shipwreck'd in the *Wager*, now in England to give any relation of the matter.

The gentleman who commanded in the long-boat on his arrival before us at Lisbon, represented us to the English merchants in a very vile light, we were even advised by some of our friends there not to return to our country, lest we should suffer death for mutiny. But when the gentlemen of the factory had perus'd our journal, they found, if there was any mutiny in the case, the very person who accused us, was the ringleader and chief mutineer. We were confident of our own innocence, and determin'd to see our country at all events, being positive that we have acted to the best of our understandings, in all respects, for the preservation of our lives and liberties; and when our superiors shall think proper to call us to an account, which we expect will be at the commodore's arrival, we do not doubt but we shall clear ourselves in spite of all invidious reflections and malicious imputations.

It has been hinted to us, as if publishing this journal would give offence to some persons of distinction. We can't conceive, how any transactions relating to the *Wager*, although made ever so publick, can give offence to any great man at home. Can it be any offence to tell the world that we were shipwreck'd in the *Wager*, when all people know it already? Don't they know that the *Wager* was one of his majesty's storeships? That we had on board not only naval stores, but other kind of stores of an immense value? Don't they also know that we went abroad with hopes of acquiring great riches, but are return'd home as poor as beggars? We are guilty of no indecent reproaches, or unmannerly reflexions; though, it is certain, we cannot but lament our being engaged in so fatal an expedition. When persons have surmounted great difficulties, it is a pleasure for them to relate their story; and if we give ourselves this satisfaction, who has any cause to be offended? Are we, who have faced death in so many shapes, to be intimidated, lest we should give offence to the – Lord knows whom? We never saw a satyrical journal in our lives, and we thought that kind of writing was the most obnoxious to give offence.

It has been a thing usual, in publishing of voyages, to introduce abundance of fiction; and some authors have been esteem'd merely for being marvellous. We have taken care to deviate from those, by having a strict regard to truth. There are undoubtedly in this book some things which will appear incredible. The account we give of the Patagonian Indians, and our own distresses, tho' ever so well attested, will not easily obtain credit; and people will hardly believe that human nature could possibly support the miseries that we have endured.

All the difficulties related we have actually endur'd, and perhaps must endure more: till the commodore's arrival we cannot know our fate; at present we are out of all employment, and have nothing to support ourselves and families, but the profits arising from the sale of our journal; which perhaps may be the sum total we shall ever receive for our *Voyage to the South Seas.*

A Voyage to the South Seas

ON Thursday the 18th of September 1740, sailed from St Hellens his majesty's ship *Centurion,* Commodore Anson, with the *Gloucester, Pearl, Severn, Wager,* and *Tryal,* and two storeships; this squadron was design'd round Cape Horn into the South Seas, to distress the Spaniards in those parts. The ships were all in prime order, all lately rebuilt. The men were elevated with hopes of growing immensely rich, and in a few years of returning to Old England loaden with the wealth of their enemies.

Saturday the 20th, the Ram-head bearing N by W half W distant four leagues, the commodore hoisted his broad pendant, and was saluted by every ship in the squadron, with thirteen guns each. This day join'd company with us his majesty's ships, *Dragon, Winchester, Chatham, South-Sea-Castle,* and *Rye Galley,* with a large convoy of merchant ships.

Thursday the 25th, we parted company with the *Winchester* and the *South-Sea-Castle,* with their convoys, bound for America.

On Monday, we parted company with the Streights and Turky convoys.

Friday, October the 3rd, at eight in the morning, we saw two brigantines to the south-east; the commodore gave a signal to chace; at nine fired two shot to bring 'em to; at ten spoke with the chace, being two brigs from Lisbon, bound for New York.

Sunday the 26th, about five in the *morning,* the *Severn* showed lights, and fired several guns ahead; soon after we saw the land bearing W by S and at noon the east end of Madeira bore north, distant five leagues.

Wednesday we moored in Fonchiale [Funchal] road, so called from a city of that name, which is the metropolis of the island of Madeira; here we employ'd most of our time in getting aboard water, and stowing our dry provisions between decks.

Tuesday, November the 4th, Captain Kidd our commander was removed on board the *Pearl,* and the Honourable Captain Murray succeeded him in the *Wager.* Captain Norris of the *Gloucester* having obtained leave to return to England, on account of his ill state of health, occasioned the above removals.

While we lay at Madeira, we were informed of ten sail of ships cruising off and on, to the westward; these ships were judg'd to be French, and had been seen every day for a week before our arrival: the commodore sent out a privateer sloop, but she returned the day following, without seeing 'em; so that we can give no account of 'em.

On Wednesday the 5th, we sailed from Madeira. On the 20th the *Industry* storeship parted company; and on Friday the 28th, by account, we cross'd the Equinoctial.

On the 17th of December we saw the island of St Catharine, at noon; the northmost land in sight bore WNW and the southmost SW by W. Variation per amplitude 13 : 57 easterly.

On the 18th, the north end of the island of St Catharine bore NW by W distant seven leagues; and the island of Gaul bore NW distant six leagues.

On the 19th we anchor'd in St Catharine's Bay, in upward of twelve fathom water, the island Gaul on the coast of Brazil bearing N by E distant four leagues. On the 20th we anchor'd in St Catharine's road, and the day following we moored between the island of St Catharine and the main.

On Monday the 22nd, the commodore ordered fresh beef for the sick people.

On the 27th came in a Portuguese brig from Rio Janeiro, for the Rio Grand: while we lay here, the people were generally employ'd in overhauling the rigging, and getting aboard water.

On the 17th of January 1741, we sailed from St Catharine's; the commodore saluted the fort with eleven guns, the fort returned the same number.

On Thursday the 22nd we lost sight of the *Pearl*.

On Tuesday the 17th of February, the *Pearl* join'd the squadron; and on the 19th we came to anchor off the river of St Julian's, on the coast of Patagonia, St Julian's Hill bearing SW by W and the southmost land in sight S by E distant from the shore three leagues. This day our captain, the Honourable George Murray, took command on board the *Pearl*, Captain Kidd having died on the voyage since we left St Catharine's.

Captain Kidd was heard to say, a few days before his death, that this voyage, which both officers and sailors had engag'd in, with so much cheerfulness and alacrity, would prove in the end very far from their expectations, notwithstanding the vast treasure they imagined to gain by it; that it would end in Poverty, Vermin, Famine, Death, and Destruction. How far the captain's words were prophetick, will appear in the course of our journal. Captain Cheap succeeded Captain Murray on board the *Wager*.

On the 26th of February we sent on board the *Pearl* twelve butts and two puncheons of water; the *Pearl* having, while she was separated from us, been chased by five large Spanish men-of-war, the commander-in-chief being distinguish'd by a red broad pendant with a swallow's tail at his main-top-masthead, and a red flag at his ensign-staff: during the chace, the *Pearl,* in order to clear ship, threw overboard and stove fourteen tons of water; she likewise stove the long-boat, and threw her overboard, with oars, sails and booms, and made all clear for engaging; but night coming on, at seven o'clock lost sight of the enemy; at five in the morning saw the Spanish ships from the mast-head, two points on the lee-quarter, still giving chace, and crowding all the sail they could; but at nine the *Pearl* lost sight of 'em entirely. We judged this to be Admiral Pizarro's squadron, sent out in pursuit of Commodore Anson. Had our ships united fallen in with 'em, 'tis probable we might have given a good account of 'em. While we lay at St Julian's, we saw the sea full of shrimps, and red as if they were boiled; the water appeared tinctured to that degree, that it look'd like blood.

On the 27th, we sent on board the *Pearl* four puncheons of water more; at six in the morning, the commodore made signal to weigh; at eight weigh'd, and came to sail; this day we lost sight of the *Gloucester*.

The 28th, the *Gloucester* came into the squadron again.

On the 7th of March we pass'd through the Streights of Le Mair; Cape Diego on the island of Terra del Fuego bore NW by W three leagues, and the west end of the island, Staten Land, bore ENE distant four leagues, the squadron under reeft courses.

On the 10th we lost sight of the *Ann [Anna]* pink,* on the 12th carried away the rails and timbers of the head on both sides.

On the 16th the *Ann [Anna]* pink join'd the squadron again. The 30th the *Gloucester* broke her mainyard in the slings. April the 1st, the commodore order'd Mr Cummins, the carpenter, on board the *Gloucester*.

On the 8th carried away the mizen-mast, two feet above the awning; there was no sail on the mast. Upon the rowl of a sea, all the chain-plates to windward broke, lat. 56 : 31, long. 87 : 4 west. At noon Cape St Bartholomew bore north, 84 deg. E distant 229 leagues.

The 10th lost sight of the *Severn* and *Pearl*, lat. 56 : 29, long. 85 west. At ten last night fell in with two small islands; at eight in the morning the islands bore NNW by the compass distant eight leagues, in the latitude 54 : 00 south; we took 'em for the islands which lay off Brewer's Streights, latitude 54 : 50 south, long. 84 : 56 west.

* A pink was a small, flat-bottomed sailing vessel with bulging sides, often used as a victualler. [C.H.]

On the 12th we had very hard gales at west, with the largest swell I ever saw; I was officer of the watch (tho' I was gunner of the ship, I had the charge of a watch during the whole voyage); we had our larboard tacks on board: between six and seven in the morning, holding by the topsail hallyards to windward, there broke a sea in the ship, which carried me over the wheel, bilg'd the cutter, and canted her off the skeet's bottom up athwart the barge; it likewise half filled the long-boat; the boat-swain was for heaving the cutter overboard, I order'd him to do nothing with her till I had acquainted the captain, who was then very ill in his cabbin: the captain desired me to use all means to save the cutter; at the same time I asked leave to scuttle the long-boat, and get the spritsail yard and jib in, for fear of endangering the bowsprit; which he ordered to be done, and told me, it was a very great misfortune that he should be ill at such a time. When I came from the captain, I found the lieu-tenant on the deck, got the cutter in her place, scuttled the long-boat, and got the spritsail yard and jib-boom in. The carpenter was still aboard the *Gloucester*.

The 13th, under reeft courses, the larboard tacks; the commodore being on the weather-quarter, bore down under our lee, and spoke with us. He ask'd the captain, if the carpenter was return'd from the *Gloucester?* The captain answer'd, no; and am surprized the captain should detain him, when he knows I must want him about my mizen-mast. The commodore told him he would speak with the *Gloucester*, and order him on board. He then ask'd the captain, why he did not set the maintopsail, and make more sail? Captain Cheap made answer, my rigging is all gone, and broke fore and aft, and my people almost all taken ill, and down; but I will set him as soon as possible. The commodore desired he would, and make what sail he could after him.

The 14th, the carpenter return'd from the *Gloucester,* it being the only day this fortnight a boat could live in the sea. As soon as the carpenter came on board, he waited on the captain, who order'd him to look on the chain-plates and chains, and to give his opinion of the mast's going away. The carpenter look'd as order'd, and gave Captain Cheap for answer, that the chainplates were all broke. The captain shook his head, and said, Carpenter! that is not the reason of the mast's going away. The carpenter, not willing, as the mast was gone, to lay it to any one's misman-agement, or to occasion any uneasiness about what was now past prevention, fitted a capp on the stump of the mizen-mast, got up a lower studding-sail-boom of 40 feet, and hoisted a sail to keep the ship to.

Today, being the 19th, and the finest day we had in these seas, we were employ'd in repairing the rigging; we bent a new mainsail and reeft him, as did the *Anne* [*Anna*] pink; the *Gloucester* at the same time fix'd her main yard; the commodore and *Tryal* keeping ahead, and at a considerable distance; between four and six at night saw the commodore's light. At six, being reliev'd by the master, he could not see the com-modore's light, tho' it was visible to every one else on the quarterdeck: the master still persisted he could not see it; on which I went and acquainted the captain, who came upon deck, and seeing the light, ask'd the master, where his eyes were? This was the last time I ever saw the commodore. The lieutenant having the first watch lost sight of him at nine o'clock, and at ten was oblig'd to hand the foresail; in doing of which we lost a seaman overboard. We saw the *Gloucester* and *Anne* [*Anna*] pink astern in the morning; but they were soon gone ahead, and out of sight.

The 21st, as I was in the steward's room, Joseph King, seaman, came for a pound of bread. I heard him ask the steward, if he thought they would be serv'd with the same quantity of water as before? Without waiting for an answer, no, G–d d—n 'em; as the commodore was parted, they should find the difference. Not knowing the consequence of this, or by whom the fellow might be spirited up, I acquainted the captain with the affair, who order'd me to deliver a brace of pistols charg'd with a brace of balls to every officer in the ship who wanted 'em, and to take no farther notice of the matter.

May the 1st. This day the officers were call'd, and their opinions ask'd concerning the best bower-anchor; resolv'd to cut the anchor away, for fear of endangering the ship, there being no possibility of securing it without putting our foremast in extreme danger, the shrouds and chain-plates being all broke.

Fourteen days before the loss of the ship, the wind at S and SSW steer'd NW by N and NNW by the compass: laid the ship to for the first four nights; the meaning of this I could not learn. I ask'd the lieutenant the reason of our bearing for the land on a lee shore, when we had a fair wind for our rendezvous, which I had always thought was for the island of Juan Ferdinandez [Juan Fernandez]. The lieutenant told me the rendezvous was alter'd to an island in the latitude of 44 : S. Upon this I said to the lieutenant, this is a very great misfortune to us; that we can do nothing with the ship in the condition she is in upon a lee shore; and am surpriz'd, that we should be oblig'd to go there. The lieutenant told me, he had said every thing he could to dissuade the captain from it, but found him determin'd to go there. The fifth night, and every night after, made sail; the wind to the westward. I never reliev'd the lieutenant, but I ask'd him, what he thought of a lee shore with the ship in this condition? He always reply'd, he could not tell. We saw rockweed in abundance pass by the ship. The Honourable John Byron, midshipman, being on the quarterdeck, said, we can't be far off the land by these weeds. The lieutenant and mate being by, I said, gentlemen, what can we do with the ship in the miserable condition she is in on a lee shore? The lieutenant answer'd, whenever I have been with the captain since our first lying to, I always persuaded him to go for Juan Ferdinandez; therefore I would have you go to him, he may be persuaded by you, tho' he will not by me. I said, if that was the case, my going to him is needless. In a quarter of an hour afterwards, the captain sent for me, and said, gunner! What longitude have you made? I told

7

him 82 : 30. What distance do you reckon yourself off the land? I answer'd, about 60 leagues: but if the two islands we saw are those which are laid down in your chart to lay off Brewer's Streights, and the same current continues with the western swell, we can't be above a third part of the distance off the land. The captain made answer, as for the currents, there is no account to be given for 'em; sometimes they set one way, and sometimes another. I said, sir, very true; but as the ship has been always under reeft courses, with the mizen-mast gone, she must wholly drive to leeward, and nigher the land than expected. The captain then told me, I suppose you are not unacquainted of my rendezvous for the island of Nostra Signora de Socora [Nuestra Señora de Socorro], in the latitude of 44. I reply'd, sir, the ship is in a very bad condition to come in with the lee shore; and if it is possible to bring the ship to an anchor, we shall never purchase him again. The captain answer'd, I don't design to come to an anchor; for there are no soundings until you come within seven leagues of the land. I purpose to stand off and on twenty-four hours; and if I don't see the commodore, or any of the squadron in that time, we will go for Juan Ferdinandez. To this I said, sir, the ship is a perfect wreck; our mizen-mast gone, with our standing rigging afore and abaft, and all our people down; therefore I can't see what we can do in with the land. The captain's answer was, it does not signify, I am oblig'd and determin'd to go for the first rendezvous.

On the 13th, at eight in the morning, the straps of the forejeer blocks broke; reev'd the top ropes, and lower'd the yard; went to strapping the blocks. At nine, the carpenter going forward to inspect the chain-plates, saw the land from the fore-castle; on which he ask'd the boatswain's mate, who was by him, if he saw the land? He answer'd, no. The carpenter shew'd it him, and he saw it plain. The carpenter then shew'd it to the lieutenant; but he would not believe it to be land, because it bore NNW and said it was impossible; therefore he never inform'd the captain of the sight of land, as the Honourable Mr

Byron hath heard the captain say. At two in the afternoon lower'd the foreyard, and hawl'd the foresail up. Notwithstanding I was officer of the watch, I was oblig'd to go upon the foreyard, where was Mr Campbell midshipman, one boatswain's mate, four seamen, and the master's servant; which were all the hands we could get out of the ship's company to assist. Whilst on the yard I saw the land very plain, on the larboard-beam bearing NW half N nearest high land, with hillocks, and one remarkable *hommacoe* like a sugar-loaf, very high. At the sight of land I came off the foreyard, and acquainted the captain. He immediately gave orders to sway the foreyard up, and set the foresail; then we wore ship with her head to the southward. The captain coming forward unhappily received a fall, which dislocated his shoulder, so that he was obliged to be put into the surgeon's cabbin. Some time after he sent for the lieutenant and myself, acquainting us of the necessity there was for making sail, as being on a lee shore; therefore desired we would use our utmost endeavours to crowd the ship off. You see, gentlemen, said he, my misfortune will not permit me to continue on the deck: as for the master, he is not worthy of the charge of a watch; therefore I must desire you, Mr Bulkeley, to be in the watch with him, and to make but two watches: keep a good look-out, and, if possible, set the main-topsail. Mr Baynes, I must desire Mr Cummins to be with you; and beg you will take all the care you can. I having the first watch, set the main, fore and mizen staysail; it blew so hard I found it impossible to set the maintopsail; of which I acquainted the captain: all the hands we could muster in both watches, officers included, were but twelve; the rest of the ship's company were all sick below: I very often could get no more than three seamen in my watch. The ship for these three weeks hath been no better than a wreck; the mizen-mast gone; the standing rigging and chain-plates, afore and abaft, mostly broke and ruin'd. The topsails now at the yards are so bad, that if we attempt to loose 'em for making sail, we are in danger of splitting 'em; and we have not a spare sail in the ship that can be brought to the yard without being repair'd. This is the present deplorable situation of the ship. All the first and middle watch it blow'd and rain'd; and withal so very dark, that we could not see the length of the ship: for the greatest part of the night she came up no nearer than S by W and SSW. At four in the morning she came up with her head west; so that her head was then off the shore.

Thursday, May the 14th, 1741, at half an hour past four this morning, the ship struck abaft on a sunken rock, founded fourteen fathom; but it being impossible to let go the anchor time enough to bring her up, being surrounded on every side with rocks (a very dismal prospect to behold!), the ship struck a second time, which broke the head of the tiller; so that we were obliged to steer her with the main and foresheets, by easing off one, and hawling aft the other, as she came to, or fell off. In a short time after, she struck, bilged, and grounded, between two small islands, where providence directed us to such a place as we could save our lives. When the ship struck it was about break of day, and not above a musket-shot from the shore. Launch'd the barge, cutter, and yawl over the gunnel; cut the main and foremast by the board, and the sheet-anchor from the gunnel. The captain sent the barge ashore, with Mr Snow the mate, to see if the place was inhabited, and to return aboard directly; but, without any regard to his duty, or the preservation of the lives of the people, he staid ashore. The barge not returning as expected, the lieutenant was sent in the yawl, with orders to bring off the barge. The lieutenant tarried ashore, but sent off the boat. As soon as the boat came on board, the captain, being very ill, was persuaded by the officers to go ashore: with the captain went the land-officers, mate, and midshipmen; the officers remaining on board were the master, boatswain, gunner, and carpenter: the boatswain, who was laid up a month before the loss of the ship, became of a sudden very vigorous and active. At night it blow'd very hard at north, with a great tumbling sea; we expected every moment that the ship would part, fetching such jirks and twistings as shock'd every person aboard, who had the least care for the preservation of life; yet, in the dismal situation we were in, we had several in the ship so thoughtless of their danger, so stupid, and insensible of their misery, that upon the principal officers leaving her, they fell into the most violent outrage and disorder: they began with broaching the wine in the lazaretto; then to breaking open cabbins and chests, arming themselves with swords and pistols, threatning to murder those who should oppose or question them: being drunk and mad with liquor, they plunder'd chests and cabbins for money and other things of value, cloathed themselves in the richest apparel they could find, and imagined themselves lords paramount.

Friday the 15th the ship was bilged in the midships on a great rock; we took care to secure some powder, ball, and a little bread. In the afternoon, the carpenter and myself went ashore with several of those imaginary lords in the rich attire they had plunder'd yesterday; but upon the purser and Lieutenant Hamilton of marines presenting pistols to some of their breasts, those grandees suffer'd themselves very quietly to be disrob'd of all their greatness, and in a few minutes look'd like a parcel of transported felons. On our coming ashore, we found the captain had taken his lodging in a little hut, supposed to be built by Indians; as for our parts, we were forced to take shelter under a great tree, where we made a large fire; but it rain'd so hard, that it had almost cost us our lives; an invalid died that very night on the spot. Before I left the ship I went to my cabbin for my journal, but could not find it; I believe it is destroy'd with the rest, for there is not one journal to be produced; we have good reason to apprehend there was a person employ'd to destroy them; I afterwards found part of the master's journal along shore, tore to pieces: whatever is related in this book, preceding the loss of the *Wager*, is extracted from a journal belonging to a gentleman lately an officer on board the *Pearl*. After we lost sight of the *Pearl*, I was obliged to have recourse to my memory, which I believe has been very faithful to me. From the time we were shipwreck'd, the carpenter and myself were exceeding careful in writing each day's transactions: had other persons taken the same care, there would be no necessity of imposing upon the publick a partial and inconsistent narrative, instead of a faithful relation of facts.

On the 16th, the weather very boisterous and a great sea, the boatswain wanted a boat; but finding no appearance of any coming aboard, brought a quarterdeck gun, a four-pounder, to bear on the captain's hut, and fir'd two shot, which went just over the captain's tent. This day, being resolv'd to contrive something like a house, to secure us from the inclemency of the rain, and severity of the weather, we hawl'd up the cutter, and propping her up we made a tolerable habitation. As for food this island produces none; nor is there any vegetable upon it but cellery, which grows here in abundance, and is of great use to us, the men being in general very much troubled with the scurvy.

On the 17th of May, being Whitsunday, got several wild fowls, and plenty of mussels, limpetts, and other shellfish, which we find very refreshing, having subsisted a long time on nothing but salt-provisions.

The 18th went on board the ship, to see if it was possible to come to any provisions; got out of the lazaretto two casks of flour and some wine, which were very useful.

On the 19th went aboard again to scuttle the decks, in order to get some beef and pork out of the hold; we also scuttled the carpenter's store-room, for nails and other things of service.

The 20th cut away the gunnel, to get the long-boat out; which was done. Today we found several men dead, and some drowned, in the ship; suppos'd to have drank till they were not able to get from the water, as it flowed into the ship. While we were aboard working on the wreck, there came alongside a canoe with several Indians, bowing and crossing themselves, giving us to understand they were inclineable to the Romish religion; we gave 'em out of the ship two bales of cloth, and sent them ashore to the captain; he gave them hats, and presented each of them with a soldier's coat. They had abundance of the largest and best mussels I ever saw, or tasted. This day was the first time of the boatswain's coming ashore; the captain called him rogue and villain, and felled him to the ground with his cane, so that he was motionless, and to appearance dead; when he had recovered the blow, and saw a cockt pistol in the captain's hand, he offered his naked breast; the captain told him, he deserved to be shot, and said no more to him. The captain, Lieutenant Hamilton of marines, the surgeon, and purser, always appear'd in arms on the beach, on the coming ashore of every boat, in order to prevent the people bringing any thing from the ship in a clandestine manner; they were so cautious of any thing being imbezzled, that they would not suffer the boats to go off and work by night, notwithstanding the moon, tides, and fairness of weather were more favourable to us by night than day; by this we omitted several opportunities of getting out provisions, and other useful things, which we shall shortly stand in great need of.

The 21st, continue to scuttle between decks, in getting necessaries out of the ship; found several men dead.

The *22nd,* the Indians brought us three sheep, and some mussels. They are a people of a small stature, well shaped, of an olive complexion, with black hair; in behaviour very civil they have little cloaths, except about their waists, notwithstanding the climate is excessive cold. They stay'd all night, it being very rainy weather, and has been ever since we have been here, the wind blowing from north to NW.

Saturday the 23rd, the wind from the ENE to north, fell abundance of snow, insomuch that the mountains are cover'd with it. It freezes very hard, and we find it extreamly cold. The next day, the same weather, we went aboard, and scuttled for flour in the forehold.

The 25th, little wind at NE and frosty weather, went aboard

again, and got out of the forehold eight barrels of flour, one cask of pease, with some brandy and wine. This day went to allowance, of half a pound of flour per man, and one piece of pork for three men, it being the first time of serving since on shore.

The 26th, we got out more casks of flour, one cask of oatmeal, with some brandy and wine. In the evening the Indians came with their wives, we gave the women hats, and the men breeches; they made signs as if they would bring more sheep.

On the 27th, we scuttled over the captain's store-room, got out several casks of rum and wine, and brought them ashore. This was the first time of the lieutenant's being between decks since the loss of the ship. The following day we went aboard, cut down and tost overboard the ship's awning, to make a deck for the long-boat.

Since the 27th, we have been employ'd in getting up the long-boat, and repairing the barge which had been stove ashore. Rainy weather.

On Wednesday, the 3rd of June, hard gales of wind at NNW, with abundance of rain; deserted this day James Mitchel, carpenter's mate, John Russell, armourer, William Oram, carpenter's crew, Joseph King, John Redwood, boatswain's yeoman, Dennis O'Lary, John Davis, James Roach, James Stewart, and William Thompson, seamen. Took up, along shore, one hogshead of brandy, and several things that drove out of the ship, as bales of cloth, hats, shoes, and other necessaries. An information was given, this day, by David Buckley, to the captain, that there was a design to blow him up, with the surgeon, and Lieutenant Hamilton of marines. The train was actually found, laid by the deserters, to blow 'em up the night before they went off.

Thursday the 4th, we finished the boats, and shot several wild geese. Finding murmurings and discontents among the people, we secured the oars, and hawled up the boats, being apprehensive they would go away with them by night.

The 5th, we went on board the ship, found several casks of wine and brandy between decks, most part of the planks between decks gone, and some strakes to windward started out, part of the upper deck blown up, the stumps of the masts and pumps risen five feet; brought ashore one cask of flour, with some stuff for the use of the long-boat; and two quarter casks of wine; the wind at S by E.

Saturday the 6th, the wind at south and fair weather, we went aboard, got out of the hold eight casks of flour, two casks of wine, a quarter cask and three hogsheads of brandy. The lieutenant went to the Indians, but could not find 'em, being inform'd by the deserters that they were gone.

On Sunday the 7th, we went aboard the ship, got out a cask of pork, two barrels of flour, started one pipe of wine, and brought it ashore, with a quarter cask of pease, some bales of cloth, and carpenter's stores. This day Mr Henry Cozens, midshipman, was confin'd by the captain; the fault alledg'd against him was drunkenness. We learn from Nicholas Griselham, seaman, who was present and near the captain all the time, that as Mr Cozens was rowling up a steep beach a cask of pease, he found it too heavy for him, and left off rowling; the captain seeing this told him, he was drunk; Mr Cozens reply'd, with what should I get drunk, unless it be with water? The captain then said, you scoundrel, get more hands, and rowls the cask up: Cozens called for more hands, but no people came; with that the captain struck him with his cane. Griselham likewise says, that Cozens talked to the captain about one Captain Shelvocke; * but the words he does not remember. But the same

---

* George Shelvocke had sailed from England in the privateer *Speedwell* in 1719. The object of his expedition, financed by London merchants, was to attack shipping off the Chilean coast. However, he was wrecked off the island of Juan Fernandez. From her timbers another craft was built and in this the crew of forty men sailed away, having persuaded Shelvocke to sign new articles which took no account of the interests of the London merchants. They soon captured a large Spanish ship, and sacked and plundered various Spanish settlements. Having captured an even larger Spanish

night I heard Mr Cozens use very unbecoming language to the captain, telling him, that he was come into those seas to pay Shelvocke's debts; and also insolently added, tho' Shelvocke was a rogue, he was not a fool; and, by G–d, you are both. When he spoke this, he was a prisoner in the store-tent, and asked the captain if he was to be kept there all night? On these provocations, the captain attempted to strike him again; but the centinel said, he should strike no prisoner of his. But Cozens endeavouring to stave a cask of brandy, was soon after released. This day got out of the ship several chests of wax candles of all sizes, bales of cloth, bales of stockings, shoes, with some clocks, and mercantile wares, with which the ship was throng'd.

The 8th, Mr Cummins and myself went to the deserters; we find they are determined to go off to the northward; the reason of their stay is the want of craft to go off in. They now find themselves mistaken, they believed at first they were on the main, but are convinced they are four or five leagues from it, therefore they purpose to build a punt out of the wreck of the ship: they live on seaweed and shellfish; got up one cask of beef, which was brought on shore with a cask of brandy, found one cask of beef on the rocks.

On Tuesday the 9th, I went with the doctor's mate to the deserters, and spoke to William Oram, a carpenter, and a very useful man, desiring him to return, with a promise of pardon from the captain: in this affair I was obliged to act very secretly.

Today, Mr Cozens, the midshipman, had a dispute with the surgeon; the latter having some business in our tent, which

---

ship, they sailed from California across the Pacific to China, thence to India where the plunder was divided and the mutinous crew dispersed. On his return to England, Shelvocke was sued by the merchants and was arrested and imprisoned. But he managed to escape from the King's Bench prison and to leave England. His book *A voyage Round the World by way of the Great South Sea* was written to exculpate himself. Captain Cheap had a copy with him on the voyage, and the boat in which Bulkeley made his way back to civilisation was named after the *Speedwell* (see p. 57 below).

when he had done, on his going away, Mr Cozens followed him; they soon fell to blows, but the surgeon had so much the advantage of the midshipman, that he tied his hands behind him and left him. In the evening the captain sent for me and the carpenter to his tent: we found with the captain, the lieutenant, purser, surgeon, and Lieutenant Hamilton of marines. Here we had a consultation, which was chiefly concerning the disturbances among the people, as well in our tent as in the rest. Mr Cummins and I assured the captain, that the people in our tent were generally very well affected to him, and that we never would engage in any mutiny against him, or any other officer that would act for the publick good, and his majesty's service the captain said, he had no reason to suspect us, for we were the only two in the ship, that he put any trust or confidence in; strict orders were given the centinel to keep a good look-out, and have a watchful eye on the provisions; notwithstanding all this precaution and care, there was one third part of a barrel of flour, and half a barrel of gunpowder taken away that night. It is to be observed, that this day's consultation was the first that Captain Cheap ever had with his officers; had he sometimes consulted them aboard, we might probably have escaped our present unhappy condition.

Wednesday the 10th. This day, serving the provisions, the boatswain's servant, a Portuguese boy, talking bad English, and bringing in the allowance of wine, the boatswain, Mr Cozens midshipman, and the cook his messmates, with some difficulty, understood by the boy's talk, that one of the men had his allowance stopped; Mr Cozens went to know the reason; the purser and he having some dispute two or three days before, the purser told him, when he asked for his wine, that he was come to mutiny, and, without any farther ceremony, discharged a pistol at his head, and would have shot him, had he not been prevented by the cooper's canting the pistol with his elbow, at the instant of its going off; the captain, and Lieutenant Hamilton, hearing the discharge of the pistol, the latter ran out with a firelock, then called the captain out of his tent, telling him that Cozens was come to mutiny; the captain on this jumped out, asking where the villain was, clapped a cock'd pistol to Mr Cozens's cheek, and precipitately shot him, without asking any questions; the noise of the two pistols going off, reached our tent; it was rainy weather, and not fit for gunning, so that we could not imagine the meaning of it; soon after we heard Mr Cozens was shot by the captain: the lieutenant came to call all hands to the captain; I asked if we must go armed; the lieutenant answered, yes; but, on consideration, I thought better to go without arms. When we came to the captain, he acquainted us with what he had done, and told us he was still our commander. The captain, purser, surgeon, Lieutenants Hamilton, Ewers, and Fielding of marines being all armed, I said to the captain, sir, you see we are disarmed; on this the captain dropped his firelock to the ground, saying, I see you are, and have only sent for you, to let you all know I am still your commander, so let every man go to his tent; accordingly every man obeyed him. In our tent we had eighteen of the stoutest fellows that belonged to the ship; and I believe the captain, and the gentlemen above-mentioned, have some suspicion of Mr Cummins and myself, believing we can sway most of the seamen on shore: but I think this day we have given a proof of the sincerity of our intentions, and our detestation of mutiny, by not appearing in arms at the report of Mr Cozens being shot; we walked up with the captain, where we saw Mr Cozens with his elbow on the ground resting his right cheek on the palm of his hand, alive, and to appearance sensible, but speechless; the captain ordered him to the sick tent, the surgeon's mate dressed his left cheek where he was shot, and felt a ball about three inches under his right eye; the surgeon refused dressing him; this we may impute to his having lately a quarrel with Mr Cozens, which has been already mentioned.

The shooting of Mr Cozens was a very unhappy affair; the person whose allowance was stopped, made no complaint to

him; he was too officious in the business, and his preceding behaviour, and notorious disrespectful words to the captain,
might probably make the captain suspect his design was
mutiny; tho' this we must aver, that Mr Cozens neither on this,
or any other occasion, appeared in arms since the loss of the
ship: however, his fate laid the foundation of a great deal of
mischief which afterwards followed.

Thursday the 11th, moderate gales at WNW. The carpenter
employed in laying the blocks for the long-boat, Dr O——y, of
the land forces, was desired to assist the surgeon's mate, to take
the ball out of Mr Cozens's cheek, which he then was inclinable
to do; but in the afternoon, finding it not agreeable to the
captain, refused to go, as we are informed by the surgeon's mate,
who desired some surgeon might be present, to be witness of
the operation; the ball was taken out, and for some time
supposed to be lost, but was afterwards found.

This day being the 12th, the carpenter finished the blocks for
lengthening the long-boat; in the morning he went to the
captain's tent for some bolts for the use of the long-boat, where
he saw the surgeon at the medicine chest, who asked him how
that unfortunate creature did, meaning Mr Cozens; the
carpenter told him he had not seen him today: the surgeon then
said he would have visited him, but the captain would not give
him leave. This was looked on as an act of inhumanity in the
captain, and contributed very much to his losing the affections
of the people, whose opinion was, that as Mr Cozens was very
strong and healthy, with proper assistance he might recover; the
people did not scruple to say that the captain would act a more
honourable part to discharge another pistol at him, and dispatch
him at once, than to deny him relief, and suffer him to languish
in a cold wet place in pain and misery.

On the 13th, Mr Cozens being, to all outward appearance,
likely to recover, desired he might be removed to our tent,
which was his place of residence before this unhappy accident.
We being unwilling to disoblige the captain, the carpenter and

myself waited on him; we told him, we were come to ask a favour, hoping that he would have so much mercy and compassion on the unhappy man who was in the sick tent, as to permit us to remove him to his former lodging; but the captain answer'd, no; I am so far from it, that, if he lives, I will carry him a prisoner to the commodore, and hang him.

On the 14th, went aboard the ship, but could do nothing, she working so very much; we brought ashore the fore-topsail yard; the boat went up the river, brought back abundance of geese and shaggs. Wind at west.

Monday the 15th, hard gales of wind at west, with rain and hail; drove ashore three barrels of flour, and abundance of small stuff out of the ship; took up along shore several pieces of pork and beef; John Anderson, a seaman, walking round the rocks, and reaching after a piece of beef, slipping his footing, was drown'd, but taken up directly, and that night bury'd; turn'd the boatswain out of our tent for breeding quarrels; his turbulent temper was so well known to the captain, that he express'd himself pleas'd at our turning him out, and said he was surpriz'd we ever admitted him among us.

On the 17th, the carpenter at work on the long-boat. The surgeon's mate this day took out of Mr Cozens's cheek a ball much flatted, and a piece of bone, supposed to be part of the upper jaw, which was desired by Mr Cozens to be deliver'd to me; I receiv'd it, with the first ball mention'd to have been lost.

Thursday the 18th, the carpenter cut the long-boat in two, and lengthen'd her eleven feet ten inches and half by the keel.

Sunday the 21st, went aboard the ship; but it being dangerous going about any thing, by reason of her working much, and a great sea tumbling in, the boats were employ'd in going about the rocks in search of subsistence.

The 22nd, the carpenter went with the boat up the bay to seek the Indians, but saw nothing of them; at night the boat return'd, the people having shot abundance of wild fowl.

The 23rd, the lieutenant went with the boat, and found the

Indians just come from the place where they catch seal; their canoes were loaded with seal, sheep, and oil.

Wednesday the 24th, departed this life Mr Henry Cozens, midshipman, after languishing fourteen days with the wound he had receiv'd in his cheek: we bury'd him in as decent a manner as time, place, and circumstances would allow. There have died sundry ways since the ship first struck forty-five men; seven have deserted from us, and still continue away; remain and now victual'd one hundred men.

Thursday the 25th, the wind at WNW and rainy weather; saw the Indians coming towards us in their canoes; but the deserters settling where they took their habitation when first we saw 'em, by their rowing, we thought they were design'd to go there; and knowing the deserters intended to take one of their canoes to go over to the main, we therefore launch'd the yawl and went off to them; there were five canoes of 'em, laden with seal, shellfish, and four sheep; they brought with 'em their wives and children, so that in all they were about fifty in number; they hawl'd their canoes up, and built four wiggwhams, which they cover'd with the bark of trees and sealskins ; we imagin'd by this they had an intention to settle with us; they are a very simple and inoffensive people, of a low stature, flat-nos'd, with their eyes sunk very deep in their heads; they live continually in smoak, and are never without a fire, even in their canoes; they have nothing to cover their nakedness, but a piece of an old blanket, which they throw over their shoulders: we always see 'em in this manner, notwithstanding we cloath 'em whenever they come to us. By the crosses set up in many parts of the land, one would think they had some notion of the Romish religion : we can't make 'em understand us by any speech, nor by our signs; we show'd 'em a looking-glass; when they saw the representation of themselves, they seem'd amaz'd, and show'd a thousand antick gestures; and when once they beheld themselves in the looking-glass, they could hardly be prevail'd on to look off.

On Sunday the 28th, in the afternoon, about twelve of the Indian women went off in their canoes: we thought they were gone to get mussels, but soon saw 'em diving; which we imagin'd was for pieces of beef or pork that came out of the wreck; but, when they came ashore, we found they had been only diving for sea-eggs. The women among those people seem to take more pains for the provisions of life than the men; the latter having little to do but to provide wood, and indulge themselves by the fire, while the women go every tide a fishing. Today we kill'd two Indian sheep.

Monday the 29th, launch'd the yawl to go with the Indians to shew us where they get the mussels; but being too late for the tide, we came away without any: the captain sent to our tent two quarters of mutton; the carpenter daily at work on the long-boat. Winds variable.

On the 30th, the Indian women went again for sea-eggs, and brought a great quantity, with abundance of white maggots about three quarters of an inch in length, and in circumference the bigness of a wheat-straw. These women keep an incredible time under water, with a small basket in their hands, about the size of the womens work-baskets in England, into which they put whatever they get in their diving. Among these people the order of nature seems inverted; the males are exempted from hardships and labour, and the women are meer slaves and drudges. This day one of our seamen died: we observe, the Indians are very watchful of the dead, sitting continually near the above-mention'd corpse, and carefully covering him; every moment looking on the face of the deceas'd with abundance of gravity: at the burial their deportment was grave and solemn; seeing the people with their hats off during the service, they were very attentive and observant, and continued so till the burial was over. They have nothing, as I have said before, but a blanket to cover 'em, and the boys and girls are quite naked, notwithstanding we felt it as cold here, as in the hardest frosts in England, and almost always rainy.

Wednesday, July the 1st, employ'd in cutting timbers in the woods for the long-boat; rainy weather; the wind at SW the Indian women diving for food as before.

Thursday the 2nd, last night the store-tent was broke open, and robbed of a great deal of flour.

Monday the 6th, hard gales of wind, with showers of rain and hail; came ashore from the ship one cask of beef, with several of the lower deck carlings, and plank of the upper and lower deck beams; and, what was reckon'd very odd, the cabbin-bell came ashore, without its being fasten'd to any wood, or any one thing of the ship near it.

Tuesday the 7th, hard gales of wind, with hail, rain, and lightning: the Indian women went out as usual in their canoes to dive for sea-eggs, and brought ashore abundance of 'em; they jump overboard out of their canoe about a mile from shore; they take the handle of their baskets, which I have already described, between their teeth, and dive in five or six fathom water; their agility in diving, and their continuance under water, for so long a time as they generally do, will be thought impossible by persons who have not been eye-witnesses of it; they seem as amphibious to us as seals and allegators, and rarely make use of any provision but what they get out of the sea.

Wednesday the 8th, launch'd the yawl and went on board; saw several casks, some of meat, and some of liquor; the decks and sides abaft drove out, and entirely gone; the larboard side abaft drove on shore; about two miles and a half from the tent a cask of liquor was found, and broach'd by the person who found it, which was allow'd to be a great fault; he likewise broach'd a cask of meat, which should have been preserv'd to carry away with us.

On Thursday the 9th, the Indians with their wives and children launch'd their canoes, and went away; 'tis believ'd they wanted provisions, such as seal; they are indeed never settled long in a place; it was said some of our people wanted to have to do with their wives, which was the reason of their going away so soon. Today we saw several things drive out of the ship up the lagoon, as the stump of the main-mast, one of the pumps, with one of the gun-carriages. Wind at NW.

Friday the 10th, went aboard the ship, found her broke asunder just at the gangway; saw the cables out to the windward, but could not see any casks of liquor or provisions; went to shorter allowance of flour, one pound for three men *per diem*. Last night the tent was robbed of half a barrel of flour; orders were given by the captain to watch the store-tent by night; all the officers, the marine included, with the mates and midshipmen, were oblig'd to watch, the captain and carpenter alone excus'd, the carpenter being every day at work on the long-boat.

Friday the 17th, for this week past hard gales of wind, with rain and hail as usual. Last Wednesday the ship parted her upper works from the lower deck: launch'd the boat and went off to the wreck, but could do nothing; went up the bay; took a quarter cask, about three parts full of wine; saw the Indian dogs ashore, but no people.

Saturday the 18th, launched the boat, sent her to the wreck, and brought ashore one cask of beef; it is believed some guns were heard from the sea: the watch reported they have heard them two nights past. Great disturbances among the people. Wind at ENE and frosty weather.

Sunday the 19th, launch'd the boat, sent her to the wreck, hook'd a cask supposed to be beef; but when towed ashore, we found it contained nothing but hatchets; we took up along shore, abundance of checque shirts in dozens, also caps, bales of cloth, and pieces of beef and pork.

Wednesday the 22nd. This day began to build a house to dwell in, finding our stay here, will be much longer than we at first expected.

The 23rd, took up along shore several pieces of beef and pork, shirts, caps, frocks, trowsers, pieces of cloth, with other serviceable things, and wax candles of all sizes.

Saturday the 25th, hard showers of rain and hail; the wind at north. Shot several seagulls, geese, hawks, and other birds the carpenter had this day given him by one of the people, a find large rock crab, it being the first of the kind we ever saw here.

Sunday the 26th, moderate gales and variable winds, with rain and hail: most part of our people eat a weed that grows on the rocks; it is a thin weed of a dark green colour, and called by the seamen, slaugh. It is surprising how the blackcurrant trees, which are here in great plenty, have budded within these three days. Began thatching our new house with bushes: today we caught a fine rock-fish; this is the first fish we have seen alive since our being here. Observing our new town, we find there are no less than eighteen houses in it.

Monday the 27th, launched the boat, went to the wreck, but found nothing; close weather, the wind still at north: rise the sheers for erecting a tent over the long-boat to keep the men from being exposed to the continual rains. This day we finished the thatching of our new house.

Wednesday the 29th, fresh gales at NW with rain; sure no men ever met with such weather as we have in this climate today we walked in the woods to take some notice of the trees, which we find to be very much like our beech in England; but the trees and bushes are in general of a soft free nature, and with a spicey bark.

Thursday the 30th, wind still at NW and rainy weather. This day departed this life Nathaniel Robinson, the last private man of the invalids; there are now only two left, *viz.* the captain and surgeon. Being at the Honourable Mr Byron's tent, I found him looking in Sir John Narborough's voyage* to these seas; this

---

* Sir John Narbrough's expedition of 1669 aboard the *Sweepstakes* was described in *An Account of several late Voyages and Discoveries to the South and North towards the Streights of Magellan, the South Seas,* . . . *also towards Nova Zembla, Greenland or Spitsberg* . . . (London 1694) which included accounts of voyages by other captains. His descriptions were accurate, and proved invaluable. See Byron's journal, below.

book I desired the loan of, he told me it was Captain Cheap's, and did not doubt but he would lend it me; this favour I requested of the captain, and it was presently granted. Carefully perusing this book, I conceived an opinion that our going through the Streights of Magellan for the coast of Brasil, would be the only way to prevent our throwing ourselves into the hands of a cruel, barbarous, and insulting enemy: our long-boat, when finished, can be fit for no enterprize, but the preservation of life: as we cannot act offensively, we ought to have regard to our safety and liberty. This evening proposals were offered to the officers concerning our going through the Streights of Magellan; which at this time they seem to approve of.

Friday the 31st, hard gales at NW with rain: this day was taken up along shore an otter just killed, but by what animal we could not tell; it was bleeding fresh when taken up, and proved a dainty repast. Came ashore the ship's beams, with several things of great value.

Saturday, August the 1st, hard gales at NW with rain and hail. This day put to an allowance of flour, one quarter of a pound a man *per diem,* and one pint of wine; those who like brandy, to have half a pint in lieu of wine. We have now in a manner nothing to live on but what we pick up along the shore: the ship's company agree to go through the Streights of Magellan.

Sunday the 2nd. This morning found the store-tent robbed of brandy; filled up all the ullage casks; picked up about the rocks abundance of clams, a shellfish not unlike our cockles; these fish are at present the support of our life. The people are now very quarrelsome and discontented.

Monday the 3rd, this day having fine weather (which is a prodigy in this place), launched the boat, and went about the rocks and islands of discovery. This day we also moved into our new house, it being a very commodious habitation, exceedingly well thatched; in this dwelling there are cabbins for fourteen people, which are covered inside and out with broad cloath.

This is a rich house, and, in some parts of the world, would purchase a pretty estate; there are several hundred yards of cloth about it, besides the curtains and linings, which are shalloon and camblet; in short, considering where we are, we cannot desire a better habitation. The people fall into disputes concerning the boat, where we are to proceed with her, when she is built and ready for going off. It is the opinion of the navigators, that going through the Streights of Magellan is the safest and only way to preserve life and liberty: the artists, who have worked the bearings and distance, are very pressing that it should be moved to the captain, purposing to have their reasons drawn up, and signed by all who are willing to go that way, and to be delivered to the captain for his opinion; upon this there was a paper drawn up, and as soon as the people heard it, they came flocking to sign first, crying all aloud for the Streights, seeming overjoyed, as if they were going to England directly, without any affliction or trouble; but there must be a great deal of hardship to be encountered before we arrive at our native country. This paper was signed by all the officers on the spot, except the captain, lieutenant, purser, and surgeon, and by all the seamen in general, except the captain's steward.

Tuesday the 4th, at the time of serving at the store-house, about twelve o'clock, I went to the captain, with the master, carpenter, and boatswain, and read to him the paper; he answered, he would consider of it, and give his answer: here follows a copy of the paper signed.

We whose names are under-mentioned, do, upon mature consideration, as we have met with so happy a deliverance, think it the best, surest, and most safe way, for the preservation of the body of people on the spot, to proceed through the Streights of Magellan for England. Dated at a desolate island on the coast of Patagonia, in the latitude of 47 deg. 00 min. south, and west, longitude from the meridian of London 81 deg. 40 the South Seas, this 2nd day of August 1741.

John Bulkeley, gunner
John Cummins, carpenter
Thomas Clark, master
John King, boatswain
John Jones, master's mate
John Snow, ditto
Robert Elliot, surgeon's mate
The Hon. John Byron,
  midshipman
Alexander Campbell, ditto
Isaac Morris, ditto
Thomas Maclean, cook
John Mooring, boatswain's
  mate
Richard Phipps, ditto
John Toung, cooper
Richard Noble, quarter-
  master
William Rose, ditto
William Hervey, quarter-
  gunner
John Bosman, seaman
William Moore, ditto
Samuel Stook, ditto

Samuel Cooper, seaman
David Buckley, quarter-
  gunner
Henry Stevens
Benjamin Smith
John Montgomery
John Duck
John Hayes
James Butler
John Hart
James Roach
Job Barns
John Petman
William Callicutt
George Smith
Peter Deleroy
James Mac Cawle
John George
John Shorclan
Richard East
William Lane
William Oram
Moses Lewis
Nicholas Griselham
} seamen

We whose names are under-mention'd, have had sufficient reasons, from the above-mention'd people, to consent to go this way. Sign'd by

Capt. Robert Pemberton
Commander of His Majesty's Land Forces
William Fielding, Robert Ewers, Lieutenants

Wednesday the 5th, this day I went with the master, carpenter, master's mates, and midshipmen, to the captain, to acquaint him with what was done, and resolv'd on; and farther told him, it was a duty incumbent on us to preserve life before any other interest. He answer'd, gentlemen, I desire time to consider of it, and will give you my final determination; on which we took our leave, and came away.

Thursday the 6th, hard gales at WSW and rainy weather. At noon went with Mr Cummins to Captain Pemberton's tent, to have some farther conference for our future deliverance. While we were there, the captain sent his service to Captain Cheap for a pair of pocket-pistols, his own property, which had been refused him on his request some time before. The servant was answer'd, by the captain's favourite and prime minister the steward, the captain is ill, and I can't let you have 'em. This answer not being satisfactory to Captain Pemberton, he sent a second time, and insisted on the delivery of his pistols; but was answer'd, they could not be come at before the captain was up; but a little time after it was judg'd proper to send Captain Pemberton his pistols. From Captain Pemberton's we went to the lieutenant's tent; while there, the lieutenant was sent for to Captain Cheap; about an hour after the carpenter and myself were sent for; when we came to him, he said, gentlemen, I have maturely consider'd the contents of your paper, so far as it regards the preservation of the people on the spot: this paper has given me a great deal of uneasiness, insomuch that I have not clos'd my eyes till eight o'clock this morning, for thinking of it; but, I think, you have not weigh'd the thing rightly; do you know we are above one hundred and sixty leagues distant SW from the Streights of Magellan, with the wind against us? Then think on the distance to be run afterwards on the other side the Streights, with the wind always against us, and where no water is to be had. I answer'd, sir, you say it is above one hundred and sixty leagues to the Streights; but let the navigators work it, and they will find it not above ninety leagues; yourself and lieutenant are undoubtedly navigators and judges, therefore will certainly find it as I say. Mr Cummins acquainted him, according to his calculation, the vessel would carry a month's water, at a quart a manger *diem;* and, sir, do you consider, after running along shore to the northward this side the land, that we have one hundred leagues to run right out to sea to the island of Juan Ferdinandez; and five hundred chances to one, if we meet the commodore there, or any of the squadron; nor do we know but the commodore may have shared the same fate with ourselves, or perhaps worse? The captain answer'd, it's a thousand to one if we see the commodore at Juan Ferdinandez; for, gentlemen, to let you into a secret, which I never discover'd before, we shall meet him at Baldavia, his orders were to go there with the squadron, it being a place of little or no force. Mr Cummins answer'd, sir, 'tis agreed, the commodore is at Baldavia; but we make it in our bargain, when we go from hence, that we will put ashore at every place when we want water, whenever the weather will permit, without any obstruction. The captain reply'd, there is no occasion for that; we will water at the islands, and take a vessel going along. Mr Cummins said, sir, what shall we do with a vessel, without provisions, for ninety souls? The captain answer'd, we will take a vessel loaden with flour from Chili, there being a great many trading vessels that way; and then we will proceed through the Streights of Magellan. Mr Cummins said, how shall we take a vessel without guns? not having any but muskets; and our enemies know, as well as ourselves, that we have a squadron in these seas, therefore undoubtedly are well arm'd, and keep a good look-out. The captain's answer to this was, what are our small arms for, but to board 'em? The carpenter said, sir, if a shot should take the boat under water, it would not be in my power to stop a leak of that kind, where the plank is so thin, that in some places it is not above three quarters of an inch thick. The captain then said, gentlemen, I am agreeable to any thing, and willing to go any way, for the preservation of the people; but at the same time would have you consider of it, the wind being always against us on the other side the land, and we have above seven hundred leagues to the River Plate. I answer'd the captain, 'tis not above five hundred and ninety leagues from hence to Cape St Antonio's; and, as I have before said, let the navigators work it, and reason take place, which is what we chiefly desire to be govern'd by: another inducement we have to go the way propos'd is, that we may be assur'd of water and provision. I allow that, says the captain, and we may save our own; but how do you know whether we may not meet enemies in the Streights? I reply'd to the captain, we can have no enemies to encounter there, but Indians in their canoes, and those we can master at our pleasure. The captain then seem'd to countenance our opinion again; and said, when we come to St Julian's we shall be sure of salt in plenty for our provisions, without which our fowls will not keep above two or three days: besides, when we come to the River Plate, we may meet with a prize, they not being acquainted with any English vessel like ours, with schooner's sails; by which means we may run up the river, and take a larger vessel: if we fail here, we may go ashore, and get what cattle we please; but what business have we at the Rio Grand? We must go to the Rio Janeiro. I told him, we should be oblig'd to stop at every place along shore for supplies; at St Catharine's the governor will give us a certificate, so that we shall be known to be the people that were there in the squadron. The captain said, that's true, and I can get bills of credit in any part of Brazil; besides, the people may be separated, some in the *Flota,* and some in other ships; with less hands we may go to Barbadoes. Mr Cummins told him, we might venture to England with twelve hands. Yes, you may, says the captain, with thirty. It is to be observ'd, during all this debate, the lieutenant spoke not a word. The carpenter asking him the reason of his silence in all the consultation, he answer'd, I'll give my opinion hereafter. The captain said, I knew nothing of his being acquainted with it, till Mr Bulkeley told me yesterday; but at the same time, Mr Baynes, I expect you will be the first that will sign the paper. I imagin'd the captain meant our paper, and immediately answer'd, with some warmth, as he had refus'd signing at first, and at the same time agreed to the proposal, that I had sign'd so close, that there was no room left for his name, and now it was too late for him to sign. The captain surpriz'd me, by saying, I don't mean your paper. I told him, any other, which should be contrary to ours, would never be sign'd by us. Mr Cummins said to the captain, sir, 'tis all owing to you that we are here; if you had consulted your officers, we might have avoided this misfortune; considering the condition the ship was in, she was not fit to come in with the land, all our men being sick, and not above three seamen in a watch; suppose the mast had gone by the board, as was every moment expected. The captain made answer, gentlemen, you do not know my orders, there never were any so strict given to a commander before; and had I but two men living besides myself, I must, and was obliged to go to the first rendezvous, which was the island of Nostra Senhora di Socora: I was obliged to go there at all events. I made answer to this, sir, if that is the case, it seems plain, the thing was design'd we should be here: but, sir, I am of opinion, notwithstanding the commodore had his orders to go with the squadron to Baldavia, that at the same time those orders were so far discretional, that if the squadron was disabled, care was to be taken not to endanger his majesty's ships. Yes, that (says the captain) was settled at St Julian's: notwithstanding what has been said, gentlemen, I am agreeable to take any chance with you, and to go any way; but would have you consider of it, and defer your determination till all is ready to go off the spot. I then told the captain, you have known, sir, from the time you saw the proposal, that the people are uneasy, and the work is at a stand, and in this situation things will be until this affair is settled; therefore the sooner you resolve, the better. The captain reply'd, I design to have a consultation among my officers have you any more objections to make? I answer'd, yes, sir, one more; which is, when you go from hence, you are not to weigh, come to an anchor, or alter course, without consulting your officers. The captain said, gentlemen, I was your commander till the ship parted, or as long as any stores or provisions were getting out of her. We told him, we had always taken care to obey his orders in the strictest manner; which he allow'd us to have done; and he added, you were the officers that I placed my whole dependence in. We answer'd, sir, we will support you with our lives, as long as you *suffer* reason to rule; and then we parted. After this consultation the captain seldom came out of his tent, which occasion'd great disturbances among the people.

Friday the 7th, the wind at WNW with rain. This day the navigators work'd the bearings and distance along shore, from one place to another, to know the true distance: hereupon it was agreed to proceed through the Streights of Magellan, according to Sir John Narborough's directions, which give us great encouragement to go that way. Captain Pemberton draw'd his men up, and dismiss'd 'em again. Great uneasiness among the people.

Saturday the 8th, this morning went to the lieutenant, for him to acquaint the captain all his officers were ready to give sufficient reasons for going through the Streights of Magellan, desiring a consultation might be held in the afternoon. At three o'clock the captain sent for me and Mr Cummins; when we came, the master and boatswain were sent for, but they were gone in search of subsistence, as limpetts, mussels, &c. The captain said, gentlemen, I don't doubt but you have consider'd upon the business you are come about; therefore I am determin'd to take my fate with you, or where the spirit of the people leads, and shall use my best endeavours for their preservation; but I am afraid of meeting contrary winds, for after the sun has cross'd the line we must expect to meet 'em. I made answer, by all accounts, the wind hangs from NW to the SW above three parts of the year; which is in our favour. Mr Cummins told him, there was fresh water to be got as well on one coast as the other; and if Sir John Narborough's treatment was so ill in a profound peace, what must we expect in a time of open war? The captain said, I am afraid, very bad. Then Mr

Cummins spoke in this manner to the captain: sir, I always took you for an honourable gentleman, and I believe you to be such; on your honour, sir, I beg you will give the true sentiments of your mind, whether thro' the Streights is not the surest and safest way to preserve our lives, notwithstanding we have a thousand difficulties to encounter with any way? The captain answer'd, I really think going to the northward is the safest way; for suppose we should be drove off to sea, when on the other side the land, what is to be done then? I said, sir, it is our business to keep the shore, to prevent all accidents that may happen that way. Then Lieutenant Baynes made an objection, suppose you have the wind blowing right in, and a tumbling sea, as to endanger the boat, what are we to do? I made answer, sir, if you remember, when we were riding at St Julian's, it blow'd a very hard gale of wind right in from the sea; yet, even then, the sea did not run so high as to endanger a boat riding at anchor another instance I bring you from St Catharine's, when we had such hard gales, that the *Tryal* lost her masts, and the *Pearl* separated from the squadron; yet, at that time, there was no sea comparable to what we have met with this side the land. The lieutenant allow'd this to be fact. Then the captain said, I will allow you to have water at Port Desire; but do you consider the lengthening your distance, by keeping along shore, and rounding every bay, and some of those bays are very deep. I told him, that undoubtedly there was water all along the coast, and that we had no business to round the bays, but to steer from one headland to the other. Then Lieutenant Baynes made a second objection, suppose we are forced into a bay, and shoalwater? I answer'd, we should always have a boat ahead, and our draught of water will not be above four or five feet at most; and if we should be so unfortunate as to lose our boat, we must keep the lead a going. The Lieutenant reply'd, that was true, and there could not be a great deal of difficulty in it. This was the only time the lieutenant ever spoke in publick on the affair; he always allow'd, when absent from the captain, that going through the Streights was the best way; but in the captain's presence he sided with him, and was for going to the northward.

Sunday the 9th, at three this afternoon, I went with Mr Cummins, the master, and boatswain, as desir'd, to the captain, to give him our opinions, believing, going thro' the Streights the surest way to preserve life: it was therefore agreed, that if the wind did not set in against us, at the sun's crossing the line, that the captain would go that way. The captain ask'd every man's opinion, and found the people unanimous for the Streights of Magellan. Today, being fair weather, launch'd the yawl to go a fowling; shot several geese, ducks, shaggs, and sea-pies. Heel'd the long-boat for planking.

Monday the 10th, wind at N and NNW. Rainy weather. Eat slaugh and seaweed fry'd with tallow-candles, which we pick'd up along shore; this we reckon at present exceeding good eating, having nothing to live on but a quarter of a pound of flour a man per day, and what we can get off the rocks; for many days the weather has been so bad, that we have not been able to stir abroad, tho' almost starv'd for want of food.

Tuesday the 11th, hard gales at SW with heavy rains. This afternoon the people came in arms to acquaint us of the stores being robbed; they therefore wanted our consent for moving the stores to our tent; on which we desir'd they should desist from offering any violence; we told 'em of the ill consequence of mutiny, which, as we always abhor'd, we took all imaginable care to prevent: the people, on our persuasions, instantly quitted their arms. The captain presently sent for me and Mr Cummins, to acquaint us with what had happen'd: he told us the purser, accidentally coming by, saw the prisoner Rowland Crusset, marine, crawling from the bushes, and from under the store-tent, and found on him upwards of a day's flour for ninety souls, with one piece of beef under his coat, and three pieces more, which were conceal'd in the bushes, to carry off when an opportunity offer'd; and the centry, Thomas Smith, his messmate, a marine, undoubtedly was privy to the robbery. The captain farther said, we have nothing to do with them; but I shall send to Captain Pemberton, to insist on a court-martial I really think, that for robbing the store-tent (which, in our present circumstances, is starving the whole body of people), the prisoners deserve death. This was not only the captain's opinion, but indeed the sentiments of every person present. After we parted from the captain, we were sent for by Captain Pemberton: he acquainted us, he would go as far as the martial law would allow him, and in conjunction with the sea-officers I look (said he) on the lieutenant as nothing, and the captain in the same light: as for you two (meaning the gunner and carpenter), I confide in, and shall have regard to your opinions. When the articles of war were read, we found their crime did not touch life, but that they were to suffer corporal punishment. Whilst Mr Cummins was laying open the nature of their guilt, and the ill consequence of lenity in the circumstances we were in, I propos'd a way, next to death; which was, if judg'd proper by Captain Pemberton and Captain Cheap, to carry 'em off to an island where the ship parted, there being mussels, limpetts, and clams in abundance, and no want of water, and there to be left till we should be ready for sailing; and, to strike a terror in all for the future, that if any man should be guilty of the like offence, without any respect of person, he should share the same fate. This proposal was approved of by both the captains. At night Lieutenant Baynes surpriz'd us with a new kind of proposal we little dreamt of, which was, to have a proper place of devotion, to perform divine service in every Sabbath Day: for this sacred office our tent was judg'd the most commodious place. The duty of publick prayer had been entirely neglected on board, tho' every seaman pays fourpence per month towards the support of a minister; yet devotion, in so solemn a manner, is so rarely perform'd, that I know but one instance of it during the many years I have belong'd to the navy. We believe religion to have the least share in this proposal of the lieutenant. If our tent should be turn'd into a house of prayer, and this project takes, we may, perhaps, in the midst of our devotion, be surpriz'd, and our arms taken from us, in order to frustrate our designs, and prevent our return to England through the Streights of Magellan, or any other way.

Wednesday the 12th, hard gales from SW to W with heavy showers of hail and rain. Serv'd out provisions today, a piece of beef for four men; some time past we have had but a quarter of a pound of flour per man *per diem,* and three pieces of beef; we live chiefly on mussels, limpitts, and clams, with *Saragraza* and *Thromba;* one is a green broad weed, common on the rocks in England; the other is a round seaweed, so large, that a man can scarce grasp it; it grows in the sea, with broad leaves; this last we boil, the *Saragraza* we fry in tallow; in this manner we support life: even these shellfish and weeds we get with great difficulty; for the wind, the rain, and coldness of the climate in this season, are so extremely severe, that a man will pause some time whether he shall stay in his tent and starve, or go out in quest of food.

Friday the 14th, very hard gales at W and NW with showers of rain and hail, which beat with such violence against a man's face, that he can hardly withstand it; however, one of our mess-mates today shot three gulls and a hawk; which gave us a very elegant repast. This day was held a court-martial on the centry who is believ'd confederate with the marine that robbed the store-tent: sentence was pass'd on 'em to receive six hundred lashes each: Captain Cheap, not thinking the punishment adequate to the crime, cut 'em short of their allowance; so that they have now but half the provisions they had before: the day following the offenders receiv'd two hundred lashes each, as part of their punishment. We hawl'd the long-boat higher up, for fear the sea should wash the blocks from under her. We have found out a new way of managing the slaugh; we fry it in thin batter with tallow, and use it as bread.

Sunday the 16th, fresh gales of wind at SW with heavy showers of hail: the people generally complain of a malady in their eyes; they are in great pain, and can scarce see to walk about. The last tide flowed nine feet perpendicular; today we picked up shellfish in abundance, with pieces of beef and pork. The prisoners received two hundred lashes more.

Tuesday the 18th, this day the carpenter, who has all along been indefatigable in working about the long-boat, saw one of the seamen cutting up an anchor-stock for fire-wood, which had been designed for a particular use for the boat; at sight of the fellow's folly he could not contain himself: this affair, added to the little concern and intolerable indifference that appeared in the generality of the people, for some time impaired his understanding, and made him delirious; all possible methods are used to restore him, as he is the only man, who, through the assistance of providence, can compleat the means of our deliverance.

Wednesday the 19th, the carpenter was so much recovered, that he went to work as usual; at night, the lieutenant acquainted us, that the captain desired to speak with the carpenter and me tomorrow at noon, to consult what should be done with the two prisoners, having received but four hundred lashes out of the six, to which they were sentenced by a court-martial, the other two hundred being remitted by their own officers.

Thursday the 20th, we waited on the captain, who acquainted us with what the lieutenant had mentioned last night relating to the prisoners: we told him the people were very uneasy about this mitigation of the punishment inflicted on them by a court-martial; therefore it was agreed they should provide for themselves as well as they could; but to have no sort of provisions out of the store-tent for the future.

Saturday the 22nd, we begun upon several contrivances to get provisions, such as building punts, cask-boats, leatherboats, and the like.

On Sunday the 23rd, the store-tent was again robbed, and, on examination, was found a deficiency of twelve days brandy for ninety men: the lieutenant, myself, and carpenter went to the captain to consult some way which might effectually prevent those villainous practices for the future; the captain desired us to make a nice enquiry into this robbery, being determined to inflict the severest punishment on the offenders; tho' it would give him the greatest concern if any innocent person should suffer. This day we confined one of the centinels for being drunk on his post; the day following the boatswain gave us information of the persons who had robbed the tent; they were two centinels, Smith and Butler; those very persons were the first who insisted, that the seamen, as well as themselves, should watch the store-tent; their own officers, as yet, have brought them to no examination: we have also information that the purser holds frequent conversation with the rebels, contrary to all the laws of the navy, supplying them with liquors in abundance, to the great distress of his majesty's faithful subjects, who have but half a pint per day to subsist on. There are now great disturbances among the people concerning going to the northward; they believe Captain Cheap never intended to return to England by his proposing this way, in opposition to the opinion of all the navigators, who have given reasons for going thro' the Streights of Magellan. There is a sort of a party rage among the people, fomented by a kind of bribery that has more influence on the seamen than money; there are some daily bought off by rum, and other strong liquors. Unless a stop is put to these proceedings, we shall never go off the spot.

Tuesday the 25th, this day felt four great earthquakes, three of which were very terrible; notwithstanding the violent shocks and tremblings of the earth, we find no ground shifted. Hard gales of wind at north, with heavy showers of rain.

Thursday the 27th, the disturbances increase among the people; we plainly see there is a party raised to go to the northward; we went to the lieutenant, and consulted with him what was to be done in the present exigence; myself being reckoned the projector of the scheme for going through the Streights was threatened to be shot by Noble the quarter-master. After having some discourse with the lieutenant, he told me, if I would draw up a paper for the captain to sign, in order to satisfy the people, that he would go to the southward, and every officer to have a copy of it, to justify himself in England, it would be as proper a method as we could take. The paper was immediately drawn up in these words, *viz:*

Whereas upon a general consultation, it has been agreed to go from this place through the Streights of Magellan, for the coast of Brazil, in our way for England: we do, notwithstanding, find the people separating into parties, which must consequently end in the destruction of the whole body; and as also there have been great robberies committed on the stores, and every thing is now at a stand; therefore, to prevent all future frauds and animosities, we are unanimously agreed to proceed as above-mention'd.

This paper was deliver'd to the lieutenant, who said that he was sure the captain would sign it; but in case of refusal, he should be confin'd for shooting Mr Cozens, and he would take the command on himself: and, to prevent further disturbances, the purser, as he much convers'd with the rebels, it is agreed, by the body of officers, to send him off the island, for acting so contrary to his duty, in contempt of the articles of war, the laws of his country, and the known rules of the navy. It was likewise agreed, that any person, who engaged himself in raising parties, should be disarm'd. By this day's proceedings, we thought the lieutenant a gentleman of resolution; but the words and actions of people do not always concur.

Friday the 28th, today the officers and people all appear'd in arms. The master, boatswain, gunner, and carpenter, with Mr Jones mate, and Mr Campbell midshipman, went into the captain's tent, the lieutenant being with him. As soon as the officers were seated, a consultation was held concerning Smith and Butler robbing the store-tent; they were sentenced to be transported to the main, or some island. As soon as this affair was over, we talk'd to the captain of the uneasiness among the people; that there had been a long time a visible inquietude among 'em, and that we could not help seeing there were schemes form'd to obstruct our design in going to the southward. The captain answer'd, gentlemen, it is time enough to think of this when we are ready to go off: have not I told you before, that I do not care which way I go, southward or northward? I will take my fate with you. Every body now expected the lieutenant to reply, especially after the zeal he express'd himself with the day before; but he sate speechless, without any regard to the welfare of the people, or to his own proposals. Finding he did not move in the affair, I took out the paper which was agreed to by the lieutenant and the rest of the officers, and read it to the captain, and ask'd him to sign it, which he strenuously oppos'd, and seem'd very much enrag'd that it should be propos'd to him. Upon this we dropt the matter, and began to discourse concerning the provisions. We thought it necessary, that ten weeks subsistence should be secur'd to carry with us, and that the liquor should be buried underground; but he gave us no answer. Finding no relief here, we went to Captain Pemberton's tent, to consult with him what we should do in the present exigence. On our coming out from the captain, we saw a flag hoisted on Captain Pemberton's tent, the captain himself seated in a chair, surrounded by the people. On seeing this, all the officers present at the consultation, except the lieutenant, went over to Captain Pemberton. Here it was agreed, in case the captain persisted to refuse signing the paper, to take the command from him, and to give it the lieutenant, according to the lieutenant's own proposal. At the same time Captain Pemberton told the people, he would stand by 'em with his life, in going through the Streights of Magellan, the way propos'd in the paper. The people gave three cheers, crying aloud for England. The captain hearing the noise, got out of bed to his tent door, and call'd the people, enquiring what they wanted; then sent for all the officers: he was then told, since he refus'd signing the paper, and had no regard to the safety of our provisions, the people unanimously agreed to take the command from him, and transfer it to the lieutenant. Hearing this, with an exalted voice, Captain Cheap says, who is he that will take the command from me? Addressing himself to the lieutenant, is it you, sir? The lieutenant reply'd, no sir. The terror of the captain's aspect intimidated the lieutenant to that degree, that he look'd like a ghost. We left him with the captain, and return'd to Captain Pemberton's tent, to acquaint him of the lieutenant's refusing the command. We had not been long here before Captain Cheap sent for us. I was the first person call'd for; at my entering his tent, I saw him seated on a chest, with a cock'd pistol on his right thigh; observing this, I desir'd Mr Jones, who was the mate he always rely'd on for navigation, to tell the captain, I did not think proper to come before a cock'd pistol : notwithstanding I was arm'd, I drew back, altho' I had my pistol cock'd, and there were several men near me arm'd with muskets. The captain's personal bravery no man doubted of; his courage was excessive, and made him rash and desperate ; his shooting Mr Cozens was a fatal proof of it; he was grown more desperate by this unhappy action, and was observ'd since seldom to behave himself with any composure of mind. It is a piece of human prudence to retreat from a man in a phrenzy, because he who does not value his own life, has another man's in his power. I had no desire of falling by the hand of Captain Cheap, and should be greatly disturb'd to be compell'd, for my own preservation, to discharge a pistol at a gentleman against whom I never had any spleen, and who was my commander. When Mr Jones acquainted him with what I desired him, the captain threw his pistol aside, and came out of his tent; he told the people, he would go with them to the southward; he desired to know their grievances, and he would redress them: they all call'd out for their sea-store of provisions to be secur'd, and the rest equally divided. Here the captain show'd all the conduct and courage imaginable; he was a single man against a multi-tude, all of 'em dissatisfy'd with him, and all of 'em in arms: he told 'em the ill consequence of sharing the provisions, that it was living today and starving tomorrow; but the people were not to be satisfy'd, the officers had now no authority over 'em, and they were some time deaf to their persuasions; nay, it was with difficulty that they could dissuade 'em from pulling down the store-tent, and taking away the provisions by force; they remov'd the provisions out of the store-tent, then fell to digging a hole to bury the brandy; the sea-store to be secur'd, the remainder to be immediately shar'd. Had this been comply'd with, the consequences might have been very terrible: however, to pacify 'em in some shape, it was agreed, that every man should have a pint of brandy per day, which, by calculation, would last 'em three weeks. On this they seem'd very easy, and went to their respective tents. The captain told his officers, that he would act nothing contrary to what was agreed on for the welfare and safety of the community. Finding the captain in a temper of mind to hearken to reason, I said to him, sir, I think it my duty to inform you, that I am not the person whom you imagine to be the principal in this affair. The captain answer'd, how can I think otherwise? I reply'd, sir, the paper I read to you was your lieutenant's projection: there sits the gentleman, let him disown it, if he can. The captain turning himself to the lieutenant, says, Mr Bulkeley has honestly clear'd himself. We then drank a glass of wine, and took our leaves. At night the captain sent for Mr Cummins and me to sup with him; we were the only officers present with him: when I was seated, I said, sir, I have my character at stake, for drawing back from your cock'd pistol: had I advanc'd, one of us must have dropt. The captain answer'd, Bulkeley, I do assure you, the pistol was not design'd for you, but for another; for I knew the whole before. We then talk'd of indifferent things, and spent the evening in a very affable manner.

Saturday the 29th, came here five Indian canoes, loaden with mussels; men, women and children were about fifty: these Indians had never been with us before; they are not so generous and good-natur'd as our friends I have already mention'd; they were so mercenary, that they would not part with a single muscle without something in exchange; their stay was but short with us, for the next morning they launch'd their canoes, and went off.

Tuesday, September the 1st, the carpenter was shot in the thigh with several large pewter sluggs by the captain's cook; but he being at a great distance, the sluggs did not enter his skin: whether this was design'd, or accidental, we don't know; however, we thought it proper to disarm him.

Wednesday the 2nd, wind at N and N by W with rain. This day we were inform'd that three of the deserters, *viz.* James Mitchel, carpenter's mate, Joseph King and Owen Thomson, seamen, were gone over to the main in a punt of their own building; the others were here yesterday, and I believe would be gladly received again, but am of opinion there are few voices in their favour.

Friday the 4th, some disorders among the people about watching the provisions; some taking all opportunities to rob the stores. Our living now is very hard; shellfish are very scarce, and difficult to be had; the seaweeds are our greatest support; we have found a sort of seaweed, which we call *dulse*; it is a narrow weed, growing on rocks in the sea, which, when boil'd about two hours, thickens the water like flour; this we esteem a good and wholesome food.

Sunday the 6th, last night the store-tent was robbed of brandy and flour: the people at hearing this were greatly enrag'd, and insisted on searching the marines' tents; on search they found four bottles of brandy, and four small parcels of flour. The captain sent for the lieutenant, master, gunner, carpenter, and surgeon, with Lieutenants Hamilton, Ewers, and Fielding, of the army; Captain Pemberton was also sent for, but was so ill that he could not be present, but desir'd all might pass according to the judgment of the above-mention'd officers. A consultation was held: five of the accus'd marines did not appear, dreading the punishment due to their crime; they march'd off to the deserters: four more, who staid to be try'd, receiv'd sentence, on the first opportunity, to carry them off to the main, and there to shift for themselves with the former deserters. The seamen insisted on a pint of brandy each man *per diem*, which was agreed on. The provisions being found were put into the store.

Monday the 7th, I was invited to a dog-feast at Mr Jones's tent: there were present at this entertainment, the lieutenant, the Honourable John Byron, Mr Cummins, Mr Campbell, Mr Young, Lieutenants Ewers and Fielding, and Dr Oakley of the army. It was exceeding good eating; we thought no English mutton preferable to it.

Tuesday the 8th, in the afternoon, William Harvey, quarter-gunner, came to our tent, with a paper sign'd by seven people; the contents as follow, *viz:*

These are to acquaint you, the gentlemen, officers, and seamen of the ship *Wager*, that, for the easement of the boat now building, we do agree to go in the yawl, after she is fitted up, with allowing us our share of provisions, and other conveniencies, to go in her to the southward, through the Streights of Magellan, for the coast of Brazil.

David Buckley, quarter-gunner   *William Rose*, quarter-master
William Harvey, ditto   *John Hayes*, seaman
Richard Noble, quarter-master   *John Bosman*, ditto
William Moor, captain's cook

The next day, the above-mention'd added one more to their number, *viz.* Peter Plastow, captain's steward: he came to acquaint us, he was willing to go with them, and hoped we would give our consent; we told him we had nothing to do with it, therefore he must apply to the captain.

Thursday the 10th, hard gales at WNW with rain and hail. The captain sent for the lieutenant, master, myself, the carpenter, and boatswain: when we were all met, the captain ask'd us, if Plastow had mention'd any thing to us about going off in the yawl. We told him he had. Plastow being sent for, the captain said, Peter! I hear you are for going in the boat. He answer'd, yes, sir; I will take my chance, for I want to get to England. The captain bade him be gone for a villain, and said no more. This Plastow was a mighty favourite with the captain, and had often been admitted to his conversation: he above all men ought to have stood stedfast to him, because the captain regarded him above the whole body of people, and hath been heard to say as much. It was this day agreed, that the sentence put off on the 6th should be executed the first opportunity, without any delay; and that no boat should go off from hence before all was ready, believing some have a design to go to the northward.

Friday the 11th, wind at NNW. The people very uneasy; scarce any work done for this week past; every thing is at a stand; we have now among us no command, order, or discipline; add to our uneasiness, the uncomfortableness of the climate; we have been inhabitants of this island sixteen weeks, and have not seen ten fair days; the murmurings of the people, the scarcity of provision, and the severity of the weather, would really make a man weary of life.

Monday the 14th, last night very hard gales at NW and WNW with large showers of hail, with thunder. The wind today is much abated. As to the article of provisions, nothing comes amiss; we eat dogs, rats, and, in short, every thing we can come at.

Friday the 18th, Dennis O'Lary and John Redwood, seamen, with six marines, were put off to the main, according to their sentence; it being a fine summer's day. This day the lieutenant, bringing a pair of pistols to the carpenter, and complaining they were in bad order, did not imagine they were loaded, snapping the first it miss'd fire, the second went off, but providentially did no harm, tho' the lieutenant had then a crowd of people about him.

Sunday the 20th, little wind, and clear weather. Launch'd the barge, and went off to the wreck; we took up four casks of beef, with a cask of pease, which was stav'd; we serv'd out to each man five pieces of beef, and pease to such as would have 'em, but there were none to take 'em; having now plenty of meat, our stomachs are become nice and dainty.

Wednesday the 23rd, the people went to the captain with a two-gallon cagg, and ask'd it full of wine: the captain refus'd 'em; but apprehending that they would make no ceremony of filling it without leave, and carrying it off by force, he thought proper to order it to be fill'd: they brought it to the long-boat, and drank it in her hold. Stept the long-boat's mast forward. The people very much disorder'd in liquor, and very quarrelsome.

Thursday the 24th, I was sent on a week's cruize in the barge; the officers with me were Mr Jones the mate, and the Hon. Mr Byron midshipman, and Mr Harvey the purser, who was a good draughtsman; we went in order to discover the coast to the southward, for the safety of the long-boat; we were informed on our return, that the people in our absence went to the captain, and got two gallons of wine which they mixed with their half pints of brandy; they got all drunk and mad, but no great mischiefs ensued. Six Indian canoes, likewise came in our absence loaden with men, women, and children; they brought with them clams out of the shells strung on lines: the Indian women dived for mussels, and brought them ashore in abundance; the men went to the fresh water river, and caught several fish like our English mullets. The people bought dogs of the Indians, which they kill'd, and eat, esteeming the flesh very good food: the next day the Indians went out and caught a vast quantity of fish out of a pond, where they sent in their dogs to hunt; the dogs dived, and drove the fish ashore in great

47

numbers, to one part of the pond, as if they had been drawn in a seyne; the Indians sold the fish to the people. This method of catching fish, is, I believe, unknown any where else, and was very surprising; and, what is also very strange, after the Indians went away, we hauled the seyne over the pond, and could never get a fish.

Monday the 28th, returned with the barge; the first evening we were out we had a good harbour for the barge, which we put into; the first animal we saw was a fine large bitch big with puppies; we killed her; we then roasted one side and boiled the other, were exceedingly well pleased with our fare, supped heartily, and slept well: the next morning we got up at daybreaking, and proceeded on our cruize, finding all along the coast to be very dangerous; at evening put into a place of very good shelter for the barge: here we found the Indians had been very lately, the shore being covered with the offals of seal: in an hour's time we killed ten wild fowl; we roasted three geese and two ducks, the rest we put into a sea-pye, so that we fared most elegantly; got up at daylight next morning, but seeing the weather hazy and dirty, thought it not proper to put out with the barge, fearing we should not get a harbour before night; we took a walk five miles in the country cross the land to the southward, but could not see any shelter for the boat, being then twelve leagues from the place we came from; so we returned back in the evening, and got into a fine sandy bay; I think it as good a harbour for shipping as any I ever saw: coming into this bay, saw the southmost land, which we had seen before, bearing about SSW right over an inlet of land, about two miles. After landing, lived as we did last night; in the morning we walked over, where we found a deep bay, it being eighteen leagues deep, and twelve leagues broad; here we had a very good prospect of the coast; we found here the green pease that Sir John Narborough mentions in his book.

Saturday the 3rd of October, after our return from the

cruize, the lieutenant, the master, myself, the boatswain, and Mr Jones the mate, went to the captain, to acquaint him how forward the boat was, and to consult some measures to be observ'd on board the boat, to prevent mutiny; he desir'd a day or two to consider of it.

On Monday the 5th, the carpenter sent his case bottle, as usual, to the captain, to be filled with wine; but it was sent back empty, with this answer, I will give him none. This sudden change of the captain's behaviour to the carpenter, proceeded from some words which the latter dropt, and were carried to the captain: the words the carpenter spoke were to this purport, that he was not to be led by favour or affection, nor to be biassed by a bottle of brandy. Today we heeled the long-boat, and caulked the starboard side, paid her bottom with wax, tallow, and soap that came out of the ship.

Tuesday the 6th, hard gales at NW and N with rain: this morning the lieutenant acquainted us of the captain's resolution, which was to be captain as before, and to be governed by the rules of the navy, and to stand or fall by them; it was objected in the present situation, the rules of the navy are not sufficient to direct us, several rules being requisite in our circumstances which are not mention'd there; that the whole body of officers and people are determin'd not to be govern'd by those rules at present. This objection was started, not from a disrespect to those rules; but we imagin'd, if Captain Cheap was restor'd to the absolute command he had before the loss of the *Wager*, that he would proceed again upon the same principles, never on any exigence consult his officers, but act arbitrarily, according to his humour and confidence of superior knowledge: while he acts with reason, we will support his command with our lives; but some restriction is necessary for our own preservation. We think him a gentleman worthy to have a limited command, but too dangerous a person to be trusted with an absolute one. This afternoon the people insisted to be serv'd brandy out of the casks that were buried underground;

accordingly they were serv'd half a pint each man. Got the long-boat upright.

Thursday the 8th, this day the master went to the captain concerning ten half barrels of powder more than can be carried off, which will make good water-casks for the boats: the captain told him not to start the powder, or destroy any thing, without his orders; and said, he must have time to consider of it. In the afternoon, Captain Pemberton, of the land forces, came on the beach, and desired the assistance of the seamen to take Captain Cheap a prisoner, for the death of Mr Cozens, the midshipman; telling us, he should be call'd to an account, if he did not. This evening the carpenter went up to the hill-tent, so called from its situation; the people were shooting balls at marks; some of 'em were firing in vollies, without shot or sluggs: one of the men on the beach fir'd at the tent while the carpenter was in it, who was standing with a book in his hand; there was a piece of beef hung close at his cheek, the ball went through the tent and the beef, but the carpenter receiv'd no damage. Today I overhaul'd the powder, and told the lieutenant that I had twenty-three half barrels in store, and that we could not carry off in the vessel about six half barrels; therefore purpose to start the overplus into the sea, and make watercasks of the half barrels, they being very proper for that purpose. I desired him to acquaint the captain with my intention; that since he had no regard for the publick good, or to any thing that tended to promoting it, the carpenter and I had determin'd never to go near him again. The lieutenant declin'd going, fearing the captain would murther him; but he sent the master to him, to let him know the necessity of starting the powder: the captain's answer to the master was, I desire you will not destroy any one thing without my orders. We now are convinc'd the captain hath no intention of going to the southward, notwithstanding he had lately given his word and honour that he would; therefore Captain Pemberton, in order to put an end to all future obstructions, demanded our assistance to make him a prisoner for the shooting Mr Cozens, intending to carry him as such to England; at the same time to confine Lieutenant Hamilton with him; which was readily agreed to by the whole body. It was reckon'd dangerous to suffer the captain any longer to enjoy liberty; therefore the lieutenant, gunner, carpenter, and Mr Jones the mate, resolv'd next morning to surprize him in his bed.

Friday the 9th, this morning went in a body and surpriz'd the captain in bed, disarm'd him, and took every thing out of his tent. The captain said to the seamen, what are you about? Where are my officers? At which the master, gunner, carpenter and boatswain, went in. The captain said, gentlemen, do you know what you have done, or are about? He was answer'd, yes, sir; our assistance was demanded by Captain Pemberton, to secure you as a prisoner for the death of Mr Cozens; and as we are subjects of Great Britain, we are oblig'd to take you as such to England. The captain said, gentlemen, Captain Pemberton hath nothing to do with me; I am your commander still; I will shew you my instructions; which he did to the people; on this we came out. He then call'd his officers a second time, and said, what is this for? He was answer'd, as before, that assistance was demanded by Captain Pemberton to take him prisoner for the death of Mr Cozens. He still insisted, Captain Pemberton has no business with me; I could not think you would serve me so. It was told him, sir, it is your own fault; you have given yourself no manner of concern, for the publick good, on our going from hence; but have acted quite the reverse, or else been so careless and indifferent about it, as if we had no commander; and if other persons had given themselves no more trouble and concern than you have, we should not be ready to go from hence as long as provisions lasted. The captain said, very well, gentlemen, you have caught me napping; I do not see any of you in liquor; you are a parcel of brave fellows, but my officers are scoundrels. Then turning himself to me, he said, gunner, where's my lieutenant? Did not he head you? I told him, no, sir; but was here to see it executed, and is here now. One of you (says the captain) call Mr Baynes. When Mr Baynes came, he said, what is all this for, sir? Sir, it is Captain Pemberton's order. Captain Pemberton hath no business with me, and you will answer for it hereafter; if I do not live to see England, I hope some of my friends will. On this the lieutenant left him. The captain then address'd himself to the seamen, saying, my lads, I do not blame you; but it is the villainy of my officers, which they will answer for hereafter. He then call'd Mr Baynes again, and said, well, sir, what do you design to do by me? The lieutenant answer'd, sir, your officers have design'd the purser's tent for you. Hum! I should be obliged to the gentlemen, if they would let me stay in my own tent. The lieutenant came to acquaint the officers of the captain's request; but they judg'd it inconvenient; as Mr Hamilton's tent join'd the purser's, one guard might serve 'em both; accordingly all his things were mov'd to the purser's tent: as he was coming along, he said, gentlemen, you must excuse my not pulling my hat off, my hands are confin'd. Well, Captain Baynes! you will be call'd to an account for this hereafter. The boatswain, after the captain's confinement, most barbarously insulted him, reproaching him with striking him, saying, then it was your time; but now, G–d d–n you, it is mine. The captain made no reply but this, you are a scoundrel for using a gentleman ill when he is a prisoner. When the captain was a prisoner, he declared, he never intended to go to the southward, having more honour than to turn his back on his enemies; and farther, he said, gentlemen, I do not want to go off in any of your craft; for I never design'd to go for England, and would rather chuse to be shot by you; there is not a single man on the beach dare engage me; but this is what I fear'd.

It is very odd, that Captain Cheap should now declare he never intended to go to the southward, when he publickly gave his word and honour he would go that way, or any way where the spirit of the people led: but he afterwards told his officers, he knew he had a severe trial to go through, if ever he came to

England; and as for those who liv'd to return to their country, the only favour he requested from them, was to declare the truth, without favour or prejudice; and this we promis'd faithfully to do: his words, in this respect, were as much regarded by us as the words of a dying man, and have been most punctually observ'd.

Saturday the 10th, little wind at N and NW. Getting all ready for going off this afternoon, the captain sent for the lieutenant and me, desiring us both to go to Captain Pemberton, to know what he intended to do with him. We accordingly came, and both promis'd to go directly, and bring him his answer. When we came out, went to the lieutenant's tent; from thence I expected, and made no doubt, but he would go to Captain Pemberton's: but when I ask'd him, he refus'd; which very much surpriz'd me. I thought it very ungenerous to trifle with Captain Cheap, or any gentleman in his unhappy situation; therefore went alone to Captain Pemberton. When I deliver'd him Captain Cheap's message, the answer was, I design, and must carry him prisoner to England. I return'd, and acquainted Captain Cheap with Captain Pemberton's answer: he ask'd me then, if the lieutenant was with me. I told him, no; and I believe did not design it. He said, Mr Bulkeley, I am very much oblig'd to you, and could not think the lieutenant would use me thus. In the evening the lieutenant and I were sent for again: the captain said to the lieutenant, sir, have you been with Captain Pemberton? He answer'd, no, sir. I thought, sir, you promis'd me you would: however, I have his answer from Mr Bulkeley; I am to be carried a prisoner to England. Gentlemen, I shall never live to see England, but die by inches in the voyage; and it is surprizing to me to think, what you can expect by going to the southward, where there are ten thousand difficulties to be encounter'd with: I am sorry so many brave fellows should be led to go where they are not acquainted, when, by going to the northward, there is the island of Chili, not above ninety leagues, where we need not fear taking prizes, and may have a chance to see the commodore. I made answer, sir, you have said, that we shall be call'd to an account for this in England: I must tell you, for my part, had I been guilty of any crime, and was sure of being hang'd for it in England, I would make it my choice to go there, sooner than to the northward: have not you given your word and honour to go to the southward? It is true, there is a chance in going to the northward, by delivering us from this unhappy situation of life to a worse, *viz.* a Spanish prison. The captain said no more but this, gentlemen, I wish you well and safe to England.

Sunday the 11th, this morning the captain sent for me, and told me, he had rather be shot than carried off a prisoner, and that he would not go off with us; therefore desired me to ask the people to suffer him to remain on the island: the people readily agreed to his request; and also consented to leave him all things needful for his support, as much as could be spar'd. Lieutenant Hamilton and the surgeon chose to stay with him. We offer'd him also the barge and yawl, if he could procure men to go with him. The question was propos'd before the whole body; but they all cry'd aloud for England, and let him stay and be d—n'd; does he want to carry us to a prison? There is not a man will go. The captain being depriv'd of his command in the manner above-mention'd, and for the reasons already given, it was resolv'd to draw some articles to be sign'd for the good of the community, and to give the lieutenant a limited command. The paper was drawn up in this manner

Whereas Captain David Cheap, our commander in his majesty's ship the *Wager,* never consulted any of his officers for the safety and preservation of the said ship, and his majesty's subjects thereto belonging; but several times, since the unhappy loss of the said ship, he has been solicited in the most dutiful manner, promising him at the same time to support his command with our lives, desiring no more than to go off heart in hand from this place to the southward, which he gave his word and honour to do; and being almost ready for sailing, did apply to him, some few days past, to draw up some proper articles, in order to suppress mutiny, and other material things, which we thought necessary to be agreed to before we went off; but he, in the most scornful manner, hath rejected every thing propos'd for the publick good; and as he is now a prisoner, and the command given to the lieutenant, upon his approbation of the following articles.

FIRST, as we have no conveniency for dressing provisions on board the vessel for a third part of the number to be carried off the spot, therefore this day serv'd out to every man and boy twelve days provision, for them to dress before we go off; and also it is agreed, that whoever is guilty of defrauding another of any part of his allowance, on sufficient proof thereof, the person found guilty (without any respect of person) shall be put on shore at the first convenient place, and left there.

SECONDLY, in regard to the boats going off with us, we think proper to allow one week's provision for each man appointed to go in them, in order to prevent separation from each other, which would be of the worst consequence of any thing that can happen to us; to prevent which, we do agree, that when underway they shall not separate, but always keep within musket-shot, and on no pretence or excuse whatsoever go beyond that reach. The officer, or any other person, that shall attempt a separation, or exceed the above-mention'd bounds, shall, on proof, be put on shore, and left behind.

THIRDLY, it is agreed, in order to suppress mutiny, and prevent broils and quarrels on board the vessel, that no man shall threaten the life of another, or offer violence in any shape; the offender, without any respect of station or quality, being found guilty, shall be put on shore, and left behind.

FOURTHLY, we do agree, whatever fowl, fish, or necessaries of life, we shall happen to meet with in our passage, the same shall be divided among the whole; and if Captain David Cheap shall be put on board a prisoner, it shall not be in the lieutenant's power to release him.

The aforesaid articles were agreed to, and sign'd by the under-mention'd

Robert Beans [Baynes], lieutenant
Thomas Clark, master
John King, boatswain
John Bulkeley, gunner
John Cummins, carpenter
Thomas Harvey, purser
Robert Elliot, surgeon's mate
John Jones, master's mate
John Snow, ditto
The Hon. *John Byron*, midshipman
Alexander Campbell, ditto
Isaac Morris, ditto
Thomas Maclean, cook
Richard Phipps, boatswain's mate
Benjamin Smith, seaman
William Oram, carpenter's mate
John Hart, joiner
John Bosman, seaman
William Harvey, quarter gunner
Richard East, seaman
Samuel Cooper, ditto
Job Barns, ditto
James Butler, ditto
William Rose, quarter master

John Mooring, boatswain's mate
Matthew Langley, gunner's mate
Guy Broadwater, coxswain
Samuel Stook, seaman
Joseph Clinch, ditto
John Duck, ditto
Peter Plastow, captain's steward
John Pitman, butcher
David Buckley, quarter gunner
Richard Noble, quarter master
William Moore, captain's cook
George Smith, seaman
John Shoreham, seaman
John Hayes, ditto
Henry Stephens, ditto
William Callicutt, ditto
John Russel, armourer
James Mac Cawle, seaman
William Lane, ditto
James Roach, ditto
John George, ditto
John Young, cooper
Moses Lewis, gunner's mate
Nicholas Griselham, seaman

Monday the 12th, at daylight, launch'd the long-boat, and gave her the name of the *Speedwell* (which God preserv'd to deliver us); we got all the provision on board, and other necessaries. The captain sent for the lieutenant, myself, and the carpenter, desiring us to leave him what could be spar'd, and to send to the deserters to know if they will go in the yawl to the northward; we promis'd to grant him his request. Today every body got on board. The captain, surgeon, and Mr Hamilton, had their share of provisions equal with us.

Tuesday the 13th, we sent the barge to the deserters, with Mr Snow the mate, to know if they were willing to tarry, and go with the captain to the northward; to acquaint them what provision and necessaries should be allow'd 'em: they readily agreed to tarry. On the return of the boat, deliver'd to the captain the share of provision for the deserters, and sundry necessaries, as under-mention'd, *viz:*

Six hand-grenadoes
Five half barrels of powder
Two caggs of musket-balls
Lieutenant Hamilton's pistols and gun
One pair of pistols for the captain
Twelve musket-flints
Six pistol-flints
Sundry carpenters tools
Half a pint of sweet oil
Two swords of the captain's own
Five muskets
Twelve pistol-balls
One Bible
One azimuth compass
One quadrant
One Gunter's scale

Provision deliver'd to the captain, surgeon, and Lieutenant

Hamilton, with eight deserters; which last are to be at half allowance of the quantity made out to the people, which make the whole number seven at whole allowance.

To the captain, surgeon, and Lieutenant Hamilton:
  Six pieces of beef
  Six pieces of pork
  Flour ninety pound
For the deserters:
  Eight pieces of beef
  Eight pieces of pork
  Flour one hundred weight

As soon as the above things were deliver'd, we got ready for sailing. I went and took my leave of the captain: he repeated his injunction, that at my return to England, I would impartially relate all proceedings: he spoke to me in the most tender and affectionate manner; and, as a token of his friendship and regard for me, desir'd me to accept of a suit of his best wearingapparel: at parting, he gave me his hand with a great deal of chearfulness, wishing me well and safe to England. This was the last time I ever saw the unfortunate Captain Cheap. How ever, we hope to see him again in England, that Mr Cummins and myself may be freed from some heavy imputations to our prejudice laid on us by the gentleman who succeeded him in command, and who, having an opportunity of arriving before us in England, not only in the places he touch'd at abroad, but at home, has blacken'd us with the greatest calumnies; and, by an imperfect narrative, has not only traduc'd us, but made the whole affair so dark and mystical, that till the captain's arrival the Lords of the Admiralty will not decide for or against us. But if that unfortunate captain never returns to his country, let us do so much justice to his character, to declare, that he was a gentleman possess'd of many virtues; he was an excellent seaman himself, and lov'd a seaman; as for personal bravery, no man had a larger share of it; even when a prisoner he preserv'd the dignity of a commander; no misfortunes could dispirit or deject him, and fear was a weakness he was entirely a stranger to; the loss of the ship, was the loss of him; he knew how to govern while he was a commander on board; but when things were brought to confusion and disorder, he thought to establish his command ashore by his courage, and to suppress the least insult on his authority on the first occasion; an instance of this was seen on the boatswain's first appearing ashore; shooting Mr Cozens, and treating him in the manner he did after his confinement, was highly resented by the people, who soon got the power in their own hands, the officers only had the name, and they were often compell'd, for the preservation of their lives, to comply sometimes with their most unreasonable demands; and it is a miracle, amidst the wildness and distraction of the people, that there was no more bloodshed.

At eleven in the forenoon, the whole body of people embark'd, to the number of eighty-one souls; fifty-nine on board the vessel, on board the cutter twelve, and in the barge ten: at noon got under sail, the wind at NW by W. The captain, surgeon, and Mr Hamilton, being on the shoreside, we gave them three cheers; which they return'd. Coming out of Wager's Bay split the foresail, and very narrowly escap'd the rocks; with the assistance of the barge, and our own oars, tow'd her clear, and bore away, into a large sandy bay, on the south side of the lagoon, which we call'd by the name of the Speedwell Bay. At four in the afternoon anchor'd in ten fathom fine sand; the barge and cutter went ashore, there not being room on board the boat to lodge the people.

Wednesday the 14th, fresh gales at SW and W with rain. At three this afternoon, being fair weather, weigh'd, and came to sail to take a cruize up the lagoon, to try the vessel; it being smooth water, she work'd very well; after three or four trips return'd, and anchor'd where we came from.

These are to certify the Right Honourable the Lords Commissioners for executing the office of Lord High Admiral of Great Britain, &c. that we, whose names are undermention'd do beg leave to acquaint your lordships, that Captain David Cheap, our late commander in his majesty's ship *Wager*, having publickly declar'd, that he will never go off this spot, at his own request desires to be left behind; but Captain Pemberton, of his majesty's land forces, having confined him a prisoner for the death of Mr Henry Cozens midshipman, with Lieutenant Hamilton for breaking his confinement, did insist on delivering them up on the beach to the charge of Lieutenant Beans [Baynes]; but he, with his officers and people, consulting the ill consequences that might attend carrying two prisoners off in so small a vessel, and for so long and tedious a passage as we are likely to have, and that they might have opportunities of acting such things in secret as may prove destructive to the whole body; and also in regard to the chief article of life, as the greatest part of the people must be oblig'd, at every place we stop, to go on shore in search of provisions, and there being now no less than eighty-one souls in this small vessel, which we hope to be deliver'd in; we therefore, to prevent any difficulties to be added to the unforeseen we have to encounter with, think proper to agree, and in order to prevent murther, to comply with Captain David Cheap's request: the surgeon also begs leave to be left with him. Dated on board the *Speedwell* schooner in Cheap's Bay, this 14th day of October, 1741.

Robert Beans [*Baynes*],
   lieutenant
Thomas Clark, master
John King, boatswain
John Bulkeley, gunner
John Cummins, carpenter
Robert Elliot, surgeon's mate

John Jones, master's mate
John Snow, ditto
Captain *Pemberton*, of his
   majesty's land forces
Vincent Oakley, surgeon of
   ditto

Thursday the 15th, this morning, it being calm, made a signal for the boats to come off, by firing five muskets. At daylight came to sail, with the wind at W by N. It blowing hard, and a great swell, the vessel would not work; therefore we were oblig'd to put into a small bay, laying SW of Harvey's Bay, where we had very good shelter, there being a large ledge of rocks without us, which broke the sea off. At eleven we sent the barge to Cheap's Bay for what canvass could be found serviceable, having left a sufficient quantity behind, to supply us with sails, in case we wanted 'em. Went in the barge the Hon. John Byron, at his own request, Alexander Campbell midshipman, William Harvey quarter-gunner, David Buckley ditto, William Rose quartermaster, Richard Noble ditto, Peter Plastow captain's steward, Joseph Clinch seaman, and Rowland Crusset marine. This afternoon the carpenter went ashore in the cutter, with several of the people, to look for provender. Shot several geese, and other sea fowl. Rainy weather. Wind WNW.

Friday the 16th, continual rain, and hard gales all night at SW. This morning the carpenter came on board, and acquainted us that he saw an anchor of seven feet in the shank, the palm of each arm filed off just above the crown: this anchor we suppose to have belong'd to some small vessel wreck'd on the coast. The cutter brought off abundance of shellfish ready dress'd for the people.

Sunday the 18th, at noon, the cutter came off, and brought aboard plenty of shellfish and greens. The Honourable Mr Byron, Mr Campbell, and three of the barge's crew, came from where the barge lay. Mr Byron came aboard, and inform'd us of the barge's being safe in the bay, where we left her, and only waited the opportunity of weather to come round with her. At the same time he desired to know, if we would give him, and those who would stay with Captain Cheap, their share of provisions. This question of Mr Byron's very much surpriz'd us; and what surpriz'd us more was, that he should be influenc'd by Mr Campbell, a person whom he always held in contempt. As for my part, I believe Mr Byron left us because he could not get any accommodation aboard the vessel that he lik'd, being oblig'd to lie forward with the men; as were also the carpenter and myself, when below: it is very certain, that we are so closely pent up for want of room, that the worst jail in England is a palace to our present situation.

Tuesday the 20th, serv'd out to the people eight days flour, to be dress'd ashore. I went in the cutter to command in my turn for a week.

Wednesday the 21st, close weather; the wind from W to NW with rain and hail. Brought aboard shellfish in abundance. At noon the Honourable Mr Byron came with some of the crew overland; he ask'd me, whether the boat's crew were gone off, and if we had serv'd the provision, for he wanted to return to the barge. I told him all the people were out a fishing, and that the first who came in should carry him off. On which he said, I think we will go and get some fish too, having nothing else to live on. This was the last time I ever saw his honour. When the people return'd from fishing, they told me Mr Byron had lost his hat, the wind blowing it off his head. I said, rather than he should want a hat, I would give him my own. One of the seamen forced a hat on his head; his name was John Duck: but Mr Byron would by no means wear it; saying, John! I thank you; if I accept of your kindness, you must go bare-headed; and, I think, I can bear hardships as well as the best of you, and must use myself to them. I took eight people, and went overland to the place where the barge lay, to get the canvass that we stood so much in need of; but found she was gone from thence. The people in the barge told our men, that they would return to us again; but it is plain they never intended it.

Thursday the 22nd, this day we saw sea-fowl in vast flocks flying to the southward, where was a dead whale. Look'd out all this day for the barge, but to no purpose. The barge not returning was a very great misfortune, having no boat but the cutter; and if by an unlucky accident we lose her, we must be reduc'd to the greatest extremities to get provision. The persons in the barge, except the captain's steward, always approv'd of going to the southward; but it seems Mr Campbell the patroon prevail'd on 'em to return to Captain Cheap.

Friday the 23rd, saw thousands of sea-fowl; in the morning they fly to the northward, and in the evening come back to the south; they are birds of a very large size, but of what kind we do not know. Since we have been here we saw several Indian graves; they are dug just within the surface of the earth, with a board on each side, and a cross stuck up at the head. The day following a gun, a four pounder, was seen near the anchor in Clam Bay; we call it by this name, because of the vast quantities of this sort of shellfish which are found there.

Monday the 26th, it being very calm, and fair weather, I went ashore to bring off the people; weigh'd the long-boat, and took her in tow over a bar, where was ten feet water, but a great swell; as soon as we got over the bar, there sprung up a breeze of wind at NW steer'd away S half E for the southmost part of land, which bore S by E distant fourteen leagues. The two points of land make a large and deep sandy bay; we sounded, but found no ground; it is a bald shore close to. I kept ahead in the cutter, in order to provide a harbour for the long-boat; providence directed us to a very good one: it blew so hard, with thick hazy weather, that we could not keep the sea. At eight at night we anchor'd in eight fathom water, abreast of a fine sandy bay, and land-lock'd not above three boats length from the shores. At the entrance of the harbour, which lies about a league up the lagoon, I set the land; the northmost point bore by the compass N by E distant twelve leagues, and the southmost S by W distant five leagues; the entrance lies E.

Tuesday the 27th, fresh gales at W and cloudy weather, with a great swell without, insomuch that we could not put out to sea; we therefore sent the people ashore to dress their provisions; each man is allow'd but a quarter of a pound of flour per day, without any other subsistence, but what providence brings in our way.

Thursday the 29th, early this morning, it being calm and thick weather, with small rain, we rowed out of the lagoon; at five it cleared up, with a fresh breeze at SSE steer'd SW and SW by W saw a small island bearing S by W the southmost end S by E. This island we call the rock of Dundee, it being much like that island in the West Indies, but not so large; it lieth about four leagues distant from the southmost point of land out at sea. This day it blow'd so hard, that we were oblig'd to take the cutter in tow.

Friday the 8oth, hard gales, and a great sea; saw some islands and some sunken rocks; at six saw the main in two points of land, with a large opening; on each side the sunken rocks are innumerable; the entrance is so dangerous, that no mortal would attempt it, unless his case was desperate, as ours; we have nothing but death before our eyes in keeping the sea, and the same prospect in running in with the land: we ran in before the wind to the opening that appear'd between the two points, the northmost of which bore N by E and the southmost S by E. We steer'd in E and found the opening to be a large lagoon, on the southmost side, running into a very good harbour; here our small vessel lay secure in a cove, which nature had form'd like a dock; we had no occasion to let go an anchor, but ran alongside the land, and made fast our head and stern. The people went ashore in search of provision; here we found plenty of wood and water, and fine large mussels in great quantities. Serv'd to each man half a piece of beef.

Saturday the 31st, this morning cast loose, and row'd towards the mouth of the lagoons, designing to put out to sea; but the wind blew so hard, that we were oblig'd to come to an anchor. This afternoon, in weighing the grapenel, in order to go to the cove, we found it foul among some rocks; all hands haul'd, took a turn round the main-mast, and went aft; which weigh'd the grapenel, but streighten'd one of the flukes: here the land is very high and steep on each side; the carpenter and cooper were on the highest of these hills, and found deep ponds of water on the top of them; these hills are very rocky, and there are great falls of water all along the coast: the whole navy of England may lay with safety in many of those lagoons; but the coast is too dangerous for any ship to fall in with the land. The people today were very much afflicted with the gripes, and pains in their side. Here are abundance of trees, not unlike our yew trees; they are not above seven or eight inches in diameter, and the bark is like cedar. The land is to appearance very good; but on digging beneath the surface, we find it almost an entire stone. We saw no people here, tho', it is plain, here have been some lately, by their wiggwhams or huts. We are so closely pent up for want of room, that our lodging is very uncomfortable; the stench of the mens wet cloaths make the air we breathe nauseous to that degree, that one would think it impossible for a man to live below. We came to sail, and steer'd out of the lagoon west; went into a sandy bay, one league to the southward of the lagoon. Indian huts to be seen, but no natives.

Monday, November the 2nd, at five in the morning, came to sail with the wind at S and S by E. At noon the wind came to the W and WNW in small breezes. This day I had a very good observation, it being the first since we left Cheep's Island. We found ourselves in the latitude of 50 : 00 S. After observing, bore away, and ran into a fine smooth passage between the island and the main. These islands I believe to be the same that are taken notice of in Cook's Voyage. From the entrance to the north-ward, to the going out of the Cape of Good Hope (as we call it), the distance is about six leagues, and the depth of water is from two fathom to twelve; the northmost land before we came into the passage bore N by W and the southmost, or Cape of Good Hope bore S by E. In the evening anchored in a fine sandy bay: here we also saw Indian huts, but no people; today we shot wild geese in abundance, and got of shellfish, as limpets and mussels.

Tuesday the 3rd, at four this morning weighed, and came to

sail with the wind at W till we got about the Cape of Good Hope, then at WNW steering S and a tumbling sea from the W. The cutter steer'd S by E into a deep bay; supposing them not to see the southmost land, we made the signal for her, by hoisting an ensign at the topping list; as the cutter was coming up to us, her square sail splitted; we offered to take them in tow, but they would not accept it; we lay with our sails down some time before they would show any signal of making sail; coming before the wind, and a large sea, we ordered them to steer away for the southmost point of land after us, and to keep as near us as possible; but instead of observing our directions, they steered away into the cod of a deep bay, supposed to be King's Bay: the cutter being much to leeward, and the weather coming on very thick, we were obliged to steer after her, but soon lost sight of her. The place being exceeding dangerous, we could not venture any farther after the cutter; therefore we hauled by the wind to the southward; it continued blowing hard, with thick weather, with sunken rocks and breakers, so that we were obliged to bear away before the wind into a large bay, the tide running rampant, and in a great swell, every where surrounded with sunken rocks, that we thought nothing but a miracle could save us; at last we got safe into the bay, and came to in two fathom water, we steered in E. At four this morning rowed out between the islands; after we got out, had a fresh breeze at NW steered out SSW then S and S by E the cutter ahead. At seven in the morning abreast of Cape Good Hope, saw a large high rock bearing S steered S by E going within it, and the main abreast of the rocks; saw a long point making into islands bearing S by E steer'd S until abreast of them: the same day saw a very high land, with a low point running off, in small hommacoes, bearing from the northmost point S by E about eighteen leagues; between those two points, is a large deep bay, all within surrounded with rocks and small islands; steered S and S by W for the outermost point, the cutter keeping within, and we considering the ill consequence of being embay'd, to prevent which we hauled the mainsail and foresail down, and kept the vessel before the wind; at eleven the cutter came alongside, with her mainsail split; we called to them to take hold of a towe rope, but they refused, telling us that the boat would not bear towing, by reason of the swell of the sea, therefore they would have us nearer the shore, where we should have smooth water; we answered them that the water was smoother without, and nothing nigh the sea that runs within; besides, we shall be embay'd, therefore we desire you to come on board the vessel, and we'll take the boat in tow: they had no regard to what we said; we at the same time, for above a quarter of an hour, lay in the trough of the sea, with a fair wind: the people in the cutter would neither make sail, nor row; at last, finding them obstinate, we hoisted a skirt of the mainsail, and edged farther off, S by W. When they found we would not go into that bay, they hoisted their mainsail, and went ahead; being some distance ahead, we made sail, the cutter still keeping ahead till one o'clock; then she bore away S by E and SSE the reason of which we could not tell, it blowing very hard, with a great sea, nothing before us but rocks and breakers, therefore of consequence the farther in, the sea must be the greater. At half an hour past two, the cutter, being on the beam, and four miles within us, we bore away after them; and in a very heavy squall of wind and rain we lost sight of her: after the squall was over, it cleared up, but we saw nothing of the cutter, nor could we clear the shore to the northward, being not above two miles off the breakers; therefore we were under a necessity of hauling to the southward for self-preservation, and very narrowly escaped clearing the rocks: after running about three leagues, saw an opening, where we hoped to find a good harbour; bore away for the opening; we were here again surrounded with rocks and breakers, with a hard gale of wind, and a great sea, the oldest seaman on board never saw a more dismal prospect; we ran in before the wind for about two leagues, expecting every rise and fall of the sea to be a wreck, but providence at length conducted us to an indifferent place of shelter: we are now in a most wretched condition, having no boat to go ashore in, to seek for provender: and the greatest part of the people on board are so regardless of life, that they really appear quite indifferent whether they shall live or die; and it is with much intreaty that any of them can be prevailed on to come upon deck, to assist for their preservation.

The people's names in the cutter are as follow, *viz*:

Names	Quality	Age	Where born
Thomas Harvey	purser	25	*Westminster*
John Mooring	boatswain's mate	34	*Gosport*
William Oram	carpenter's crew	28	*Philadelphia*
Richard Phipps	boatswain's mate	30	*Bristol*
Matthew Lively	gunner's mate	34	*Exeter*
John George	seaman	22	*Wandsworth*
Nicholas Griselham	ditto	31	*Ipswich*
James Stewart	ditto	35	*Aberdeen*
James Roach	ditto	21	*Cork*
James Butler	ditto	32	*Dublin*
John Allen	ditto	18	*Gosport*

Wednesday the 4th, hard gales at WNW and a great sea without; served out flour and a piece of beef to two men for a week's subsistence; the weather is so bad that there is no other food to be got.

Thursday the 5th, little wind at SW with heavy rains; at six this morning went under sail, but could make no hand of it, therefore were obliged to put back again: as soon as we came to an anchor, the boatswain employed himself in making a raft to get ashore with; this raft was made with oars and water barrels, when it was made, and over the side it would carry three men; but it was no sooner put off from the vessel's side but it canted, and obliged the people to swim for their lives; the boatswain got hold of the raft, and, with some difficulty, reached the shore;

when he came off in the evening, he informed us he had seen a beef puncheon, which gave us some reason to apprehend some other ship of the squadron had suffered our fate.

Friday the 6th, this morning went under sail, the wind at WNW with fresh gales and heavy rain; the wind came to the westward, and a great sea, so that we could not turn out over the bar: in our putting back we saw the cutter, a very agreeable sight, which gave us new life; in the evening anchored at the place sailed from; the carpenter and others went ashore to get shellfish, which we stood in great need of; at night the proper boat's crew would not go ashore with the boat as usual, but made her fast astern of the vessel, with only two men in her, she never being left without four before; at eleven at night one of the men came out of her into the vessel, it blowing very hard at NNE in half an hour shifted to NW and rainy weather, that we could not see a boat's length: at two the next morning the cutter broke loose from the stern of the vessel; we called from on board to James Stewart, the man that was in her, but he could not hear us; in a short time we lost sight of her, believing she must be stove among the rocks. The loss of the cutter gives the few thinking people aboard a great deal of uneasiness; we have seventy-two men in the vessel, and not above six of that number that give themselves the least concern for the preservation of their lives, but are rather the reverse, being ripe for mutiny and destruction; this is a great affliction to the lieutenant, myself, and the carpenter; we know not what to do to bring them under any command; they have troubled us to that degree, that we are weary of our lives; therefore this day we have told the people, that, unless they alter their conduct, and subject themselves to command, that we will leave them to themselves, and take our chance in this desolate part of the globe, rather than give ourselves any farther concern about so many thoughtless wretches: divided the people into four watches, to make more room below. The people have promis'd to be under government, and seem much easier.

69

Sunday the 8th, this morning the people requested provisions to be serv'd; it being four days before the usual time, we think the request very unreasonable. We laid the inconveniencies before them of breaking in upon our stores, considering the badness of the weather, and the length of our passage; that if we are not exceedingly provident in regard to serving out provisions, we must all inevitably starve. They will not hearken to reason; therefore we are obliged to comply with their demands, and serve out provisions accordingly. Several of the people have desir'd to be put on shore, desiring us to allow them some few necessaries: we wanted to know what could induce them to request our putting them ashore in this remote and desolate part of the world: they answer'd, they did not fear doing well, and doubted not but to find the cutter, which if they did, they would go back to the northward, otherwise they would make a canoe; therefore insisted on going ashore. On their earnest intreaties, the body of people agreed to their request: we haul'd the boat close in shore; the people who chose to stay behind were eleven in number; we supply'd them with proper necessaries, and they sign'd a certificate, to inform the Lords of the Admiralty that they were not compell'd to stay, but made it their own choice, and that they did it for the preservation of themselves and us.*

A Copy of their Certificate

These are to certify the Right Honourable the Lords Commissioners for executing the office of Lord High Admiral of Great Britain, &c. that we, whose names are undermention'd, since the misfortune of losing the cutter, have consider'd the ill conveniences and difficulties to be attended, where so great a number of people are to be carried off; therefore we have requested, and desired the officers and company remaining of the same vessel to put us on shore, with such necessaries of life

---

* The fate of this group is unknown. .

as can be conveniently spar'd out of the vessel. We, of our own free will and choice, do indemnify all persons from ever being call'd to an account for putting us on shore, or leaving us behind, contrary to our inclinations. Witness our hands, on board the *Speedwell* schooner, in the latitude 50 : 40 S this 8th day of November, 1741. Which was sign'd by the following people, *viz*:

Matthew Langley, gunner's
   mate
John Russel, armourer
George Smith, cook's mate
William Callicutt, washerman
John Williamson, marine
John McCleod, boatswain's
   servant
John Hart, joiner
Joseph Turner, captain's
   servant

Luke Lyon, gunner's
   servant
Richard Phipps,
   boatswain's mate
Henry Mortimer, marine
Witness:
John Cummins, carpenter
John Snow, master's
   mate
Vincent Oakley, surgeon
   of the army

Monday the 9th, at ten at night, we weigh'd, and row'd out of the bay; at daylight got about four leagues right out, every way surrounded with rocks and breakers, with a great western swell: we found it a very difficult matter to get clear of those rocks and breakers; they reach alongshore eighteen leagues, and without us at sea eight leagues; I take it, that from the land they are fourteen leagues in the offing; those sunken rocks appear like a low level land. This coast is too dangerous for shipping, the wind being three parts of the year to the westward, which blows right on the shore, with a large western swell, that seldom or never ceases; it always blows and rains; it is worse here than in the rainy season on the coast of Guinea; nor can we as yet distinguish summer from winter, only by the length of the days. Steer'd out of the bay W by N then S by W then S. At noon I had a good observation in the latitude of 50 : 50 south; the northmost part of the bay bore NE by E seven leagues; the southmost point of land SSE twelve leagues. This coast, as far as we have come, lies N by E and S by W by the compass.

Tuesday the 10th, at four this morning made all the sail we could, steering SE in order to make the land; at six steer'd in ESE at seven made the land; at eight saw a point of land bearing SE distant six leagues, which, when abreast, seeing no land to the S I take the point for Cape Victory, and the four islands we see I believe to be the islands of Direction, which Sir John Narborough gives an account of; excepting the distance, they exactly answer his description; therefore, by the latitude in yesterday's observation, and by the distance we have run since, we are now at the opening of the Streights of Magellan. At ten in the morning, hard gales at NW steer'd SE the cape bearing E distant four leagues; at noon bore E by N distant six leagues; haul'd the mainsail down, and went under a foresail. I never in my life, in any part of the world, have seen such a sea as runs here; we expected every wave to swallow us, and the boat to founder. This shore is full of small islands, rocks, and breakers; so that we can't haul further to the southward, for fear of endangering the boat; we are oblig'd to keep her right before the sea. At five broach'd to, at which we all believ'd she would never rise again. We were surrounded with rocks, and so near that a man might toss a bisket on'em: we had nothing but death before our eyes, and every moment expected our fate. It blew a hurricane of wind, with thick rainy weather, that we could not see twice the boat's length; we pray'd earnestly for its clearing up, for nothing else could save us from perishing; we no sooner ask'd for light, but it was granted us from above. At the weather's clearing up, we saw the land on the north shore, with islands, rocks, and breakers all around us; we were obliged to put in among 'em for shelter, finding it impossible to keep the sea; we were in with the land amongst them, and compell'd to push thro', looking death in the face, and expecting every sea to bury us; the boldest men among us were dismay'd, nor can we possibly give an account in what manner we have been this day deliver'd. After sailing amidst islands, rocks, and breakers, for above a league, we got safe into a good harbour, surrounded with small islands, which kept the sea off; here the water was as smooth as in a mill-pond. We call this harbour the Port of God's Mercy, esteeming our preservation this day to be a miracle. The most abandon'd among us no longer doubt of an almighty Being, and have promis'd to reform their lives.

Wednesday the 11th, the wind much abated, with rain. This morning weigh'd, and ran farther in. In the evening we saw two Indians lying on their bellies on the top of a steep rock, just over the vessel, peeping with their heads over the hill. As soon as we discover'd them, we made motions to them to come down; they then rose up, and put on their heads white feather'd caps; we then hoisted a white sheet for an ensign; at this they made a noise, pronouncing *Orza, Orza*; which we took for a signal to come ashore. We would not suffer above two men to go ashore, and those disarm'd, lest we should put them in fear. The Indians had nothing in their hands but a club, like to our cricket batts, with which they kill their seal. As soon as they saw the two men come ashore, they walk'd away; and when they perceiv'd our men follow'd them, and gain'd ground of them, they took to their heels, frequently looking back, crying *Orza, Orza*, beckoning the people to follow, which they did for a mile or two along shore, out of sight of the vessel: then the Indians fled to the woods, still wanting our people to follow them; but being disarm'd, they were apprehensive the Indians would bush-fight them; so they thought proper to give over the pursuit, and to return to the boat.

Thursday the 12th, hard gales at WNW with rain. At six this morning we again saw the two Indians; they made the same noise and motions to come ashore; at which I went with four of the people; the Indians walk'd and ran as before, looking back, and making signs to follow, which we did till we got to the place where the canoe lay with four Indians in her. The two Indians got into the canoe, and put her off the shore before we could get nigh them; as soon as we got abreast of the canoe, they made signs as if they wanted cloathing; we endeavour'd to make them understand we wanted fish, and would truck with them; they had none, but signified to us they would go and get some: they had a mangey dog, which they parted with to one of the people for a pair of cloth trowzers; this dog was soon kill'd, dress'd, and devour'd. Here we found plenty of mussels, which gave us great relief, having scarce any thing to subsist on for this week past.

Friday the 13th, very uncertain weather, and squally; the wind variable from WNW to SSW. This morning all hands ashore a fishing. Lieutenant Ewers of the marines kill'd a large seal or sea-dog; it is exceeding good food, and we judg'd it to have weigh'd seventeen score.

Saturday the 14th, little wind at WNW and close weather, with rain. At five this morning cast loose, and steer'd south out between the islands; the weather clearing up, we saw the south shore; it first appear'd like a large island, stretching away to the westward, and at the west end two *hommacoes* like sugar-loaves, and to the southward of them a large point of rocks; steer'd SE until the point bore W then steer'd SE by E.

I took the point for Cape Pillar, and was fully assur'd of our being in the Streights.

Sunday the 15th, at three this morning cast loose, and row'd, but could not get out, so were oblig'd to put back, and make fast, it blowing hard, with thick weather all day; in the evening it clear'd up. This day several people drove a trade with their allowance, giving silver buckles for flour, valued at twelve shillings per pound, and before night it reach'd to a guinea, the people crying aloud for provisions, which are now so scarce, that several on board are actually starving through want.

Monday the 16th, at three this morning cast loose, being little wind, and steer'd up the Streights SE by E the wind at NW. At eight o'clock got abreast of Cape Monday; at nine the cape bore W distant four leagues; at noon running alongshore, made two openings, which put the rest of the officers to a stand, not knowing which to take for the right passage. Asking my opinion, I gave it for keeping on the ESE passage, the other lying SE by S. On which they said, Sir John Narborough bids us keep the south shore on board. I answer'd, that Sir John tells us ESE is the direct course from Cape Pillar; I'll venture my life that we are now in the right passage; so we kept on E by S half S. After running a league or two up, and not seeing Cape Quod, nor any outlet, the wind blowing hard, we were for running no farther, whereas one league more would have convinc'd every body; but they all gave it against me, that we were not in the right passage. The wind being at WNW we could not turn back again; so that we were oblig'd to put into a cove lying on the north shore, where we found good anchoring in four fathom water; no provisions to be got here, being a barren rocky place, producing not any thing for the preservation of life. This afternoon died George Bateman, a boy, aged sixteen years: this poor creature starv'd, perish'd, and died a skeleton, for want of food. There are several more in the same miserable condition, and who, without a speedy relief, must undergo the same fate.

Tuesday the 17th, at five this morning weigh'd, and row'd out, it being calm; at seven a fresh breeze right up the sound; we could not turn to windward not above a mile from where we last lay; we made fast alongside the rocks; all hands ashore a fishing for mussels, limpetts, and clams; here we found those shellfish in abundance, which prov'd a very seasonable relief. Just before we got in, one of the men gave a guinea for a pound of flour, being all the money he had.

Wednesday the 18th, the wind at WNW in hard squalls, with hail and snow. This morning cast loose, and stood over to the southward, believing the tide to run stronger and more true than on the north shore, hoping shortly to get out of the sound, which is not above a league in the wind's eye. At two o'clock got into a cove on the south side; made fast alongside of the rocks; all hands on shore getting mussels, and other fish.

Thursday the 19th, fresh gales at WNW with hail and snow. This morning cast loose, and sail'd out, but could make no hand of it; our boat will not work to windward; put back from whence we came, and sent the people ashore to get mussels. This night departed this life Mr Thomas Caple, son of the late Lieutenant Caple, aged twelve years, who perish'd for want of food. There was a person on board who had some of the youth's money, upwards of twenty guineas, with a watch and silver cup. Those last the boy was willing to sell for flour; but his guardian told him, he would buy cloaths for him in the Brazil. The miserable youth cry'd, sir, I shall never live to see the Brazil; I am starving now, almost starv'd to death; therefore, for G–d's sake, give me my silver cup to get me some victuals, or buy some for me yourself. All his prayers and intreaties to him were vain; but heaven sent death to his relief, and put a period to his miseries in an instant. Persons who have not experienc'd the hardships we have met with, will wonder how people can be so inhuman to see their fellow-creatures starving before their faces, and afford 'em no relief: but hunger is void of all compassion; every person was so intent on the preservation of his own life, that he was regardless of another's, and the bowels of commiseration were shut up. We slip no opportunity, day or night, to enter into the supposed right Streights, but can get no ground. This day we serv'd flour and a piece of beef between two men for a week. Captain Pemberton, of his majesty's land forces, gave two guineas for two pounds of flour; this flour was sold him by the seamen, who live on mussels. Many of the people eat their flour raw as soon as they are serv'd it. The wind and weather not permitting us to go out, the men were employ'd in getting wood and water.

Tuesday the 24th, this morning, it being calm, row'd out; at eight o'clock had the supposed right Streights open, having a breeze at WNW, SE by E through the first reach, and SSE through the second; then saw three islands, the largest of which lies on the north shore; and there is a passage about two miles broad between that and the islands to the southward; there is also another passage between that island and the north shore, of a mile and a half broad. Before you come to those islands there is a sound lying on the south shore: you can see no seapassage until you come close up with the island, and then the imaginary Streights are not above two miles broad. Steer'd away for the island SE about two leagues; then came into a narrow passage, not above a cable's length over, which put us all to a stand, doubting of any farther passage. The wind took us ahead, and the tide being spent, we put into a small cove, and made fast. At seven in the evening, being calm, cast loose, being willing to see if there was any opening; but, to our great misfortune, found none; which very much surpriz'd us. The lieutenant is of opinion, that we are in a lagoon to the northward of the Streights. This I cannot believe; and am positive, if ever there was such a place in the world as the Streights of Magellan, we are now in them, and above thirty leagues up. If he, or any of the officers, had given themselves the trouble of coming upon deck, to have made proper remarks, we had been free from all this perplexity, and by this time out of the Streights to the northward. There is not an officer aboard, except the carpenter and myself, will keep the deck a moment longer than his watch, or has any regard to a reckoning, or any thing else. It is agreed to go back again.

Wednesday the 25th, little wind, with rain. At eight this morning row'd out, and got about a league down; here we could get no ground, and were oblig'd to put back again.

Thursday the 26th, little wind; row'd out, got about five leagues down. This day we were in such want of provisions, that we were forc'd to cut up the seal-skin and broil it, notwithstanding it has lain about the deck for this fortnight.

Friday the 27th, little wind, and close weather. This morning cast loose, and row'd down; had a fresh breeze at north; steer'd WSW up into another opening on the south shore, hoping to find a passage out of the lagoon, as the lieutenant calls it, into the right Streights. After going two leagues up, saw there was no opening; put back, and made fast, where we came from; being determin'd to go back, and make Cape Pillar a second time; which is the south entrance of the Streights. Got abundance of large mussels, five or six inches long; a very great relief to us at present.

Sunday the 29th, hard gales from NW to SW with heavy rains. Great uneasiness among the people, many of them despairing of a deliverance, and crying aloud to serve provisions four days before the time. Finding no way to pacify them, we were oblig'd to serve them. We endeavour'd to encourage and comfort them as much as lay in our power, and at length they seem'd tolerably easy.

Monday the 30th, fresh gales at W with continual rain. This day died three of our people, *viz:* Peter Delroy barber, Thomas Thorpe and Thomas Woodhead, marines; they all perish'd for want of food: several more are in the same way, being not able to go ashore for provisions; and those who are well can't get sufficient for themselves; therefore the sick are left destitute of all relief. There is one thing to be taken notice of in the death of those people, that some hours before they die, they are taken light-headed, and fall a joking and laughing; and in this humour they expire.

Tuesday, December the 1st, 1741, little wind, and fair weather; which is a kind of prodigy in those parts. In the morning put out of the cove, and got four leagues down; then the wind took us ahead, and we put into another cove, where we got mussels and limpetts. At four this afternoon saw an Indian canoe coming over from the north shore; they landed two of their men to leeward of the cove; they came opposite to us, and view'd us; then went back, and came with the canoe within a cable's length of our boat, but no nearer; so that we had no opportunity to truck with them.

Wednesday the 2nd, little wind, with rain. At nine this morning row'd out, and got about a league farther down; the wind beginning to blow fresh, we put into another cove, and found plenty of shellfish, which kept up our spirits greatly; for it is enough to deject any thinking man, to see that the boat will not turn to windward; being of such length, and swimming so boyant upon the water, that the wind, when close haul'd, throws her quite to leeward. We have been seventeen days going seven or eight leagues to windward, which must make our passage very long and uncomfortable.

Friday the 4th, little wind at S and fair. This morning row'd out; at ten got down, where we saw a smoak, but no people; we saw a dog running along shore, and keeping company with the boat for above a mile; we then put in, with a design to shoot him; but he soon disappointed us, by taking into the woods. We put off again with a fine breeze, steering NW by W down the Streights. The carpenter gave a guinea this day for a pound of flour, which he made into cakes, and eat instantly. At six in the evening abreast of Cape Munday; at eight abreast of Cape Upright, being fair weather. Intend to keep under sail all night.

Saturday the 5th, little wind, and fair: at four this morning I saw Cape Pillar, bearing W by N distant eight leagues; saw a smoak on the south shore, and at noon we saw a smoak on the north shore, but we did not care to lose time: at three o'clock saw Cape Desseada, bearing from Cape Pillar SW distant four leagues; at four o'clock wore the boat, and steered ESE. The lieutenant was now fully convinced we have been all along in the right Streights, and had we run but one league further, on Monday, November 17, we had escaped all this trouble and anxiety: as for my own part, I was, very well assured, from the first entrance, that we were right; but the lieutenant would not believe that it was Cape Pillar on the south shore coming into the Streights, but thought we were in a lagoon to the northward; so that we have been above a fortnight coming back to rectify mistakes, and to look at Cape Pillar a second time: at eight o'clock came abreast of the smoak seen in the morning.

The people being well assured that we are actually in the Streights of Magellan, are all alive. Wind at WSW.

Sunday, little wind at W with rain: at three this morning abreast of Cape Munday; at six abreast of Cape de Quad opposite to which, on the south shore, saw a smoak, on which, we went ashore to the Indians, who came out on a point of land, at the entrance of a cove, hollowing, and crying, *Bona! Bona!* endeavouring to make us understand that they were our friends; when ashore, we traded with them for two dogs, three Brant geese, and some seal; which supply was very acceptable to us; we supped on the dogs, and thought them equal in goodness to the best mutton in England: we took from the Indians a canoe, made of the bark of trees, but soon towed her under water, and were obliged to cut her loose; steer'd NE by E. At eight o'clock abreast of St Jerom's Sound; at twelve, breast of Royal Island.

The Indians we saw in the Streights of Magellan, are people of a middle stature, and well-shaped; their complexion of a tawney olive colour, their hair exceeding black, but not very long; they have round faces, and small noses, their eyes little and black; their teeth are smooth and even, and close set, of an incomparable whiteness; they are very active in body, and run with a surprizing agility; they wear on their heads white feathered caps; their bodies are covered with the skins of seals and guianacoes: the women, as soon as they saw us, fled into the woods, so that we can give no description of them.

Monday the 7th, fresh gales at WNW and fine weather; at six this morning abreast of Cape Forward, steered N by E. At nine abreast of Port Famen; at twelve at noon, put in at Freshwater Bay, and filled one cask of water, having none aboard; at one o'clock put out again, steer'd N by E expecting plenty of wood and water at Elizabeth's Island; at nine at night passed by Sandy Point; it bore SSE and the island St George ENE distant three leagues.

Tuesday the 8th, at four this morning, being calm, weighed, and rowed towards Elizabeth's Island, it bearing WNW. At four in the afternoon anchor'd off the northmost in eight fathom water, fine sand, about half a cable's length from the shore, put the vessel in, and landed some people to see for wood and water: in the evening the people came aboard, having been all over the island in search of wood and water, but found none; here indeed we found shaggs and seagulls in great numbers, it being breeding time; we got a vast quantity of their eggs, most of them having young ones in the shell: however, we beat them up all together, with a little flour, and made a very rich pudding. Elizabeth's Island is a beautiful spot of ground to appearance, with very good pasture; but it is intirely barren of any thing for the support of man. This day John Turner, marine, perished for want of food.

Wednesday the 9th, at four this morning weighed, and steered ENE for the narrows, with the wind at SSW when abreast of the Sweepstakes Foreland, steered SSE on purpose to look for water; after going alongshore about six leagues into a deep bay, we saw a fine delightful country: here we saw the guianacoes in great numbers, ten or twelve in a drove; they are to be seen in such droves all along the shore for several leagues.

The guianacoe is as large as any English deer, with a long neck; his head, mouth, and ears, resembling a sheep; he has very long slender legs, and is cloven-footed like a deer, with a short bushy tail, of a reddish colour; his back is covered with red wool, pretty long; but down his sides, and all the belly part, is white wool: those guianacoes, though, at a distance, very much resembling the female deer, are probably the sheep of this country: they are exceeding nimble, of an exquisite quick sight, very shy, and difficult to be shot; at noon, finding neither wood nor water, wore to the northward: at three got abreast of the foreland, hauled in for Fish Cove, which lieth just round the eastern point; here we expected to land, and shoot some of those guianacoes; but when abreast of the cove, the wind blew so hard right out, that we were obliged to bear away for the first narrow, it being impossible to get in. At eight this evening entered the first narrow, meeting the flood, which runs here very strong: at twelve came to an anchor in five fathom, about a mile off shore: the tide floweth on the western shore seven hours, and ebbs five. This day Robert Vicars marine perished with want.

Thursday the 10th, at four this morning weighed, and came to sail; at six got out of the first narrow, hauled in for a deep bay on the N shore to seek for water: the boatswain swam ashore, and in half an hour afterwards came down on the beach, and brought us the news of finding fresh water. It being rocky ground, and ebbing water, the vessel struck; we were oblig'd, in this exigence, to slip the cable, time not permitting us to haul up the anchor; we stood off and on the shore till half flood; then went in, and took the cable on board: after landing some people with casks to fill, haul'd the anchor up, and went about two miles farther out.

Friday the 11th, at three this morning the boat struck upon the tide of ebb; it ebbing so fast, we could not get her off; in a quarter of an hour's time the boat was dry; we were favour'd with little wind and smooth water, otherwise she must have stove to pieces, the ground being very foul; it ebbs dry above a league off, and there is shoal water a great deal further out; so that it is dangerous for a ship to haul into this bay. While the boat was dry, got all the water-casks out of the hold, and put them ashore to be fill'd. At six haul'd the boat off, having receiv'd no damage; at eight, it being four feet flood, run the boat close in shore, and took off our water, the whole quantity being four tons, out of which we were oblig'd to leave two puncheons, one quarter-cask, with three muskets, a funnel, and some other necessaries; and were very much concern'd, lest we should also leave some of the people ashore. The wind blowing hard, and the sea tumbling in, we were under a necessity of hauling off, and putting to sea, for fear of losing the boat. Since we left the island where the *Wager* was lost, we have several times very narrowly escap'd being made a wreck, and some times have been preserv'd when we have seen our fate before our eyes, and every moment expected it, and when all the conduct and ability of men could have avail'd nothing. Any one, who has been a witness of those providential deliverances, and doubts the being of a supreme power, disqualifies himself from any title to all future mercy, and justly deserves the wrath of an incens'd deity. This day, at noon, being well out of the bay, and nigh mid-channel over, steer'd ENE for Cape Virgin Mary, with a fine gale at SW. At one we saw the cape bearing NE by E distant nine leagues; at seven in the evening saw a low point of flat land, stretching away from the cape SSE two leagues; at eight, little or no wind, steer'd E by S at twelve at night doubled the point, the wind at W right in the middle of the bay, where we fill'd the water; in land lie two peaks, exactly like asses ears. We would advise all vessels from hauling into this bay, it being shoal water and foul ground. As for every other part of the Streights of Magellan, from Cape Victory to Cape Virgin Mary, we recommend Sir John Narborough, who in his account is so just and exact, that we think it is impossible for any man living to mend his works. We have been a month in those Streights, from our first sight of Cape Pillar to Cape Virgin Mary. The whole length of the Streights, the reaches and turnings included, is reckon'd one hundred and sixteen leagues.

Saturday the 12th, little wind, and fair weather. At one this morning steer'd N by W. At four the wind came to NW. Tack'd and stood to the westward; the two points stretching off from the cape bore NW by W distant two leagues. At noon, the wind being at NE steering along shore from the cape, saw on the shore three men, on mules or horses, riding towards us; when they came abreast of us, they stop'd and made signals, waving their hats, as tho' they wanted to speak with us; at which we edg'd close to the shore, where we saw to the number of twenty; five of them rode abreast, the others were on foot, having a large store of cattle with them. On sight of this, we anchor'd within a mile of the shore. The cape bore WSW distant seven leagues; the swell tumbling in from the sea, would not permit us to speak with 'em; by their motions, actions, cloathing, and by their whole behaviour, we took them for Christians: it being a plain level land, they rode backwards and forwards like racers, waving white handkerchiefs, and making signs for us to go into a bay, which lay about a league to the northward; which we design'd to do on the tide of ebb. The flood being very strong against us, they waited on the shore till the tide was spent; we weigh'd and stood to northward; the wind blowing right in from sea, and a great swell, we could not clear the land; so that we wore and stood to the southward, and very narrowly escap'd clearing the breakers off the pitch of the cape, which lay about two leagues out at sea to the southward. At nine at night the cape bore W distant six leagues; stood out to sea till eleven o'clock, then wore and stood in the wind, shifting to NNE. The next morning we steer'd in for the bay, and saw those people again; but the wind soon afterwards veering to the westward, and blowing strong, we were oblig'd to bear away: we could not by any means come to the knowledge of these people; whether they are unfortunate creatures that have been cast away, or whether they are inhabitants about the River Gallegoes, we can't tell.

Tuesday the 15th, fresh gales, and fair weather. This morning saw the land; the southmost point bore WSW the northmost point NNE. At eight saw two ledges of rocks, running two leagues out from a point of land which makes like an old castle. At noon the extreams of the land bore W by N distant three leagues; had a good observation, latitude 49 : 10 S course made this twenty-four hours is N by E half E distant 104 miles, longitude in 74 : 05 W.

Wednesday the 16th, at noon abreast of Penguin Island, not above half a mile from shore. We saw on this island seals and penguins without number, the shore being entirely cover'd with them. We find the penguin exactly to answer Sir John

Narborough's description; therefore we beg leave to give it the reader in that excellent navigator's own words:

'The penguin is a fowl that lives by catching and eating of fish, which he dives for, and is very nimble in the water; he is as big as a Brant goose, and weighs near about eight pounds; they have no wings, but flat stumps like fins; their coat is a downy stumped feather; they are blackish grey on the backs and heads, and white about their necks and down their bellies; they are short-legg'd like a goose, and stand upright like little children in white aprons, in companies together; they are full-neck'd, and headed and beaked like a crow, only the point of their bill turns down a little; they will bite hard, but they are very tame, and will drive in herds to your boat-side like sheep, and there you may knock 'em on the head, all one after another; they will not make any great haste away.'

We steer'd N W by N for the harbour of Port Desire: the going into this harbour is very remarkable; on the south side lies, one mile in the land, an high peak'd-up rock, much like a tower, looking as tho' it was a work of art set up for a landmark to steer into this harbour; this rock is forty feet high. At five o'clock got into the harbour; run up to Seal Island, which lieth about a league up; here we kill'd more seal in half an hour, than we could carry off, being oblig'd to leave the greatest part of what we kill'd behind. The people eating greedily of the seal, were seiz'd with violent fevers and pains in their heads. While we were at Port Desire we had seal and fowl in abundance. The carpenter found here a parcel of bricks, some of 'em with letters cut in them; on one of those bricks these words were very plain and legible, *viz:* 'Captain Straiton, 16 Cannons, 1687.' Those we imagine have been laid here from a wreck. The carpenter with six men went in search of water; a mile up the water's side they found Peckett's Well, mention'd in Sir John Narborough's book; the spring is so small, that it doth not give above thirty gallons per day; but the well being full, supplied us. The people grow very turbulent and uneasy, requiring flour to be serv'd out; which, in our present circumstances, is a most unreasonable request; we have but one cask of flour on board, and a great distance to run into the Brazil, and no other provision in the boat but the seal we have kill'd here: nay, they carry their demands much higher, insisting that the marine officers, and such people as cannot be assisting in working the boat, shall have but half the allowance of the rest; accordingly they have pitch'd upon twenty to be serv'd half a pound of flour each man, and themselves a pound. This distinction the halfpounders complain of, and that twenty are selected to be starv'd. While we were at Port Desire, one day dressing our victuals we set fire to the grass; instantly the flames spread, and immediately we saw the whole country in a conflagration; and the next day, from the watering-place, we saw the smoak at a distance; so that then the fire was not extinguish'd.

Friday the 25th, little wind, and fair weather, went up to our slaughter-house in Seal Island, and took on board our seastore, which we compleated in half an hour's time; turn'd down the harbour with the tide of ebb; in the evening, the wind at NE could make no hand of it; so bore away for the harbour again, and came to an anchor.

Saturday the 26th, at three in the morning, sail'd out of Port Desire harbour; steer'd out ENE. At six Penguin Island bore S by E distant six leagues, and Cape Blanco NW by N four leagues. This day I took my departure from Cape Blanco; I judge the cape to lie in the longitude of 71 : 00 W from the meridian of London.

Monday the 28th, moderate gales, and fair. This day serv'd out all the flour in the boat, at three pound and half to each man. We have now nothing to live on but seal, and what providence throws in our way.

Friday, January the 1st, 1741–2, fresh gales, and fair weather, with a great sea. At ten last night shifting the man at helm, brought her by the lee, broke the boom, and lost a seaman overboard. The greatest part of our seal taken in at Port Desire, for want of salt to cure it there, now stinks very much; but having nothing else we are oblig'd to eat it. We are now miserable beyond description, having nothing to feed on ourselves, and at the same time almost eaten up with vermin.

Wednesday the 6th, departed this life Mr Thomas Harvey, the purser; he died a skeleton for want of food: this gentleman probably was the first purser, belonging to his majesty's service, that ever perish'd with hunger. We see daily a great number of whales.

Sunday the 10th, this day at noon, in working the bearings, and distance to Cape St Andrew, do find myself not above thirteen leagues distant from the land; therefore haul'd in NW to make it before night. We saw today abundance of insects, particularly butterflies and horse-stingers. We have nothing to eat but some stinking seal, and not above twenty out of the forty-three which are now alive have even that; and such hath been our condition for this week past; nor are we better off in regard to water, there not being above eighty gallons aboard never were beheld a parcel of more miserable objects; there are not above fifteen of us healthy (if people may be call'd healthy that are scarce able to crawl). I am reckon'd at present one of the strongest men in the boat, yet can hardly stand on my legs ten minutes together, nor even that short space of time without holding: every man of us hath had a new coat of skin from head to foot: we that are in the best state of health do all we can to encourage the rest. At four this afternoon we were almost transported with joy at the sight of land (having seen no land for fourteen days before) the extreams of which bore NW about seven leagues; we ran in with it, and at eight anchor'd in eight fathom; fine sand about a league from the shore; the northmost point bore about NE the southmost point about SW by S. This day perish'd for want of food Serjeant Ringall.

Monday the 11th, at four this morning weigh'd, and came to sail, steering along shore NE by E. This is a pleasant and delightful country to sail by; we kept within a mile of the shore; we saw horses and large dogs in great numbers, the shore being perfectly cover'd with them. At noon I had a good observation in the latitude of 38 : 40 S. At the same time saw ahead land, which I take for Cape St Andrew's; it is a long sandy point, very low, where a shoal runs off SE about three leagues. Sounded, and had but two fathom and half at high water. When we got clear of this, we steer'd NE into a sandy bay, and anchor'd there in three fathom and half, fine sand; the north point bore NNW the south point SE by E. Here is a great swell, and shoal water. This bay we call Shoalwater Bay.

Tuesday the 12th. Lying in Shoalwater bay, the wind at SE and fair weather. Having nothing on board the vessel to eat, and but one cask of water to drink, we put her in as nigh as we could venture; so that any person, who had the least skill in swimming, might get ashore: here runs a pretty large surf, which may endanger our vessel; this puts us to a stand: to go from hence without meat or drink is certain death. A few of the healthiest were resolv'd to swim on shore, to get water and provisions; the officers, *viz.* the boatswain, carpenter, and Lieutenant Ewers, to animate the rest, first leap'd into the water; eleven of the people follow'd them; in this attempt one of the marines was unfortunately drown'd: we toss'd overboard four quarter-casks to fill with water; lashing to the cask two firelocks on each side, with ammunition for shooting. When the officers and people got on shore, they saw thousands of horses and dogs; the dogs are of a mongrel breed, and very large. They also saw abundance of parrots and seals on the rocks, but not a bush growing on the place; they made a fire with horse-dung, and shot a great many seal, which they cut up in quarters to bring aboard. One of the water-casks being leaky, they cut it up, and converted it into fuel to dress the seal. They caught four armadilloes; they are much larger than our hedgehogs, and very like them; their bodies are cased all over with shells, shutting under one another like shells of armour. In this country thirteen of his majesty's British subjects put to flight a thousand Spanish horse. Horses are more numerous here, than sheep are on the plains in Dorset and Wiltshire. We on board see abundance of seal lying on the shore cut up in pieces; but the wind blows so hard we can by no means get at it. We think ourselves now worse off than ever, for we are actually starving in the sight of plenty. We have but two people on board that can swim; to give them all the assistance we can, the lieutenant and myself, with the rest of the people, proposed to haul the vessel nearer in, and make a raft for one of the two to swim ashore on, and to carry a line to haul some of the seal aboard: with much entreaty these two swimmers were prevail'd on to cast lots; the lot falling on the weakest of 'em, who was a young lad about fifteen years of age, and scarce able to stand, we would not suffer him to go. While our brethren were regaling in the fulness of plenty ashore, we aboard were oblig'd to strip the hatches of a seal-skin, which has been for some time nail'd on, and made use of for a tarpawlin; we burnt the hair off the skin, and for want of any thing else fell to chewing the seal-skin.

Wednesday the 13th, fine weather, and calm. At six this morning the boatswain shot a horse, and the people a wild dog. The horse was branded on the left buttock with these letters AR. By this we conjecture there are inhabitants not far off. At nine veer'd the boat in, lash'd the oars to the hatches, and made a stage to haul up the seal. The people swam off three casks of water; sent on shore one quarter-cask more, and two breakers. Came aboard the boatswain, carpenter, and Lieutenant Ewers; and four men more are getting the seal and the horse on board; which was no sooner in the vessel, than a sea-breeze came in, and blow'd so hard, that we were oblig'd to weigh; leaving ashore one quarter-cask, two breakers, and eight of the people. The wind at ESE and a tumbling sea, came to an anchor about a league off the shore; we shar'd all the provisions among the company; we still see the people ashore, but can't get them off.

Thursday the 14th, hard gales at ESE and fair weather. Last

night the sea was so great, that it broke the rudder-head off; we were doubtful every moment of the vessel's parting, which if she had, we must have been all of us inevitably lost. We were oblig'd to put to sea, not being able to get the people off. We sent ashore in a scuttled puncheon some wearing apparel, four muskets, with balls, powder, flints, candles, and several necessaries; and also a letter to acquaint them of the danger we were in, and of the impossibility of our riding it out till they could get off.

In Freshwater Bay, dated on board the *Speedwell* schooner, on the coast of South America, in the latitude of 37 : 25 S, longitude from the meridian of London, 65 : 00 W, this 14th day of January, 1741–2.

These are to certify the Right Honourable the Lords Commissioners for executing the office of Lord High Admiral of Great Britain, &c. that we, whose names are undermention'd, having nothing left on board the vessel but one quarter-cask of water, were oblig'd to put into the first place we could for subsistence, which was in Freshwater Bay; where we came to an anchor, as near the shore as we could, without endangering the vessel, having no boat aboard, and a large surf on the shore; therefore Mr King the boatswain, Mr Cummins the carpenter, and Lieutenant Ewers, with eleven of the people, jump'd overboard, in order to swim ashore, with three casks for water; in which attempt James Greenham was drown'd in the surf, off the shore: the sea breeze coming on, prevented the people getting on board the same night; therefore, on Wednesday morning, it being then calm, they brought to the beach the casks fill'd with water, with seal and other provisions in great quantities, which we haul'd on board. The boatswain, carpenter, Lieutenant Ewers, and three of the people swam off; but the sea breeze coming in, and the surf rising, the rest were discourag'd from coming off; we haul'd a good birth off the shore, where we lay the remainder of the day, and all the night. The greatness of the sea broke off our rudder-head, and we expected every minute the vessel would founder at her anchor. Thursday morning we saw no probability of the people coming aboard; and the wind coming out of the sea, and not one stick of firewood in the vessel to dress our victuals, and it being every man's opinion that we must put to sea or perish, we got up a scuttled cask, and put into it all manner of necessaries, with four small arms lash'd to the cask, and a letter to acquaint them of our danger; which cask we saw them receive, as also the letter that was in it; they then fell on their knees, and made signals wishing us well; at which we got under sail, and left our brethren, whose names are under-mention'd. Sign'd by

Robert Beans, lieutenant	*John Cummins,* carpenter
John King, boatswain	*Robert Elliot,* surgeon's mate
John Bulkeley, gunner	*John Jones,* master's mate
Thomas Clark, master	*John Snow,* ditto

The names of the people left on shore in the lat. of 37 : 25 S, long. 65 : 00 W.

Names	Where born
Guy Broadwater	Blackwall
John Duck	London
Samuel Cooper	Ipswich
Benjamin Smith	Southwark
Joseph Clinch	ditto
John Allen	Gosport
John Andrews	Manchester
Isaac Morris	Topsham

Those people had a good prospect of getting provisions, and we believe inhabitants are not far off; they have all necessaries for shooting; we hope to see them again, but at present we leave 'em to the care of providence and the wide world.* At noon sail'd hence; at four in the afternoon could not, clear the land, and

---

* See *Epilogue,* below.

were oblig'd to anchor in five fathom, two leagues from the shore; the northmost point of land bore NE by N, and the southmost point S by W. Hard gales at ENE and a great sea. At noon latitude in 38 : 00 S.

Friday the 15th, fresh gales at NNW and a great sea tumbling into the bay. We are not able to ride it out; therefore, at four in the afternoon, got under sail, and stood off to sea; the southmost land bore SW by S distant five leagues.

Monday the 18th, in the latitude of 36 : 29 S the north point of Freshwater Bay bearing SW distant forty-four leagues, we went to an allowance of water, at a pint a man per day, having on board not above twenty gallons for thirty-three souls.

Tuesday the 19th, little wind at S and clear weather. At four this morning saw breakers right ahead; sounded, and found five fathom; saw the land making like an island, bearing NE by E distant twelve leagues; steer'd N for about a mile or two; shoal'd the water from two fathom to nine feet; then steer'd NNE and deepen'd the water to five fathom. By the appearance of the land, we are well up the River of Plate, and do take the breakers for the English bank. Steer'd and sail'd all day ENE along shore; in the evening anchor'd in a fine sandy bay; saw two men coming down on horseback; the boatswain swam ashore, and got up behind one of them, and rode away to their caravans. When we made the land, we had not one drop of water on board: several people swam ashore to fill water; one of 'em, when ashore, drank very plentifully of water; in attempting to come off, was so weak, that he could not reach the vessel, but was unfortunately drown'd. Got one cask of water aboard, which reviv'd us exceedingly.

Wednesday the 20th, Mr Cummins and myself went ashore; four of the inhabitants came down to us on horseback. As I could talk Portugueze, I fell into discourse with them. They told me the English were still at war with the Spaniards; that they had two fifty-gun ships up the River of Plate, and one sixty-gun ship cruizing off Cape St Mary's; and not above six weeks ago a seventy-gun ship lying at anchor, parted from her anchors and drove on shore; that the ship was lost, and every man perish'd. They also told me they were Spaniards, Castilians, and fishermen; that they came here a fishing; the fish they took they salted and dried, then sold them at Buenos Aires. The town they belong'd to, they call'd Mount de Vidia, two days journey from hence. I ask'd 'em how they came to live in the King of Portugal's land. They said there were a great many Spanish settlements on this side, and gave us an invitation to their caravan. We got up behind them, and rode about a mile to it; where they entertain'd us with good jurk-beef, roasted and boil'd, with good white bread. We sought to buy some provisions of 'em; but they had none but twenty-six loaves, about as big as twopenny loaves in England; which they would not part with under four guineas. We being in a weak condition, scarce able to stand on our legs, and without bread for a long time, gave them their price. Their patroon told us at the same time, if it should be known that they had supplied us, they should be all hang'd. He promis'd, if we would give him a firelock, he would get us some wild fowl, and as many ducks in an hour or two as would serve all the people aboard. Mr Cummins sent for his firelock, and gave it him, with some powder and sluggs. On our coming away, finding one of their company missing with a horse, we were apprehensive of his being gone to betray us; therefore immediately went on board, got our water in, and made all ready for sailing to the Rio Grand.

Thursday the 21st, little wind at NW and fair weather. At four this morning got under sail; steer'd ENE. At twelve saw low land stretch off to the eastward, which bore E by S. At four the tide of flood flowing strong in oblig'd us to come to an anchor in a large bay, in eight fathom water; the south point bore SSW, the east point ESE, at eight at night got under sail, steering ESE.

Friday the 22nd, little wind at N and fair weather. At eight this morning saw Cape St Mary's, bearing NW distant ten leagues; at noon it bore WSW and the north land SE by E.

Saturday 23rd, little wind, and calm. In the morning, not seeing the land, steer'd in N at noon saw Cape St Mary's, bearing NW distant ten leagues; latitude per observation 34 : 53 S. At seven in the evening, being in shore and calm, anchored in fourteen fathom water, sandy ground; the cape bearing W by N and the northmost land N by E. This day departed this life Mr Thomas Clark the master; as did also his son the day following.

Sunday the 24th, the wind at S and hazy weather. At two in the morning weighed and came to sail; steering NE within a league of the shore. At three in the afternoon saw three islands; the northmost of which is the most remarkable one I ever beheld, appearing like a church with a lofty tower; at four we saw three islands more, steer'd N quarter W between those islands, until we saw the mainland. The most remarkable of these islands is about four miles from the main; they are all steep. At eight anchor'd in fourteen fathom, fine sand.

Monday the 25th, a fresh gale at ENE and cloudy weather. At nine this morning got under sail, in order to go back to those islands to get some seal, there being great numbers on the rocks, and we in great want of provision, with the wind against us. We took the opportunity of the wind back to the islands, but were disappointed, being not able to get ashore for provisions, came to an anchor in fourteen fathom, sandy ground. Hard gales at NNE with thunder, lightning and rain all night.

Tuesday the 26th, this morning, moderate gales at NW and fair weather, got under sail; after clear of the islands, steer'd NE by N keeping alongshore; it is a fine level land, and regular soundings fifteen fathom, five leagues off the land. We have no seal, nor any other kind of food on board. We have a fair wind, and not far from our desir'd port; so that we are in pretty good spirits. This day died the oldest man belonging to us, Thomas Maclean, cook, aged 82 years.

Wednesday the 27th, moderate gales at W, steer'd N and sail'd all day within a cable's length of the shore in three fathom water. We have now nothing but a little water to support nature. At noon had an observation, latitude in 82 : 40 south: I reckon myself 18 leagues from the Rio Grand, and hope to see it in the morning.

Thursday the 28th, kept the shore close aboard, and sounded every half hour, not caring to go within three fathom, nor keep without five, sailing along by the lead all night. At six in the morning saw the opening of the River Grand; kept within the breakers of the bar, having at sometimes not above seven feet water at half flood; steer'd NE by E until the river's mouth was fairly open; then steer'd N and NNW until abreast of the town; anchor'd on the east shore in two fathom water. There presently came a boat from the shore, with a serjeant of the army, and one soldier. The lieutenant, myself, and Mr Cummins, with Captain Pemberton of the land forces, went on shore with them. The commandant, the officers, and people of the place, receiv'd us in a most tender and friendly manner. They instantly sent on board to the people four quarters of beef, and two bags of farine bread. We were conducted to the surgeon's house, the handsomest habitation in the place; where we were most hospitably entertain'd. At four in the afternoon the governor came to town; after a strict enquiry into our misfortunes, and the reasons of our coming into this port, being somewhat doubtful that we might be inspectors of their coast, he began to examine me, the lieutenant having reported me to him as pilot. He ask'd me if there was a chart of the coast on board; and, if not, how it was possible we could hit the bar, and venture into so hazardous a place as this is? I told him, as for a chart, we had none of any kind; but I had a good observation the day before, that our vessel drew but a small draught of water; that we kept the lead always going, and in the necessity we were in, we were oblig'd, at all events, to venture; and if we had not seen the opening of the river before night, we must have been compell'd to run the vessel ashore. He examin'd me also concerning the places we stopt at, from Cape Virgin Mary to this port, and more particularly relating to the River Plate.

He was very nice in his enquiry of our putting in at Cape St Mary's, and of the bearings and distance alongshore from thence to this port. When he throughly satisfy'd himself, he embraced us, and blest himself to think of our deliverance, which he term'd a miracle. He offer'd every thing the country could afford to our relief; the sick were order'd to be taken care of in the hospital: he took the lieutenant and the land officers home with him; and desired the commandant to see that the rest of the officers and people wanted for nothing. Before he went he inform'd us, that his majesty's ships the *Severn* and *Pearl* were at Rio Janeiro, in great distress; that they had sent to England for men, and could not sail from thence until the arrival of the Flota, which would be in May or June. He also told us, that we should be dispatch'd in the first vessel which arriv'd in this port; for he did not think we could with safety go any farther in our own; and that there could not be found twelve seamen in the Brazils that would venture over the bar in her to sail to Rio Janeiro; therefore he order'd our little *Speedwell* ashore; this wonder the people are continually flocking to see; and it is now about nine months since we were cast away in the *Wager*; in which time, I believe, no mortals have experienc'd more difficulties and miseries than we have. This day may be justly stiled the day of our deliverance, and ought to be remember'd accordingly.

Sunday the 31st, little or nothing remarkable since the day we came in, only a wonderful change in our diet; we live on the best the country can produce, and have plenty of every thing. This afternoon the governor, commandant, and commissary, came on board, to see our little *Speedwell*; they were surpriz'd, that thirty souls, the number of people now living, could be stow'd in so small a vessel; but that she could contain the number which first embark'd with us, was to them amazing, and beyond all belief: they could not conceive how the man at helm could steer without falling overboard, there not being above four inches rise from the deck. I told them he sat down, and clap'd his feet against the rise; and show'd them in what manner we secured ourselves. The governor, after viewing the vessel over, told us, we were more welcome to him in the miserable condition we arriv'd, than if we had brought all the wealth in the world with us. At the same time he fully assur'd us, we should be supply'd with every thing that the country could afford; that he would dispatch us the first opportunity to Rio Janeiro; and whenever we stood in need of any thing, he order'd us to acquaint the commandant, and our wants should be instantly supply'd. He then took leave of us, and wish'd us well. All the deference and dutiful respect we could show him, to express a grateful sense of his favour, was by manning the vessel, and giving him three cheers. The next day arriv'd at this place the brigadier-governor of the island St Catharine; he came close by our vessel, we mann'd her, and gave him three cheers. The soldiers of the garrison, having twenty months arrears due to them, expected the brigadier was come to pay them; but when they found themselves disappointed, they made a great disturbance among themselves. I apply'd to the commandant for a house, the vessel, in rainy weather, not being fit to lie in; he order'd me one joining to his own, and gave me the key. I took with me Mr Cummins, Mr Jones, Mr Snow, Mr Oakley, and the cooper; we brought our trifling necessaries on shore, and remov'd to our new habitation: here we were dry and warm; and tho' we had no bedding, we lodg'd very comfortably. Since the loss of the *Wager*, we have been used to lie hard; at present we think ourselves very happily fix'd, and heartily wish that all the persons who surviv'd the loss of the ship were in so good a situation as ourselves.

Tuesday, February the 2nd, 1741–2, great murmurings among the soldiers; they detain'd the brigadier from going back, as he intended, this morning, till he promis'd to dispatch the money, cloaths, and provisions, and to see their grievances adjusted. On those terms they have agreed he shall go; and this evening he return'd for St Catharine's. We apprehended, till now, that the right officers were in place; but we find ourselves mistaken. Some time before we arrived here, there was an insurrection among the soldiers: their design was against the governor; but by his address, and fair promises of seeing them righted, he diverted the storm from himself, and got himself continued in his station; as were also the major and commissary. The soldiers dismiss'd the rest of the officers, and supply'd their places with their own people, tho' they were lately private men; they appear'd very grand, and were not distinguish'd in dress from the proper officers. The disturbance at Rio Grand is of no service to us, for we feel the effects of it; our allowance is now so small that it will hardly support nature; the people have been without farina, which is their bread, for some days past. We apply'd to the governor, who promis'd to supply us the next day; accordingly we went for a supply, which created fresh murmurings among the soldiers; however we got a small quantity of bread to supply us for ten days. The store-keeper show'd me all the provisions, which, considering there were a thousand to draw their subsistence from it, was a small stock indeed, and not above six weeks at the present allowance. He told me we were serv'd equally with the soldiers; and when more stores came, which they shortly expected, our allowance should be encreas'd. I think, in reason, this is as much as we can expect. The lieutenant not coming nigh us since our first landing, I went with the people up to him at the governor's, about two miles from this port, to endeavour to prevail with him to get us dispatch'd, acquainting him of the call and necessity there was for our assistance on board the two distress'd ships at Rio Janeiro. He said he had spoke to the governor, and could not get us dispatch'd till another vessel came in. I told him, as the garrison were in want of provisions, what we were living on here, would carry us off; and if any misfortune should attend the vessel expected in with the provisions, we should be put very hard to it for a subsistence. He promis'd to acquaint the governor; on which I took my leave.

February the 17th, this evening came into this garrison three seamen, giving an account of their belonging to a vessel with provisions and stores for this place, from Rio Janeiro; that they had been from thence three months, and had been off the bar waiting an opportunity to come in; that not having any fresh water aboard, they were oblig'd to come to an anchor ten leagues to the southward of this port; that a canoe was sent with those three men to fill the water, but the wind coming in from the sea, and blowing hard, oblig'd the vessel to put to sea, and leave them ashore, from whence they travelled here, and believ'd the vessel was gone to St Catharine's. The governor, not satisfy'd with their report, took them for spies, and kept them as such. However, in a day or two afterwards, he dispatch'd a pilot and two seamen for the island St Catharine, to bring the vessel round, in case she should be there.

I took this opportunity of sending a letter by them to the Honourable Captain Murray, commander of his majesty's ship the *Pearl* at Rio Janeiro; desiring them to order it to be dispatch'd by the first ship from St Catharine's to the Rio Janeiro.

Honourable Sir,

I take it as a duty incumbent on me to acquaint you, that his majesty's ship the *Wager* was wreck'd on a desolate island on the coast of Patagonia, in the latitude of 47 : 00 S and W longitude from the meridian of London 81 : 30, on the 14th of May, 1741. After lengthening the long-boat, and fitting her in the best manner we could, launch'd her on the 13th of October, and embark'd and sail'd on the 14th, with the barge and cutter, to the number of eighty-one souls in all. Captain Cheap, at his own request, tarried behind, with Lieutenant Hamilton, and Mr Elliot the surgeon. After a long and fatiguing passage, coming through the Streights of Magellan, we arrived here the 28th of January, 1741–2; bringing into this port alive to the number of thirty, *viz*:

Robert Beans, lieutenant
John Bulkeley, gunner
John Cummins, carpenter
Robert Elliot, surgeon's mate
John Jones, master's mate
John Snow, ditto
John Mooring, boatswain's
  mate
John Young, cooper
William Oram, carpenter's crew
John King, boatswain
Nicholas Griselham, seaman
Samuel Stook, ditto

James Mac Cawle, seaman
William Lane, ditto
John Montgomery, ditto
John George, ditto
Richard East, ditto
James Butler, ditto
John Pitman, ditto
Job Barns, ditto
John Shoreham, ditto
Thomas Edmunds, ditto
Richard Powell, ditto
Diego Findall (the
  Portugueze boy)

Captain Robert Pemberton, of his majesty's land forces
Lieutenants Ewers and *Fielding,* ditto
Vincent Oakley, surgeon of ditto
And two marines

All which are living at present, and waiting an opportunity of a passage in a Portugueze vessel, our own not being in a condition to proceed any farther, having no sails, and being so bad in all other respects, that the governor will not suffer us to hazard our lives in her; but hath promis'd to dispatch us in the very first vessel that arrives in this port; where we, with impatience, are oblig'd to tarry. We humbly pay our duty to Captain Leg, praying the representation of this to him. From,

MOST HONOURABLE SIR,
YOURS, &C.

Saturday the 20th, last night the three seamen which came here, as mention'd before, with five more of this place, attempted to run away with one of the large boats; but they were pursu'd and taken: their design was for the River Plate, the wind then favouring them. This is evident, that the governor was right in his conjecture, and did not suspect them wrongfully; they are now prisoners in the guard-house. The next morning I went to the lieutenant, desiring him to apply to the governor for a pass and horses for myself, Mr Cummins, and John Young, to go by land to St Catharine's and St Francisco; where we need not doubt of a passage to his majesty's distress'd ships at Rio Janeiro: that it was our duty to hasten to their assistance: that he, the lieutenant, ought, the very day after our arrival into this port, without any regard to expence and charges, to have dispatch'd a special messenger by land; and then we might have been assured of a vessel before now. The lieutenant answer'd, he had a thought of enquiring at first coming about what I had mention'd, and of going himself, tho' it cost him fifty pounds; but he was inform'd it was impossible to go by land. I ask'd him, if so, how came the brigadier from St Catharine's here? And how do people weekly go from hence thither? As for fatigue or trouble, whoever undertook to go, he must expect that; but there was no hardship to be encounter'd comparable to what we had already undergone. We lay here on expence to the king, without doing any service, and run the hazard of not only losing the opportunity of getting on board our own ships, but perhaps of missing the *Flota,* and of wintering here; therefore I beg'd he would entreat the governor to let us have horses and guides; which he promis'd to mention to the governor at dinner, and send me his answer in the afternoon without fail. I waited with impatience for this answer; but the lieutenant failing in his promise, was the occasion of my sending him this letter.

Sir,

    I am sorry you should give me the liberty of telling you, you have not discharg'd your promise, by letting us know the governor's answer to what we requested: which was, at our expence and charge, to go to the assistance of his majesty's ships at Rio Janeiro; since which time I am to inform you that we are in want of provision, having none of any kind allow'd us yesterday, and but one small fish per man for two days before.

The meaning of which I believe is owing to you, by the endeavouring, through the persuasions of the persons you confide in, to blacken us, and in so vile a manner, that you seem unacquainted with the ill consequence, which may attend the touching a man's character. We know, and are fully convinced, from what has been done already, that nothing will be allow'd or granted us but by your means: Mr Cummins and myself ask no favour from you, but to use your endeavours to get us dispatches to the ships at Rio Janeiro, where every man must give account of his actions, and justice take place. If I am not mistaken, you told me that what we were supply'd with here, was a bounty flowing from the generous spirit of the governor, and the gentlemen of the place. If this be the case, we ought to be very thankful indeed. I am surprized, sir, you don't see the grievances of the inhabitants here, and hear the soldiers murmurings for want of their arrears. If they should revolt at this juncture, we shall stand a very bad chance. I must acquaint you, sir, the vessel we came in, is not so much out of repair, but that, if you can get canvas out of the store for sails, we can make 'em, and get ready for sailing in ten days time. And if the vessel expected here with supplies comes in a shorter time, our vessel will be ready fix'd for the use of the governor; and if one vessel should not be large enough to carry us all off, we can go in company. I imagine you know of the stores being robb'd, and the disturbance among the soldiers, which must occasion uneasiness enough, without repeating grievances, where relief is not to be had. I beg, sir, you'll get us dispatch'd with all expedition to his majesty's service, that we may not lose the opportunity of joining the two ships and the *Flota*.

SIR, YOURS

The next morning the lieutenant came down on horseback, being the first time of his appearing among us since we have been here, which is above three weeks; we went with him to the commandant, who promised we should not want fresh beef and fish; but as for bread, there is none to be got. William Oram, one of the carpenter's crew, died this day in the hospital.

March the 6th, for several days the people very uneasy at the vessel's not arriving, the wind having been fair for above three weeks past, and little or no provisions in store, which makes them doubtful of any to be dispatch'd to their relief. This day we are resolv'd to go by land, if the governor will only allow us a guide; we acquainted the lieutenant with our resolution; he went with me and Mr Jones to the governor; we obtain'd leave to go, with the promise of a guide. Captain Pemberton, being at the governor's, desired to go with us; the governor told him the journey was so difficult and tedious, it would be impossible for him to encounter with it. The captain answer'd, that he had a company on board his majesty's ship the *Severn*, where his duty call'd him, and was determin'd, with the governor's leave, to share his fate with us by land; which was granted. The governor told us, notwithstanding the present scarcity of provisions in the place, that he had so great a regard for an Englishman, that whilst he had any thing for himself, we should not want; for which we thank'd him heartily. This governor is certainly a gentleman of a noble generous spirit, of exceeding humanity and goodness, and I believe him to have a sincere regard for an Englishman.

March the 9th, this morning Mr Jones went over with me to the north side, to make an agreement for six people to go to St Catharine's; while we were here, the governor received letters from St Catharine's, which gave an account of four vessels on their passage for this port; on the news of this we put by our journey: it was very lucky we had not set out on this journey before we heard the news: for on the nineteenth the vessels from Rio Janeiro arrived, and brought an account that the *Severn* and *Pearl* were sail'd from thence for the island of Barbadoes. Those vessels not only brought the soldiers provisions, but also a pardon.

On the 20th, the brigadier arriv'd, and had all the soldiers drawn up, where their pardon was read to them: he acquainted them with what money was come, which was not above a third part of their arrears, but the remainder was on the passage. The money he had for them should be paid directly, as far as it would go, if they would take it; but they cry'd out with one voice, the whole or none, and a great disturbance there was; some were for revolting to the King of Spain, some began to change their notes, and were for taking part of the money, and the rest insisted upon the whole. To quell this disturbance, the commandant, whom they look'd upon more than the brigadier, or the governor, used his utmost endeavours. They told the commandant they were no longer soldiers than while they were in the king's pay, and let those who are for the king, draw off one way by themselves; you are our commander, we trust in you to answer for us, what you do we will stand by with our lives: on which the commandant deliver'd his command up, shouldering his firelock, and took the place of a common soldier, telling them, since the king was so good as to pardon them, he thought it his duty to accept it; the brigadier was so well pleased with the behaviour of the commandant, that he ran to him, took him in his arms, and embraced him; the rest of the soldiers follow'd the example of their late commandant, delivering their respective commands up to their proper officers. This day put an end to the disturbance and confusion which had been some time among them, and restor'd them to tranquillity, good discipline, and order.

March the 22nd, this morning went to the lieutenant for leave to go in the first vessel, which was expected to sail in four days time; he told me he expected to go in her himself, and that we could not go off all in one vessel; there might be room for the officers, but the people must wait another opportunity. I told him that it was a duty incumbent on the officers that were in pay, particularly, to take care of the people; you, sir, have been sure of half pay ever since the ship was lost; we are not, but I will tarry myself behind with the people, and be answerable for them, if you'll give me a note under your hand to secure me the value of my pay, from the loss of the ship; otherwise I don't know any business I have but to endeavour to get to England as soon as I can, and will put it out of your power to prevent my going off in the first vessel. I left the lieutenant, and went with Mr Cummins, Mr Jones, Mr Snow, Mr King, and Dr Oakley to the governor, to obtain leave for our going; the lieutenant follow'd us, and said, but one half could go at a time. The governor told us it was order'd that the land officers, myself and the rest that apply'd to go by land, should be the first dispatch'd and might go on board when we would; but as the vessel did not belong to the king, we must buy provisions, and pay for our passage. I said, sir, we have not money to answer the expence: he then ask'd me whether I had not several times apply'd to him for leave to go by land at my own charges? I answer'd, we were obliged to dispose of our watches to raise that money, which will barely be sufficient to carry us six off that intended to go by land, therefore what must become of the rest who have not a single penny? And I hope, sir, that you are not unacquainted that the King of Great Britain allows to all his subjects, distress'd in this manner, five vintins per day to each man for subsistence. On my saying this, the governor call'd the commissary and major; he walk'd and talk'd with them aside; then came back again, and told us the account was so small, that it was not worth charging the King of England with it; therefore we must buy our own provisions, and pay our passage; and as to what we had received from them, we were welcome; upon which we thank'd them, and came away. We then consulted with the lieutenant, to know what could be done with the people; and that as the vessel we came in was not fit to proceed in any farther, it was to no purpose to leave her there; therefore we desired his consent to sell her, believing the money she would bring, would be sufficient to carry us all off. To this proposal the lieutenant consented. We then apply'd to the master of the vessel, to know what he would have for our passage; his demand was forty shillings per man; of which we acquainted the lieutenant, who told us he could not see what we could do, and, on second consideration, would not give his consent to sell the boat; for, when sold, he did not think she would fetch the money. Those words of the lieutenant put us all to a stand, especially after he had but now given his consent to sell her; and in so short time to declare the reverse, was very odd; tho' indeed it did not much surprize us, because this gentleman was never known to be over stedfast to his word. Seeing no possibility of carrying the people off without selling the boat, I told the lieutenant, if he left them behind, I could not think but so many of his majesty's subjects were sold; and believ'd he had made a present of the vessel to the governor. At this the lieutenant paus'd for a while; and then said, he had not money to carry himself off without selling his coat. I reply'd, there was no occasion for that, when he had a gold watch. The next morning went to the lieutenant again about our going off; he acquainted us, that the brigadier had order'd things in another manner; that myself, and nine more, being the persons desirous of going, should be dispatch'd in the first vessel, and every thing found us; that he, the lieutenant, was to tarry behind with the rest of the people, and to come in the next vessel, an estimate of the charges being made out; and also he told us, he had a severe check for requesting to go first himself, and offering to leave the people behind.

Sunday, March 28, I embark'd on board the St Catharine's brigantine, with the carpenter, boatswain, the two mates, the surgeon of marines, the cooper, and six of the people; the provisions laid in for us were two casks of salt beef, and ten *alcadoes* of farina.

Wednesday the 31st, we sail'd for Rio Janeiro, with the wind at W, steer'd SE and SE by E until over the bar; then E by N and ENE with a fine gale, and clear weather; there is not above two fathom and half water on the bar at high water; when you are in, it is a fine commodious harbour for small vessels; it is a low land, of a sandy soil: here is abundance of fine cattle; with freshwater fish, melons exceeding good, plenty of water, and the best milk I ever tasted.

Thursday, April the 8th, little wind at SW and fair weather. At ten this morning anchor'd before the town of St Sebastians. The Portugueze pilots, who have been in England, call the land here the Isle of Wight; and indeed it is very like it, tho' not so large, being only eight miles in length. This is a very secure harbour for shipping; a stranger may go in or out without any difficulty. At this place I was ashore, and think it as delightful and pleasant a place as ever I saw in America; abounding with fruit, as oranges, lemons, bonano's; also with yamms, potatoes, fish, and fowl.

Saturday the 10th, sail'd from St Sebastians; little wind at SW steer'd out SE between the island and the main; and at eight in the morning, on the Monday following, we anchor'd before the city of Rio Janeiro.

Tuesday the 13th, this morning we were all order'd before the governor. A Dutch surgeon was sent for, who spoke very good English. After an enquiry into our misfortunes, the governor order'd him to be our consul; telling us, that we should have a convenient house, with firing, and eight vintins a man per day subsistence money: he also desir'd we might make no disturbance among ourselves; which we promis'd to avoid. A nobleman went with the consul to look out for our habitation; they fix'd on a large magnificent house, fit for a person of quality. This being the first day of our coming ashore, they were pleas'd to order a dinner and supper out of doors, and sent us where we were to eat all together. This was the first time of the boatswain's eating with the rest of the officers since we left Cheap Island. The consul was so kind as to send us a table, benches, water-pots, and several useful things, from his own house; we thought ourselves very happily seated.

Wednesday the 14th, this morning the consul went with the officers and people to the treasury for our money. Mr Oakley, surgeon of his majesty's land forces, was desired by the consul to sign for it. The boatswain, who now look'd upon himself as our captain, was not a little displeas'd at this. When the money was received, the consul would have given it the surgeon to pay us; but he excus'd himself, telling the consul the boatswain was a troublesome man, and it might occasion a disturbance; on which the consul was so good as to come and pay it himself. Being all together, he told us the governor had order'd us eight vintins a man per day; but at the same time had made a distinction between the officers and seamen; that the money received was to be paid in the manner following, the seamen six vintins per man, and the officers ten. The reason of this distinction was, that the seamen could go to work, and get money by their labour; when the officers could not, but must be obliged to live entirely on their allowance. This distinction caused great uneasiness, the boatswain insisting that the people had a right to an equal share with us. The officers, willing to make all things easy, desir'd the consul it might be so. The consul reply'd, the money should be dispos'd of according to the governor's direction, or not at all. The boatswain then objected against the cooper, because he was no officer. The consul said, master! I believe the cooper to be a very good quiet man, and I dare say will take it as the men do; but sooner than this be an objection, I will pay the money out of my own pocket. The boatswain then began at me, abusing me in a very scandalous and abominable manner; saying, among other things, that the cooper was got among the rest of the pirates, for so he term'd me and the rest of the officers. When the money was paid, we acquainted the consul, that we had, till now, been separated from the boatswain; that he was of so perverse and turbulent a temper, and so abusive in speech, that we could not bear with him. The boatswain then chose to be with the people, and gave us the preference of the fore-room, where we desired to be by ourselves. There were two doors to our room; we lock'd both of them, and went to take a walk in the country: at our return in the evening, we found the doors broke open, and a small sword belonging to me was broken an inch off the point, and the scabbard all in pieces. The boatswain had in his room an Irishman, whom he sent in on purpose to quarrel with us. This Irishman and Richard East, one of our own people, fell upon the cooper and me: East chose to engage with me; he struck me several times; he compell'd me to stand in my own defence, and I soon master'd him. During this quarrel the carpenter call'd the guards; at sight of whom the Irishman made his escape. I desired the guards to secure East a prisoner; but the officer told me he could not, unless I would go to prison with him. I told him it was my desire, and accordingly I went. The prison was in the governor's house. I had not been there but a few minutes before the governor sent for me; he enquired of the officer concerning the disturbance, and order'd me to my habitation; but detain'd East a prisoner. When I came home, I found the boatswain, and two renegadoes with him, all about the cooper. On seeing me, he repeated his former abusive words. He made us so uneasy in our lodging, that, to prevent murder, we were oblig'd to lie out of the house. Next morning Mr Oakley and Mr Cummins went to the consul; he came with them to the house, where we were all sent for; he told us it was very strange, that people who had undergone so many hardships and difficulties, could not agree lovingly together. We answer'd, we never us'd to mess together; and sooner than we would be with the boatswain, we would make it our choice to take a house in the country at our own expence. The boatswain, on hearing this, fell again into his usual strain of slander and abusive language, calling us rogues, villains, and pirates. It was the governor's first request, that we might have no disturbance among us; yet the boatswain hath not suffer'd us to have a quiet minute since we have been here. The consul went with us two miles out of the city, at a fishing village; where we took a house, at our own expence, to pay at the rate of ten shillings per month, there being seven of us in all, viz. myself, the carpenter, surgeon, the two mates, the cooper, and a seaman. Here we thought ourselves safe and secure. The next day, in the afternoon, two of the boatswain's friends, which had lately deserted from his majesty's service, and an Irish clerk with them, came to pay us a visit. They were so impertinent, as not only to enquire into the reasons of the disturbance among ourselves, but they also instructed us in our duty, telling us, they came from our commander the boatswain, with orders to see my journal. I told them the journal should not be a secret to any person who could read; but at the same time I would never part with it to be copied out: they then drank a glass of punch with us, and left us. This is a place that a man is oblig'd sometimes to suffer himself to be used ill; if he resents all affronts, he runs a great hazard of losing his life; for here ruffians are to be hired at a small expence; and there is no place in the world where people will commit murder at so cheap a rate. Between nine and ten at night, three people came to our door; one of which knock'd, telling us that he was the person that was with me and the cooper in the afternoon. Being apprehensive that they came with no good intent, we refus'd opening the door; telling them, that it was an improper season of the night, and that we did not know they had any business with us; if they had, we told them to come in the morning: but they still insisted upon the door being open'd; saying, it would be better to do so, than to be taken away in three hours time. When they had said this, they went away. We did not know the meaning of their words, but imagin'd they were gone to bring some associates to beset the house; having nothing to defend ourselves with, we got over the back wall of the house, and took to the country for safety: in the morning apply'd to the consul, who remov'd us to a house in the midst of the village; he gave an account to the inhabitants of the design the boatswain had form'd against us, either to compel us to deliver up the journal, or to take our lives; he therefore desired that the journal and papers might be deposited in the hands of a neighbour there, till the time of our going off. The people of the place offer'd to stand by us with their lives, in opposition to any persons who should attempt to do us an injury.

Sunday the 18th, early this morning we were sent for to the consul. He said to us, gentlemen, as the lives of three of you are in danger, and I don't know what villainy your boatswain may be capable of acting, in regard to your peace and safety; I'll endeavour to get you three on board a ship bound for Bahia and Lisbon; accordingly he went to the captain of the ship, who consented that we should go with him, on these conditions, that the governor would give us a pass, and that we would work for our passage; this we agreed to: after this we requested the governor for a pass, which he was so good as to grant, and is as follows:

Rio Janeiro Grand

NAS FORTALESAS SEDEIXEM PASSAR

A 30 Abril, 1742

Podem passar par Portugal em qualquer nao que selle ofreser semque the ponha impedimento algum Bahia, 19 Mayo, 1742

Dizem Joan Bocli, e Joan Cummins, e Joan Menino, Inglezes de nasao, e cazados em Inglaterra, em quetem suas mulleres e fillios, que seudo officais de Calafate, e Condestavel, & Joneiro, de imadas fragatas Inglezas, dado a costa de Patagonia, the fesivel a portarem, a Oporto do Rio Grande, donde selhedeo faculdade para passarem aesta cidade. E como naferma do regimendo de son soberano nao vensem soldo, algum desde otempo, que nao pagau detta fragata, selhes fas presis a passarem a Inglaterra, para poderem tratar de sua vida em compania de suas familias; para oghe pretendem na naude lisensia passar a citade da Bahia, para da hi opoderem farer para Lisboa, na primera ocasiao, que the for posivell, e sim desda nao podem intentar dito transporte.

Quaime sedigne dar the lisensia que nas fortalesas selhe
nas ponha impedimento a sua passagem, come e costume
aos nacionaes decte reyne.

A. Rove

The foregoing in English thus:

Rio Janeiro Grand

FROM ALL THE FORTS LET THEM PASS

April 30, 1742

That they may pass to Portugal in any vessel that offers
itself, without any hindrance whatever, to Bahia, May 19,
1742.

John Bocli [Bulkeley], John Cummins, and John Young, of the
English nation, and married in England, where they have wives
and children, the one being an officer, the other a carpenter,
and the third cooper of the ship, being an English frigate,
arrived on the coast of Patagonia; and at their arrival in the
Great River, *i.e.* Rio Grand, leave was granted them to come to
this city; and as in the service of his majesty, they do not
advance any money, from the time that they paid off the said
ship, they are obliged to pass to England, that they may be
enabled there to seek their livelihood for their respective families: therefore they desire that they may pass in the license ship
to the city of Bahia, that they may from thence go to Lisbon, by
the first opportunity that shall offer; and that without the said
ship they will not be able to perform their intended design.

Leave is hereby granted them to pass by the said ship for
Bahia; and we command all the forts to let them pass, and
not hinder their passage, as is the custom of the nation
of this kingdom.

A. Rove

The following is a copy of the sollicitor's certificate:

Isto he para que todos sabem que os Senhores abaixo nomeados ye bem mal afortunados, nesta cidade de Rio Janeiro se comportarao com toda aboa dereysao nao dando escandalo apesoa alguma e sao dignos deque jodapessoa posa os favoreser emoque for de ajudo para sigimento de sua viagem omais breve possivel para Huropa.

John Bulkeley
John Cummins
John Young
Hoje 1 de Mayo de 1742
A sim que assiney este papel como procurador sosil da nasao Britanica.

Pedro Henriques; Delaed

In English thus:

These present:
Be it known to all persons, that the under-signed are in a deplorable condition in this city of Rio Janeiro; who have behaved themselves with decency and good decorum, not giving any scandal to any person whatsoever, and are worthy that all people may have compassion, and succour them in forwarding their voyage with all expedition to Europe.

John Bulkeley
John Cummins
John Young
The 1st of May, *1742*
I have signed this paper as a sollicitor of the British nation.

Pedro Henriq; Delaed

Tuesday, May the 20th, this evening myself, the carpenter, and cooper, went on board the *St Tubes,* one of the Brazil ships, carrying twenty-eight guns, Theophilus Orego Ferrara commander, bound for Bahia and Lisbon. The people left on shore were,

John Jones, master's mate
John Snow, ditto
Vincent Oakley, surgeon
John King, boatswain
Samuel Stook, seaman

John Shoreham, seaman
John Pitman, ditto
Job Barns, ditto
Richard East, ditto
Richard Powell, ditto

Wednesday the 21st, early this morning the captain came on board; on seeing us, he ask'd us, how we came on board without his leave? Notwithstanding he gave leave to the consul for our passage, we ought to have waited on him ashore. There was on board the ship a Spanish don, a passenger, who told the captain no Englishman should go in the same ship with him; therefore desired we might be turn'd ashore; but the captain insisted upon doing what he pleas'd aboard his own ship, and would not comply with his request. The Spanish don, when we came to converse with him, was very much mov'd with the relation of our misfortunes; and said to us, though our royal masters, the Kings of England and Spain, are at war, it was not our fault; that we were now on board a neutral ship belonging to a king who was a friend to both nations; that he would not look upon us as enemies, but do us all the service he could. He extoll'd the conduct and bravery of Admiral Vernon at Porto Bello; but, above all, applauded him for his humanity and generous treatment of his enemies. He made great encomiums on the magnificence of the British fleet, and the boldness and intrepidity of the sailors, stiling the English the Soldiers of the Sea. He supplied us in our passage not only with provisions from his table, but also with wine and brandy; and during the whole voyage appear'd so different from an enemy, that he took all opportunities of giving us proofs of his generosity and goodness.

Friday the 7th of May 1742, this morning anchor'd before the city of Bahia, went on shoar to the viceroy, shew'd him the pass we had from the governor of Rio Janeiro: he told us the pass was to dispatch us to Lisbon, and that the first ship which sail'd from hence would be the ship we came in; we petition'd him for provisions, acquainting him of our reception at Rio Grand, and Rio Janeiro, that we had hitherto been supply'd at the rate of eight vintins each manger day. He refused supplying us with any thing; upon which I told him, we had better been prisoners to the King of Spain, who would allow us bread and water, than in a friend's country to be starv'd. The captain of the ship, we came in, hearing the viceroy would not supply us, was so kind as to go with us to him, acquainting him how we were provided for at Rio Janeiro, and that he would supply us himself, if he would sign an account to satisfy the consul general at Lisbon, so that he might be reimburs'd. The viceroy answer'd, he had no orders concerning the English, that he had letters from the King of Portugal his master to supply the French, but had no orders about any other nation, and if he gave us any thing, it must be out of his own pocket, therefore he would not supply us; the captain then told him that we were officers and subjects to the King of England, and in distress; that we did not want great matters, only barely enough to support life, and beg'd that he would allow but four vintins per day, being but half the sum hitherto allow'd us. The captain's intreaties avail'd nothing, the viceroy continuing as fix'd in his resolution of giving us no relief; I don't believe there ever was a worse representative of royalty upon the face of the earth, than this viceroy; his royal master the King of Portugal is very well known to have a grateful affection for the British nation (nor can we believe he is so Frenchify'd as this viceroy makes him) his deputy differs greatly from him, he has given a proof of his aversion to the English. We think persons in the distress we were represented in to him, could in no part of the world, nay in an enemy's country, be treated with more barbarity than we were here; we work'd here for our victuals, and then could get but one meal per day, which was farina and caravances. At this place we must have starv'd, if I had not by me some money and a silver watch of my own, which I was oblig'd to turn into money to support us. I had in money fourteen guineas, which I exchang'd with the captain who brought us here for Portugueze money; he at the same time told me it would be hard upon me to be so much out of pocket, and said if I would draw a bill on the consul general at Lisbon for the sum, as if supply'd from him, upon the payment of that bill, he would return me my fourteen guineas, accordingly a bill was drawn up by an English merchant at Bahia and sign'd by us, being as follows:

Nos abaixo asignados Joam Bulkeley, Joam Cummins, & Joam Young vassalos de sua magg de Brittanica el Rey Jorge Segundo, declaramos que temos recebido de mam do Snor' Cappem de Mar e Guerra Theodorio Rodrigues de Faria a coanthia de corenta eloatro mil e oito centos reis em dinheiro decontado comque por varias vezes nos secorreo para o nosso sustento des o dia 17 de Mayo proximo passado athe odia prezente, por cuja caridade rogamos a Deos conceda mera saud born succesto e por este pedimos humildeme to ao Snor' Consul Geral da mesma nacao' que aprenzentado que este seja nao' duvide em mandar sattis fazer as sobredito snor'. Cappam de Mar e Guerra a refferida coanthia visto ser expendida em obra pia e que o estado da nossa mizeria, epobreza tre nao' pode pagar e por passar na verdade o refferido e nao' sabermos escrever pedimos a Gabriel Prynn homem de negocio nesta cidade e interprete de ambas as lingoas ou idosmas que este por nos fizese e como testemunha asignase.

Sao 44 100 re. Bahia 14 Setembro 1742
John Bulkeley
John Cummins
John Young
Como testamunha que fiz a rogo dos sobreditos,
Gabriel Prynn

The foregoing in English thus,

We the undersign'd John Bulkeley, John Cummins and John Young, subjects of his majesty King George the Second, King of Great Britain, do declare to have received from the Honourable Captain of Sea and Land, Theodore Rodrigues of Faria, the sum of forty-four thousand and eight hundred rees, in ready and lawful money, by different times, for our support and succour from the 17th of May instant to this present date and, for the said charity, we implore the Almighty to grant him health and prosperity. And on this account, we humbly desire the consul of the same nation, that, by these presents, he may not omit giving full satisfaction to the above mention'd captain of sea and land, for the said sum, it being employed on a very charitable account, being in a deplorable condition, and not able to repay the same; and we not knowing in what manner to write, to acknowledge the above favours, have desired Mr Gabriel Prynn, a merchant in this city, and interpreter of both languages, that he may act for us; and we leave it to him to do in this affair as it shall seem meet unto him; and as a witness to this matter he hath sign'd his name.

Say 44 100. Bahia the 14th September 1742
John Bulkeley
John Cummins
John Young
To the veracity of the above assertion I have sign'd my name,
Gabriel Prynn

Since our being here, we have been inform'd of one of his majesty's ships with three store-ships being arriv'd at Rio Janeiro, supply'd with stores and men for the relief and assistance of the *Severn* and *Pearl* (which were sail'd before in January last for Barbadoes), and that our people were gone on board of them, and bound for the West Indies.

Here is a very good bay for ships to ride in, with the wind from the ESE to the northward and westward back to the SW and wind to the southward, which blows in, and makes a very great sea. At the east side coming in, standeth Point de Gloria, where is a very large fortification with a tower in the mid'st; from this point the land rises gradually; about a league from hence is the city of Bahia; it is surrounded with fortifications and equally capable of defending it against any attempts from the sea or land.

Provisions here of all kinds are excessive dear, especially fish, this we impute to the great number of whales that come into this bay, even where the ships lye at anchor; the whale boats go off and kill sometimes seven or eight whales in a day. The flesh of which is cut up in small pieces, then brought to the market place, and sold at the rate of a vintin per pound; it looks very much like coarse beef, but inferior to it in taste. The whales here are not at all equal in size to the whales in Greenland, being not larger than the grampus. After living here above four months without any relief from the governor or the inhabitants, who behaved to us as if they were under a combination to starve us, we embark'd on board the *St Tubas* with our good friend the captain who brought us from Rio Janeiro; we sail'd from Bahia the 11th of September for Lisbon, in company with one of the King of Portugal's ships of war, and two East-India ships; but the *St Tubas* not being able to sail so well as the other ships, lost sight of them the first night. About 70 leagues from the westward of Madeira, we bent a new foresail; within two or three days afterwards, we had a very hard gale of wind, scudding under the foresail, and no danger happening to the ship during this gale. When the wind had ceas'd, and we had fair weather, the captain, after the evening Mass, made an oration to the people, telling them that their deliverance from danger in the last gale of wind, and that the ship though leaky making no more water than before, was owing to their prayers to Nuestra Senhora Boa Mortua and her intercession. That in gratitude they ought to make an acknowledgment to that saint for standing their friend in time of need. That he himself would shew an example by giving the new foresail, which was bent to the yard, to the saint their deliverer; accordingly one of the seamen went forward and mark'd out these words on the sail, *'Deal esta trinckado pour nostra Senhora boa mortua'* (which is as much as to say) 'I give this foresail to our Saint the deliverer from death.' The sail and money collected on this occasion amounted to upwards of twenty moydores.

On Monday the 23rd of November, in the latitude 39 : 17 north, and longitude 6 : 00 W that day at noon the rock of Lisbon bearing S by W distant sixteen leagues; we steer'd ESE to make the rock before night. At four o'clock it blew a very hard gale, and right on the shore; the ship lay to under a foresail with her head to the southward; at six it blew a storm, the foresail splitting, oblig'd us to keep her before the wind, which was running her right on the shore. The ship was now given over for lost, the people all fell to prayers, and cry'd out to their saints for deliverance, offering all they had in the world for their lives; and yet at the same time neglected all means to save themselves; they left off pumping the ship, though she was exceeding leaky. This sort of proceeding in time of extremity is a thing unknown to our English seamen; in those emergencies all hands are employ'd for the preservation of the ship and people, and, if any of them fall upon their knees, 'tis after the danger is over. The carpenter and myself could by no means relish this behaviour, we begg'd the people for God's sake to go to the pumps, telling them we had a chance to save our lives, while we kept the ship above water, that we ought not to suffer the ship to sink, while we could keep her free. The captain and officers hearing us pressing them so earnestly, left off prayers, and intreated the men to keep the pumps going, accordingly we went to pumping, and preserv'd ourselves and the ship. In half an hour afterwards the wind shifted to the WNW then the ship lay south, which would clear the course along shore had the wind not shifted; we must in an hour's time have run the ship ashore. This deliverance, as well as the former, was owing to the intercession of Nuestra Senhora Boa Mortua: on this occasion they collected fifty moydores more, and made this pious resolution, that, when the ship arriv'd safe at Lisbon, the foresail, which was split in the last gale of wind, should be carried in procession to the church of this grand saint, and the captain should there make an offering equal in value to the foresail, which was reckon'd worth eighteen moydores.

On Saturday the 28th of November, we arrived at Lisbon; and on the next morning every person who came in the ship (excepting the carpenter, myself, and the cooper), officers, passengers, the Spanish don himself, and all the people, men and boys, walk'd barefooted, with the foresail in procession, to the Church of Nuestra Senhora Boa Mortua; the weather at that time being very cold, and the church a good mile distant from the landing-place. We Englishmen, when we came ashore, went immediately on the Change. I was pretty well known to some gentlemen of the English factory. When I inform'd them that we were three of the unfortunate people that were cast away in the *Wager*, and that we came here in one of the Brazil ships, and wanted to embrace the first opportunity of going for England; they told me, that the lieutenant had been before us; that he was gone home in the packet-boat, and left us a very indifferent character. I answer'd, I believ'd the lieutenant could give but a very bad account of himself, having kept no journal, nor made any remarks since the loss of the ship, nor perhaps before; that we doubted not but to acquit ourselves of any false accusations, having with us a journal, which gave an impartial relation of all our proceedings. The journal was read by several gentlemen of the factory, who treated us, during our stay at Lisbon, with exceeding kindness and benevolence.

On the 20th of December, we embark'd on board his majesty's ship the *Stirling-Castle* for England: here we had again the happiness of experiencing the difference between a British and a foreign ship, particularly in regard to cleanliness, accommodation, diet, and discipline. We met with nothing material in our passage, and arrived at Spithead, on the 1st of January,

1742–3. Here we thought of nothing but going ashore immediately to our families; but were told by the captain, we must not stir out of the ship till he knew the pleasure of the Lords of the Admiralty, having already wrote to them concerning us. This was a very great affliction to us; and the more so, because we thought our troubles at an end. The carpenter and myself were in view of our habitations; our families had long given us over for lost; and, on the news of our safety, our relatives look'd upon us as sons, husbands, and fathers, restor'd to them in a miraculous manner. Our being detain'd on board gave them great anxiety; we endeavour'd to console 'em as well as we could; being assured, that we had done nothing to offend their lordships; that, if things were not carried on with that order and regularity which is strictly observ'd in the navy, necessity drove us out of the common road. Our case was singular: since the loss of the ship, our chiefest concern was for the preservation of our lives and liberties; to accomplish which, we acted according to the dictates of nature, and the best of our understanding. In a fortnight's time, their Lordships order'd us at liberty, and we instantly went ashore to our respective habitations, having been absent from thence about two years and six months.

After we had staid a few days with our families, we came to London, to pay our duties to the Lords of the Admiralty. We sent in our journal for their lordships inspection: they had before received a narrative from the lieutenant; which narrative he confesses to be a relation of such things as occur'd to his memory; therefore of consequence could not be so satisfactory as a journal regularly kept. This journal lay for some time in the Admiralty Office; when we were order'd to make an abstract by way of narrative, that it might not be too tedious for their lordships perusal. After the narrative was examined into, their lordships, upon our petition, were pleas'd to fix a day for examining all the officers lately belonging to the *Wager*. The gentlemen, appointed to make enquiry into the whole affair, were three commanders of ships, persons of distinguish'd merit and honour. However, it was afterwards thought proper not to admit us to any examination, till the arrival of the commodore, or else Captain Cheap. And it was also resolved, that not a person of us should receive any wages, or be employ'd in his majesty's service, till every thing relating to the *Wager* was more plain and conspicuous. There was no favour shown in this case to one more than another; so that every body seem'd easy with their lordships resolution. All that we have to wish for now is the safe arrival of the commodore and Captain Cheap: we are in expectation of soon seeing the former; but of the captain we have as yet no account. However, we hope, when the commodore shall arrive, that the character he will give of us will be of service to us: he was very well acquainted with the behaviour of every officer in his squadron, and will certainly give an account of them accordingly.

FINIS

The Narrative of
The Honourable John Byron

Preface

As the greatest pain I feel in committing the following sheets to the press, arises from an apprehension that many of my readers will accuse me of egotism; I will not incur that charge in my preface, by detaining them with the reasons which have induced me, at this time, to yield to the desire of my friends. It is equally indifferent to the public to be told how it happened, that nothing should have got the better of my indolence and reluctance to comply with the same requests, for the space of twenty years.

I will employ these few introductory pages merely to shew what pretensions this work may have to the notice of the world, after those publications which have preceded it.

It is well known that the *Wager*, one of Lord Anson's squadron, was cast away upon a desolate island in the South Seas. The subject of this book is a relation of the extraordinary difficulties and hardships through which, by the assistance of divine providence, a small part of her crew escaped to their native land; and a very small proportion of those made their way in a new and unheard of manner, over a large and desert tract of land between the western mouth of the Magellanic streight, and the capital of Chili; a country scarce to be paralleled in any part of the globe, in that it affords neither fruits, grain, nor even roots proper for the sustenance of man; and what is still more rare, the very sea, which yields a plentiful support to many a barren coast, on this tempestuous and inhospitable shore is found to be almost as barren as the land; and it must be confessed, that, to those who cannot interest themselves with seeing human nature labouring, from day to day, to preserve its existence under the continual want of such real necessaries as food and shelter from the most rigorous climate, the following sheets will afford but little entertainment.

Yet, after all, it must be allowed there can be no other way of ascertaining the geography and natural history of a country which is altogether morass and rock, incapable of products or culture, than by setting down every minute circumstance which was observed in traversing it. The same may be said of the inhabitants, their manners, religion, and language. What fruits could an European reap from a more intimate acquaintance with them, than what he will find in the following accidental observations? We saw the most unprofitable spot on the globe of the earth, and such it is described and ascertained to be.

It is to be hoped some little amends may be made by such an insight as is given into the interior part of the country; and I find what I have put down has had the good fortune to be pleasing to some of my friends; insomuch that the only fault I have yet had laid to my papers, is, that of being too short in the article of the Spanish settlements. But here I must say, I have been dubious of the partiality of my friends; and, as I think, justly fearful least the world in general, who may perhaps find compassion and indulgence for a protracted tale of distress, may not give the same allowance to a luxurious imagination triumphing in a change of fortune, and sudden transition from the most dismal, to the gayest scenes in the universe, and thereby indulging an egotism equally offensive to the envious and censorious.

I speak as briefly as possible of matters previous to our final separation from the rest of Lord Anson's squadron; for it is from this epocha that the train of our misfortunes properly commences: and though Mr Bulkeley, one of the warrant officers of the *Wager,* has long since published a journal and account of the return of that part of the ship's company, which, dissenting from Captain Cheap's proposal of endeavouring to regain their native country by way of the great continent of

South America, took their passage home in the long-boat, thro' the Streights of Magellan; our transactions during our abode on the island have been related by him in so concise a manner as to leave many particulars unnoticed, and others touched so slightly, that they appear evidently to have been put together with the purpose of justifying those proceedings which could not be considered in any other light than that of direct mutiny. Accordingly, we find, that the main substance of his journal is employed in scrutinizing the conduct of Captain Cheap, and setting forth the conferences which passed between him and the seceders, relative to the way and measures they were to take for their return home. I have, therefore, taken some pains to review those early passages of the unfortunate scene I am to represent, and to enter into a detail without which no sound judgement can be formed of any disputed point, especially when it has been carried so far as to end in personal resentment. When contests and dissensions shall be found to have gone that length, it will be obvious to every reader, why a licentious crew should hearken to any factious leader rather than to the solidity of their captain's advice, who made it evident to every unprejudiced understanding, that their fairest chance for safety and a better fortune, was to proceed with the long-boat till they should make prize of some vessel of the enemy, and thereby be enabled to bring to the commodore a supply of stout fellows to assist in his conquests, and share in the honour and rewards.

And yet it is but justice even to this ungovernable herd to explain, that though I have said above they appeared in the light of mutineers, they were not actually such in the eye of the law; for, till a subsequent act, made, indeed, on this occasion, the pay of a ship's crew ceased immediately upon her wreck, and consequently the officers' authority and command.

Having explained the foregoing particulars, I hope I may flatter myself there are few things in the following sheets, which will not be readily understood by the greatest part of my readers; therefore I will not detain them any longer.

The Narrative of
The Honourable John Byron

THE equipment and destination of the squadron fitted out in the year 1740, of which Commodore Anson had the command, being sufficiently known from the ample and well-penned relation of it, under his direction, I shall recite no particulars that are to be found in that work. But it may be necessary, for the better understanding the disastrous fate of the *Wager*, the subject of the following sheets, to repeat the remark, that a strange infatuation seemed to prevail in the whole conduct of this embarkation. For though it was unaccountably detained, till the season for its sailing was past, no proper use was made of that time, which should have been employed in providing a suitable force of sailors and soldiery; nor was there a due attention given to other requisites for so peculiar and extensive a destination.

This neglect not only rendered the expedition abortive in its principal object, but most materially affected the condition of each particular ship; and none so fatally as the *Wager*, who being an old Indiaman brought into the service upon this occasion, was now fitted out as a man of war, but being made to serve as a store-ship, was deeply laden with all kinds of careening geer, military, and other stores, for the use of the other ships; and, what is more, crowded with bale goods, and encumbered with merchandise. A ship of this quality and condition could not be expected to work with that readiness and ease which was necessary for her security and preservation in those heavy seas which she was to encounter. Her crew consisted of men pressed from long voyages to be sent upon a distant and hazardous service: on the other hand, all her land forces were no more than a poor detachment of infirm and decrepid invalids from Chelsea Hospital, desponding under the apprehensions of a long voyage. It is not then to be wondered that Captain Kid, under whose command this ship sailed out of the port, should, in his last moments, presage her ill success, though nothing very material happened during his command.

At his death, he was succeeded by Captain Cheap, who still, without any accident, kept company with the squadron, till we had almost gained the southernmost mouth of Straits Le Maire; when, being the sternmost ship, we were, by the sudden shifting of the wind to the southward, and the turn of the tide, very near being wrecked upon the rocks of Staten Land; which notwith-standing, having weathered, contrary to the expectation of the rest of the squadron, we endeavoured all in our power to make up our lost way, and regain our station. This we effected, and proceeded in our voyage, keeping company with the rest of the ships for some time; when, by a great roll of a hollow sea, we carried away our mizen-mast, all the chain-plates to windward being broken. Soon after, hard gales at west coming on with a prodigious swell, there broke a heavy sea in upon the ship, which stove our boats, and filled us for some time.

These accidents were the more disheartening, as our carpenter was on board the *Gloucester*, and detained there by the incessant tempestuous weather, and sea impracticable for boats. In a few days he returned, and supplied the loss of a mizen-mast by a lower studding-sail boom; but this expedient, together with the patching up of our rigging, was a poor temporary relief to us. We were soon obliged to cut away our best bower anchor to ease the foremast, the shrouds and chain-plates of which were all broken, and the ship in all parts in a most crazy condition.

Thus shattered and disabled, and a single ship (for we had now lost sight of our squadron) we had the additional mortifi-cation to find ourselves bearing for the land on a lee-shore; having thus far persevered in the course we held, from an error in conjecture: for the weather was unfavourable for observation, and there are no charts of that part of the coast. When those officers who first perceived their mistake, endeavoured to persuade the captain to alter his course, and bear away for the greater surety, to the westward, he persisted in making directly, as he thought, for the island of Socoro; and to such as dared from time to time to deliver their doubts of being entangled with the land stretching to the westward, he replied, that he thought himself in no case at liberty to deviate from his orders; and that the absence of his ship from the first place of rendezvous, would entirely frustrate the whole squadron in the first object of their attack, and possibly decide upon the fortune of the whole expedition. For the better understanding the force of his reasoning, it is necessary to explain, that the island of Socoro is in the neighbourhood of Baldivia; the capture of which place could not be effected without the junction of that ship which carried the ordnance and military stores.

The knowledge of the great importance of giving so early and unexpected a blow to the Spaniards, determined the captain to make the shortest way to the point in view; and that rigid adherence to orders from which he thought himself in no case at liberty to depart, begot in him a stubborn defiance of all difficulties, and took away from him those apprehensions, which so justly alarmed all such as, from ignorance of the orders, had nothing present to their minds but the dangers of a lee-shore.*

---

* Captain Cheap has been suspected of a design of going on the Spanish coast without the commodore; but no part of his conduct seems to authorise, in the least, such a suspicion. The author who brings this heavy charge against him, is equally mistaken in imagining, that Captain Cheap had not instructions to sail to this island, and that the commodore did neither go nor send thither, to inform himself if any of the squadron were there. This appears from the orders delivered to the captains of the squadron the day before they sailed from St Catharine's *(L. Anson's Voyage, B.1, C.6);* from the orders of the council on board the *Centurion,* in the bay of St Julian (C.7); and from the conduct of the commodore (C.10) who cruized (with the utmost hazard) more than a fortnight off the isle of Socoro, and along the coast in its neighbourhood. It was the second rendezvous at Baldivia, and not that at Socoro, that the commodore was forced by necessity to neglect.

We had for some time been sensible of our approach to the land, from no other tokens than those of weeds and birds, which are the usual indications of nearing the coast; but at length we had an imperfect view of an eminence, which we conjectured to be one of the mountains of the Cordilleras. This, however, was not so distinctly seen but that many conceived it to be the effect of imagination: but if the captain was persuaded of the nearness of our danger, it was now too late to remedy it; for at this time the straps of the fore jeer blocks breaking, the fore-yard came down; and the greatest part of the men being disabled through fatigue and sickness, it was some time before it could be got up again. The few hands who were employed in this business now plainly saw the land on the larboard beam, bearing NW upon which the ship was driving bodily. Orders were then given immediately by the captain to sway the foreyard up, and set the foresail; which done, we wore ship with her head to the southward, and endeavoured to crowd her off from the land; but the weather, from being exceedingly tempes-tuous, blowing now a perfect hurricane, and right in upon the shore, rendered our endeavours (for we were now only twelve hands fit for duty) entirely fruitless. The night came on, dreadful beyond description, in which, attempting to throw out our topsails to claw off the shore, they were immediately blown from the yards.

In the morning, about four o'clock, the ship struck. The shock we received upon this occasion, though very great, being not unlike a blow of a heavy sea, such as in the series of preceding storms we had often experienced, was taken for the same; but we were soon undeceived by her striking again more violently than before, which laid her upon her beam-ends, the sea making a fair breach over her. Every person that now could stir was presently upon the quarter-deck; and many even of those were alert upon this occasion, that had not shewed their faces upon deck for above two months before: several poor wretches, who were in the last stage of the scurvy, and who could not get out of their hammocks, were immediately drowned.

In this dreadful situation she lay for some little time, every soul on board looking upon the present minute as his last; for there was nothing to be seen but breakers all around us. However, a mountainous sea hove her off from thence; but she presently struck again, and broke her tiller. In this terrifying and critical juncture, to have observed all the various modes of horror operating according to the several characters and complexions amongst us, it was necessary that the observer himself should have been free from all impressions of danger. Instances there were, however, of behaviour so very remarkable, they could not escape the notice of any one who was not entirely bereaved of his senses; for some were in this condition to all intents and purposes; particularly one, in the ravings despair brought upon him, was seen stalking about the deck, flourishing a cutless over his head, and calling himself king of the country, and striking every body he came near, till his companions, seeing no other security against his tyranny, knocked him down. Some, reduced before, by long sickness and the scurvy, became on this occasion as it were petrified and bereaved of all sense, like inanimate logs, and were bandied to and fro by the jerks and rolls of the ship, without exerting any efforts to help themselves. So terrible was the scene of foaming breakers around us, that one of the bravest men we had could not help expressing his dismay at it, saying, it was too shocking a sight to bear! and would have thrown himself over the rails of the quarter-deck into the sea, had he not been prevented: but at the same time there were not wanting those who preserved a presence of mind truly heroic. The man at the helm, though both rudder and tiller were gone, kept his station; and being asked by one of the officers if the ship would steer or not, first took his time to make trial by the wheel, and then answered with as much respect and coolness as if the ship had been in the greatest safety; and immediately after applied himself with his usual serenity to his duty, persuaded it did not become him to desert it as long as the ship kept together. Mr Jones, mate, who now survives not only this wreck, but that of the Litchfield man-of-war upon the coast of Barbary, at the time when the ship was in the most imminent danger, not only shewed himself undaunted, but endeavoured to inspire the same resolution in the men; saying, 'My friends, let us not be discouraged: did you never see a ship amongst breakers before? Let us endeavour to push her thro' them. Come, lend a hand; here is a sheet, and here is a brace; lay hold; I don't doubt but we may stick her yet near enough to the land to save our lives.' This had so good an effect, that many who before were half dead seemed active again, and now went to work in earnest. This Mr Jones did purely to keep up the spirits of the people as long as possible; for he often said afterwards, he thought there was not the least chance of a single man's being saved. We now run in between an opening of the breakers, steering by the sheets and braces, when providentially we stuck fast between two great rocks; that to windward sheltering us in some measure from the violence of the sea. We immediately cut away the main and foremast; but the ship kept beating in such a manner, that we imagined she could hold together but a very little while. The day now broke, and the weather, that had been extremely thick, cleared away for a few moments, and gave us a glimpse of the land not far from us. We now thought of nothing but saving our lives. To get the boats out, as our masts were gone, was a work of some time; which when accomplished, many were ready to jump into the first, by which means they narrowly escaped perishing before they reached the shore. I now went to Captain Cheap (who had the misfortune to dislocate his shoulder by a fall the day before, as he was going forward to get the foreyard swayed up,) and asked him if he would not go on shore; but he told me, as he had done before, that he would be the last to leave the ship; and he ordered me to assist in getting the men out as soon as possible. I had been with him very often from the time the ship first struck, as he desired I would, to acquaint him with every thing that passed; and I particularly remarked, that he gave his orders at that time with as much coolness as ever he had done during the former part of the voyage.

The scene was now greatly changed; for many who but a few minutes before had shewn the strongest signs of despair, and were on their knees praying for mercy, imagining they were now not in that immediate danger grew very riotous, broke open every chest and box that was at hand, stove in the heads of casks of brandy and wine, as they were borne up to the hatch-ways, and got so drunk, that some of them were drowned on board, and lay floating about the decks for some days after. Before I left the ship, I went down to my chest, which was at the bulk-head of the ward-room, in order to save some little matters, if possible; but whilst I was there the ship thumped with such violence, and the water came in so fast, that I was forced to get upon the quarter-deck again, without saving a single rag but what was upon my back. The boatswain, and some of the people, would not leave the ship so long as there was any liquor to be got at; upon which Captain Cheap suffered himself to be helped out of his bed, put into the boat, and carried on shore.

It is natural to think that, to men thus upon the point of perishing by shipwreck, the getting to land was the highest attainment of their wishes; undoubtedly it was a desirable event; yet, all things considered, our condition was but little mended by the change. Which ever way we looked, a scene of horror presented itself; on one side, the wreck (in which was all we had in the world to support and subsist us) together with a boisterous sea, presented us with the most dreary prospect; on the other, the land did not wear a much more favourable appearance: desolate and barren, without sign of culture, we could hope to receive little other benefit from it than the preservation it afforded us from the sea. It must be confessed this was a great and merciful deliverance from immediate destruction; but then we had wet, cold, and hunger to struggle with, and no visible remedy against any of these evils. Exerting ourselves, however, though faint, benumbed, and almost helpless, to find some wretched covert against the extreme inclemency of the weather, we discovered an Indian hut, at a small distance from the beach, within a wood, in which as many as possible, without distinction, crouded themselves, the night coming on exceedingly tempestuous and rainy. But here our situation was such as to exclude all rest and refreshment by sleep from most of us; for besides that we pressed upon one another extremely, we were not without our alarms and apprehensions of being attacked by the Indians, from a discovery we made of some of their lances and other arms in our hut; and our uncertainty of their strength and disposition gave alarm to our imagination, and kept us in continual anxiety.

In this miserable hovel, one of our company, a lieutenant of invalids, died this night; and of those who for want of room took shelter under a great tree, which stood them in very little stead, two more perished by the severity of that cold and rainy night. In the morning, the calls of hunger, which had been hitherto suppressed by our attention to more immediate dangers and difficulties, were now become too importunate to be resisted. We had most of us fasted eight and forty hours, some more; it was time, therefore, to make inquiry among ourselves what store of sustenance had been brought from the wreck by the providence of some, and what could be procured on the island by the industry of others: but the produce of the one amounted to no more than two or three pounds of biscuitdust reserved in a bag, and all the success of those who ventured abroad, the weather being still exceedingly bad, was to kill one seagull, and pick some wild sellery. These, therefore, were immediately put into a pot, with the addition of a large quantity of water, and made into a kind of soup, of which each partook as far as it would go; but we had no sooner thrown this down than we were seized with the most painful sickness at our stomachs, violent reachings, swoonings, and other symptoms of being poisoned. This was imputed to various causes, but in general to the herbs we made use of, in the nature and quality of which we fancied ourselves mistaken; but a little further inquiry let us into the real occasion of it, which was no other than this: the biscuit-dust was the sweepings of the breadroom, but the bag in which they were put had been a tobaccobag; the contents of which not being entirely taken out, what remained mixed with the biscuit-dust, and proved a strong emetic.

We were in all about a hundred and forty who had got to shore; but some few remained still on board, detained either by drunkenness, or a view of pillaging the wreck, among which was the boatswain. These were visited by an officer in the yawl, who was to endeavour to prevail upon them to join the rest; but finding them in the greatest disorder, and disposed to mutiny, he was obliged to desist from his purpose, and return without them. Though we were very desirous, and our necessities required that we should take some survey of the land we were upon; yet being strongly prepossessed that the savages were retired but some little distance from us, and waited to see us divided, our parties did not make this day any great excursions from the hut; but as far as we went, we found it very morassy and unpromising. The spot which we occupied was a bay formed by hilly promontories; that to the north so exceeding steep, that in order to ascend it (for there was no going round, the bottom being washed by the sea) we were at the labour of cutting steps. This, which we called Mount Misery, was of use to us in taking some observations afterwards, when the weather would permit: the southern promontory was not so inaccessible. Beyond this I, with some others, having reached another bay, found driven ashore some parts of the wreck, but no kind of provision: nor did we meet with any shellfish, which we were chiefly in search of. We therefore returned to the rest, and for that day made no other repast than what the wild sellery afforded us. The ensuing night proved exceedingly tempestuous; and the sea running very high, threatened those on board with immediate destruction by the parting of the wreck. They then were as sollicitous to get ashore, as they were before obstinate in refusing the assistance we sent them; and when they found the boat did not come to their relief at the instant they expected it, without considering how impracticable a thing it was to send it them in such a sea, they fired one of the quarter-deck guns at the hut; the ball of which did but just pass over the covering of it, and was plainly heard by the captain and us who were within. Another attempt, therefore, was made to bring these madmen to land; which, however, by the violence of the sea, and other impediments, occasioned by the mast that lay alongside, proved ineffectual. This unavoidable delay made the people on board outrageous: they fell to beating every thing to pieces that fell in the way; and, carrying their intemperance to the greatest excess, broke open chests and cabins for plunder that could be of no use to them; and so earnest were they in this wantonness of theft, that one man had evidently been murdered on account of some division of the spoil, or for the sake of the share that fell to him, having all the marks of a strangled corpse. One thing in this outrage they seemed particularly attentive to, which was to provide themselves with arms and ammunition, in order to support them in putting their mutinous designs in execution, and asserting their claim to a lawless exemption from the authority of their officers, which they pretended must cease with the loss of the ship. But of these arms, which we stood in great need of, they were soon bereaved, upon coming ashore, by the resolution of Captain Cheap and Lieutenant Hamilton of the marines. Among these mutineers which had been left on board, as I observed before, was the boatswain; who, instead of exerting the authority he had over the rest, to keep them within bounds as much as possible, was himself a ringleader in their riot: him, without respect to the figure he then made (for he was in laced cloaths) Captain Cheap, by a blow well laid on with his cane, felled to the ground. It was scarce possible to refrain from laughter at the whimsical appearance these fellows made, who, having rifled the chests of the officers best suits, had put them on over their greasy trowsers and dirty checked shirts. They were soon stripped of their finery, as they had before been obliged to resign their arms.

The incessant rains, and exceeding cold weather in this climate, rendered it impossible for us to subsist long without shelter; and the hut being much too little to receive us all, it was necessary to fall upon some expedient, without delay, which might serve our purpose: accordingly the gunner, carpenter, and some more, turning the cutter keel upwards, and fixing it upon props, made no dispicable habitation. Having thus established some sort of settlement, we had the more leisure to look about us, and to make our researches with greater accuracy than we had before, after such supplies as the most desolate coasts are seldom unfurnished with. Accordingly we soon provided ourselves with some sea-fowl, and found limpets, mussles, and other shellfish in tolerable abundance; but this rummaging of the shore was now becoming exceedingly irksome to those who had any feeling, by the bodies of our drowned people thrown among the rocks, some of which were hideous spectacles, from the mangled condition they were in by the violent surf that drove in upon the coast. These horrors were overcome by the distresses of our people, who were even glad of the occasion of killing the gallinazo (the carrion crow of that country) while preying on these carcases, in order to make a meal of them. But a provision by no means proportionable to the number of mouths to be fed could, by our utmost industry, be acquired from that part of the island we had hitherto traversed: therefore, till we were in a capacity of making more distant excursions, the wreck was to be applied to, as often as possible, for such supplies as could be got out of her.

But as this was a very precarious fund in its present situation, and at best could not last us long; considering too that it was very uncertain how long we might be detained upon this island; the stores and provision we were so fortunate as to retrieve, were not only to be dealt out with the most frugal economy, but a sufficient quantity, if possible, laid by, to fit us out, whenever we could agree upon any method of transporting ourselves from this dreary spot. The difficulties we had to encounter in these visits to the wreck, cannot be easily described; for no part of it being above water except the quarter-deck and part of the fore-castle, we were usually obliged to purchase such things as were within reach, by large hooks fastened to poles, in which business we were much incommoded by the dead bodies floating between decks.

In order to secure what we thus got in a manner to answer the ends and purposes above-mentioned, Captain Cheap ordered a store-tent to be erected near his hut, as a repository, from which nothing was to be dealt out, but in the measure and proportion agreed upon by the officers; and though it was very hard upon us petty officers, who were fatigued with hunting all day in quest of food, to defend this tent from invasion by night, no other means could be devised for this purpose so effectual as the committing this charge to our care; and we were accordingly ordered to divide the task equally between us. Yet, notwithstanding our utmost vigilance and care, frequent robberies were committed upon our trust, the tent being accessible in more than one place. And one night, when I had the watch, hearing a stir within, I came unawares upon the thief, and presenting a pistol to his breast, obliged him to submit to be tied up to a post, till I had an opportunity of securing him more effectually. Depredations continued to be made on our reserved stock, notwithstanding the great hazard attending such attempts; for our common safety made it necessary to punish them with the utmost rigour. This will not be wondered at, when it is known how little the allowance which might consistently be dispensed from thence, was proportionable to our common exigencies; so that our daily and nightly task of roving after food, was not in the least relaxed thereby; and all put together was so far from answering our necessities, that many at this time perished with hunger. A boy, when no other eatables could be found, having picked up the liver of one of the drowned men (whose carcase had been torn to pieces by the force with which the sea drove it among the rocks) was with much difficulty withheld from making a meal of it. The men were so assiduous in their research after the few things which drove from the wreck, that in order to have no sharers of their good fortune, they examined the shore no less by night than by day; so that many of those who were less alert, or not so fortunate as their neighbours, perished with hunger, or were driven to the last extremity. It must be observed that on the 14th of May we were cast away, and it was not till the 25th of this month, that provision was served regularly from the store tent.

The land we were now settled upon was about 90 leagues to the northward of the western mouth of the Streights of Magellan, in the latitude of between 47 and 48° south, from whence we could plainly see the Cordilleras; and by two lagoons on the north and south of us, stretching towards those mountains, we conjectured it was an island. But as yet we had no means of informing ourselves perfectly, whether it was an island or the main; for besides that the inland parts at little distance from us seemed impracticable, from the exceeding great thickness of the wood, we had hitherto been in such confusion and want (each finding full employment for his time, in scraping together a wretched subsistence, and providing shelter against the cold and rain) that no party could be formed to go upon discoveries. The climate and season too were utterly unfavourable to adventures, and the coast, as far as our eye could stretch seaward, a scene of such dismal breakers as would discourage the most daring from making attempts in small boats. Nor were we assisted in our inquiries by any observation that could be made from that eminence we called Mount Misery, toward land, our prospect that way being intercepted by still higher hills and lofty woods: we had therefore no other expedient, by means of which to come at this knowledge, but by fitting out one of our ship's boats upon some discovery, to inform us of our situation. Our long-boat was still on board the wreck; therefore a number of hands were now dispatched to cut the gunwale of the ship, in order to get her out. Whilst we were employed in this business, there appeared three canoes of Indians paddling towards us: they had come round the point from the southern lagoons. It was some time before we could prevail upon them to lay aside their fears and approach us; which at length they were induced to do by the signs of friendship we made them, and by shewing some balegoods, which they accepted, and suffered themselves to be conducted to the captain, who made them, likewise, some presents. They were strangely affected with the novelty thereof; but chiefly when shewn the looking-glass, in which the beholder could not conceive it to be his own face that was represented, but that of some other behind it, which he therefore went round to the back of the glass to find out.

These people were of a small stature, very swarthy, having long, black, course hair, hanging over their faces. It was evident, from their great surprise, and every part of their behaviour, as well as their not having one thing in their possession which could be derived from white people, that they had never seen such. Their cloathing was nothing but a bit of some beast's skin about their waists, and something woven from feathers over the shoulders; and as they uttered no word of any language we had ever heard, nor had any method of making themselves understood, we presumed they could have no intercourse with Europeans. These savages, who, upon their departure, left us a few mussles, returned in two days, and surprised us by bringing three sheep. From whence they could procure these animals in a part of the world so distant from any Spanish settlement, cut off from all communication with the Spaniards by an inaccessible coast and unprofitable country, is difficult to conceive.

Certain it is, that we saw no such creatures, nor ever heard of any such, from the Streights of Magellan, till we got into the neighbourhood of Chiloe: it must be by some strange accident that these creatures came into their possession; but what that was we never could learn from them. At this interview we bartered with them for a dog or two, which we roasted and eat. In a few days after, they made us another visit, and, bringing their wives with them, took up their abode with us for some days; then again left us.

Whenever the weather permitted, which was now grown something drier, but exceeding cold, we employed ourselves about the wreck, from which we had, at sundry times, recovered several articles of provision and liquor: these were deposited in the store tent. Ill-humour and discontent, from the difficulties we laboured under in procuring subsistence, and the little prospect there was of any amendment in our condition, was now breaking out apace. In some it shewed itself by a separation of settlement and habitation; in others, by a resolution of leaving the captain entirely, and making a wild journey by themselves, without determining upon any plan whatever. For my own part, seeing it was the fashion, and liking none of their parties, I built a little hut just big enough for myself and a poor Indian dog I found in the woods, who could shift for himself along shore, at low water, by getting limpets. This creature grew so fond of me and faithful, that he would suffer nobody to come near the hut without biting them. Besides those seceders I mentioned, some laid a scheme of deserting us entirely: these were in number ten; the greatest part of them a most desperate and abandoned crew, who, to strike a notable stroke before they went off, placed half a barrel of gunpowder close to the captain's hut, laid a train to it, and were just preparing to perpetrate their wicked design of blowing up their commander, when they were with difficulty dissuaded from it by one who had some bowels and remorse of conscience left in him. These wretches, after rambling some time in the woods, and finding it impracticable to get off, for they were then convinced that we were not upon the main, as they had imagined when they first left us, but upon an island within four or five leagues of it, returned and settled about a league from us; however, they were still determined, as soon as they could procure craft fit for their purpose, to get to the main. But before they could effect this, we found means to prevail upon the armourer, and one of the carpenter's crew, two very useful men to us, who had imprudently joined them, to come over again to their duty. The rest (one or two excepted) having built a punt, and converted the hull of one of the ship's masts into a canoe, went away up one of the lagoons, and never were heard of more.

These being a desperate and factious set, did not distress us much by their departure, but rather added to our future security: one in particular, James Mitchell by name, we had all the reason in the world to think, had committed no less than two murders since the loss of our ship; one on the person found strangled on board, another on the body of a man whom we discovered among some bushes upon Mount Misery, stabbed in several places, and shockingly mangled. This diminution of our number was succeeded by an unfavourable accident much more affecting in its consequences, I mean the death of Mr Cozens, midshipman; in relating which, with the necessary impartiality and exactness, I think myself obliged to be more than ordinary particular. Having one day, among other things, got a cask of pease out of the wreck, about which I was almost constantly employed, I brought it to shore in the yawl, when, having landed it, the captain came down upon the beach, and bid me to go up to some of the tents, and order hands to come down and roll it up; but finding none except Mr Cozens, I delivered him the orders, who immediately came down to the captain, where I left them when I returned to the wreck. Upon my coming on shore again, I found that Mr Cozens was put under confinement by the captain, for being drunk and giving him abusive language; however, he was soon after released. A day or two after, he had some dispute with the surgeon, and came to blows: all these things incensed the captain greatly against him. I believe this unfortunate man was kept warm with liquor, and set on by some ill-designed persons; for, when sober, I never knew a better natured man, or more inoffensive. Some little time after, at the hour of serving provisions, Mr Cozens was at the store-tent; and having, it seems, lately had a quarrel with the purser, and now some words arising between them, the latter told him he was come to mutiny; and without any further ceremony, fired a pistol at his head, which narrowly missed him. The captain, hearing the report of the pistol, and perhaps the purser's words, that Cozens was come to mutiny, ran out of his hut with a cocked pistol, and, without asking any questions, immediately shot him through the head. I was at this time in my hut, as the weather was extremely bad; but running out upon the alarm of this firing, the first thing I saw was Mr Cozens on the ground weltering in his blood: he was sensible, and took me by the hand, as he did several others, shaking his head, as if he meant to take leave of us. If Mr Cozens' behaviour to the captain was indecent and provoking, the captain's, on the other hand, was rash and hasty: if the first was wanting in that respect and observance which is due from a petty officer to his commander, the latter was still more unadvised in the method he took for the enforcement of his authority; of which, indeed, he was jealous to the last degree, and which he saw daily declining, and ready to be trampled upon. His mistaken apprehension of a mutinous design in Mr Cozens, the sole motive of his rash action, was so far from answering the end he proposed by it, that the men, who before were much dissatisfied and uneasy, were by this unfortunate step, thrown almost into open sedition and revolt. It was evident that the people, who ran out of their tents, alarmed by the report of fire-arms, though they disguised their real sentiments for the present, were extremely affected with this catastrophe of Mr Cozens (for he was greatly beloved by them) their minds were now exasperated, and it was to be apprehended, that their resentment, which was smothered for the present, would shortly shew itself in some desperate enterprise. The unhappy victim, who lay weltering in his blood before them, seemed to absorb their whole attention; the eyes of all were fixed upon him; and visible marks of the deepest concern appeared in the countenances of the spectators. The persuasion the captain was under, at the time he shot Mr Cozens, that his intentions were mutinous, together with a jealousy of the diminution of his authority, occasioned also his behaving with less compassion and tenderness towards him afterwards, than was consistent with the unhappy condition of the poor sufferer: for when it was begged as a favour by his mess-mates, that Mr Cozens might be removed to their tent, though a necessary thing in his dangerous situation, yet it was not permitted; but the poor wretch was suffered to languish on the ground some days, with no other covering than a bit of canvass, thrown over some bushes, where he died. But to return to our story: the captain, addressing himself to the people thus assembled, told them, that it was his resolution to maintain his command over them as usual, which still remained in as much force as ever; and then ordered them all to return to their respective tents, with which order they instantly complied. Now we had saved the long-boat from the wreck, and got it in our possession, there was nothing that seemed so necessary towards the advancing our delivery from this desolate place, as the new modelling this vessel so as to have room for all those who were inclined to go off in her, and to put her in a condition to bear the stormy seas we must of course encounter. We, therefore, hailed her up, and having placed her upon blocks, sawed her in two, in order to lengthen her about twelve feet by the keel. For this purpose, all those who could be spared from the more immediate task of procuring subsistence, were employed in fitting and shaping timber as the carpenter directed them; I say, in procuring subsistence, because the weather lately having been very tempestuous, and the wreck working much, had disgorged a great part of her contents, which were every where dispersed about the shore.

We now sent frequent parties up the lagoons, which sometimes succeeded in getting some sea-fowl for us. The Indians appearing again in the offing, we put off our yawl, in order to frustrate any design they might have of going up the lagoon towards the deserters, who would have availed themselves of some of their canoes to have got upon the main. Having conducted them in, we found that their intention was to settle among us, for they had brought their wives and children with them, in all about fifty persons, who immediately set about building themselves wigwams, and seemed much reconciled to our company; and, could we have entertained them as we ought, they would have been of great assistance to us, who were extremely put to it to subsist ourselves, being a hundred in number; but the men, now subject to little or no controul, endeavoured to seduce their wives, which gave the Indians such offence, that in a short time they found means to depart, taking every thing along with them; and we being sensible of the cause, never expected to see them return again. The carpenter having made some progress in his work upon the long-boat, in which he was enabled to proceed tolerably, by the tools and other articles of his business retrieved from the wreck, the men began to think of the course they should take to get home; or rather, having borrowed Sir John Narborough's *Voyage* of Captain Cheap, by the application of Mr Bulkeley, which book he saw me reading one day in my tent, they immediately upon perusing it, concluded upon making their voyage home by the Streights of Magellan. This plan was proposed to the captain, who by no means approved of it, his design being to go northwards, with a view of seizing a ship of the enemy's, by which means he might join the commodore: at present, therefore, here it rested. But the men were in high spirits from the prospect they had of getting off in the long-boat, overlooking all the difficulties and hazards of a voyage almost impracticable, and caressing the carpenter, who indeed was an excellent workman, and deserved all the encouragement they could give him. The Indians having left us, and the weather continuing tempestuous and rainy, the distresses of the people for want of food, became insupportable. Our number, which was at first 145, was now reduced to 100, and chiefly by famine, which put the rest upon all shifts and devices to support themselves. One day when I was at home in my hut with my Indian dog, a party came to my door, and told me their necessities were such, that they must eat the creature or starve. Though their plea was urgent, I could not help using some arguments to endeavour to dissuade them from killing him, as his faithful services and fondness deserved it at my hands; but, without weighing any arguments, they took him away by force and killed him; upon which, thinking that I had at least as good a right to share as the rest, I sat down with them, and partook of their repast. Three weeks after that I was glad to make a meal of his paws and skin, which, upon recollecting the spot where they had killed him, I found thrown aside and rotten. The pressing calls of hunger drove our men to their wits end, and put them upon a variety of devices to satisfy it. Among the ingenious this way, one Phips, a boatswain's mate, having got a water puncheon, scuttled it; then lashing two logs, one on each side, set out in quest of adventures in this extraordinary and original piece of imbarkation. By this means, he would frequently, when all the rest were starving, provide himself with wild-fowl; and it must have been very bad weather indeed which could deter him from putting out to sea when his occasions required. Sometimes he would venture far out in the offing, and be absent the whole day: at last it was his misfortune, at a great distance from shore, to be overset by a heavy sea: but being near a rock, tho' no swimmer, he managed so as to scramble to it, and, with great difficulty, ascended it: there he remained two days with very little hopes of any relief, for he was too far off to be seen from shore; but fortunately a boat, having put off and gone in quest of wild-fowl that way, discovered him making such signals as he was able, and brought him back to the island. But this accident did not so discourage him, but that soon after, having procured an ox's hide, used on board for sifting powder, and called a gunner's hide, by the assistance of some hoops he form'd something like a canoe, in which he made several successful voyages. When the weather would permit us, we seldom failed of getting some wild-fowl, though never in any plenty, by putting off with our boats; but this most inhospitable climate is not only deprived of the sun for the most part, by a thick, rainy atmosphere, but is also visited by almost incessant tempests. It must be confessed, we reaped some benefit from these hard gales and overgrown seas, which drove several things ashore; but there was no dependence on such accidental relief; and we were always alert to avail ourselves of every interval of fair weather, though so little to be depended on, that we were often unexpectedly, and to our peril, overtaken by a sudden change. In one of our excursions I, with two more, in a wretched punt of our own making, had no sooner landed at our station upon a high rock, than the punt was driven loose by a sudden squall; and had not one of the men, at the risk of his life, jumped into the sea, and swam on board her, we must in all probability have perished; for we were more than three leagues from the island at the time. Among the birds we generally shot, was the painted goose, whose plumage is variegated with the most lively colours; and a bird much larger than a goose, which we called the race-horse, from the velocity with which it moved upon the face of the water, in a sort of half flying, half running motion. But we were not so successful in our endeavours by land; for though we sometimes got pretty far into the woods, we met with very few birds in all our walks. We never saw but three woodcocks, two of which were killed by Mr Hamilton, and one by myself. These, with some humming birds, and a large kind of robin red-breast, were the only feathered inhabitants of this island, excepting a small bird, with two very long feathers in his tail, which was generally seen amongst the rocks, and was so tame that I have had them rest upon my shoulders whilst I have been gathering shellfish. Indeed, we were visited by many birds of prey, some very large; but these only occasionally, and, as we imagined, allured by some dead whale in the neighbourhood, which was once seen. However, if we were so fortunate as to kill one of them, we thought ourselves very well off. In one of my walks, seeing a bird of this latter kind upon an eminence, I endeavoured to come upon it unperceived with my gun, by means of the woods which lay at the back of that eminence; but when I had proceeded so far in the wood as to think I was in a line with it, I heard a growling close by me, which made me think it advisable to retire as soon as possible: the woods were so gloomy I could see nothing; but as I retired, this noise followed me close till I had got out of them. Some of our men did assure me, that they had seen a very large beast in the woods; but their description of it was too imperfect to be relied upon. The wood here is chiefly of the aromatic kind; the iron wood, a wood of a very deep red hue, and another of an exceeding bright yellow. All the low spots are very swampy; but what we thought strange, upon the summits of the highest hills were found beds of shells, a foot or two thick.

The long-boat being near finished, some of our company were selected to go out in the barge, in order to reconnoitre the coast to the southward, which might assist us in the navigation we were going upon. This party consisted of Mr Bulkely, Mr Jones, the purser, myself, and ten men. The first night we put into a good harbour, a few leagues to the southward of Wager's Island; where finding a large bitch big with puppies, we regaled upon them. In this expedition we had our usual bad weather, and breaking seas, which were grown to such a height he third day, that we were obliged, through distress, to push in at the first inlet we saw at hand. This we had no sooner entered, than we were presented with a view of a fine bay, in which, having secured the barge, we went ashore; but the weather being very rainy, and finding nothing to subsist upon, we pitched a bell tent, which we had brought with us, in the wood opposite to where the barge lay. As this tent was not large enough to contain us all, I proposed to four of the people, to go to the end of the bay, about two miles distant from the bell tent, to occupy the skeleton of an old Indian wigwam, which I had discovered in a walk that way upon our first landing. This we covered to windward with seaweed; and, lighting a fire, laid ourselves down, in hopes of finding a remedy for our hunger in sleep; but we had not long composed ourselves before one of our company was disturbed by the blowing of some animal at his face, and, upon opening his eyes, was not a little astonished to see, by the glimmering of the fire, a large beast standing over him. He had presence of mind enough to snatch a brand from the fire, which was now very low, and thrust it at the nose of the animal, who thereupon made off: this done, the man awoke us, and related, with horror in his countenance, the narrow escape he had of being devoured. But though we were under no small apprehensions of another visit from this animal, yet our fatigue and heaviness was greater than our fears; and we once more composed ourselves to rest, and slept the remainder of the night without any further disturbance. In the morning, we were not a little anxious to know how our companions had fared; and this anxiety was increased, upon tracing the footsteps of the beast in the sand, in a direction towards the bell tent. The impression was deep and plain, of a large round foot well furnished with claws. Upon our acquainting the people in the tent with the circumstances of our story, we found that they too, had been visited by the same unwelcome guest, which they had driven away by much the same expedient. We now returned from this cruise, with a strong gale, to Wager's Island, having found it impracticable to make farther discoveries in the barge, on so dangerous a coast, and in such heavy seas. Here we soon discovered, by the quarters of dogs hanging up, that the Indians had brought a fresh supply to our market. Upon inquiry, we found that there had been six canoes of them, who, among other methods of taking fish, had taught their dogs to drive the fish into a corner of some pond, or lake, from whence they were easily taken out, by the skill and address of these savages. The old cabal, during our absence, had been frequently revived; the debates of which generally ended in riot and drunkenness. This cabal was chiefly held in a large tent, which the people belonging to it had taken some pains to make snug and convenient, and lined with bales of broad cloth driven from the wreck. Eighteen of the stoutest fellows of the ship's company had possession of this tent, from whence were dispatched committees to the captain, with the resolutions they had taken with regard to their departure; but oftener for liquor. Their determination was to go in the longboat to the southward by the Streights of Magellan; and the point they were labouring, was to prevail upon the captain to accompany them. But though he had fixed upon a quite different plan, which was to go to the northward, yet he thought it politic, at present seemingly to acquiesce with them, in order to keep them quiet. When they began to stipulate with him, that he should be under some restrictions in point of command, and should do nothing without consulting his officers, he insisted upon the full exercise of his authority, as before. This broke all measures between them, and they were from this time determined he should go with them, whether he would or no. A better pretence they could not have for effecting this design, than the unfortunate affair of Mr Cozens; which they therefore made use of for seizing his person, and putting him under confinement, in order to bring him to his trial in England. The long-boat was now launched, and ready for sailing, and all the men imbarked, except Captain Pemberton, with a party of marines, who drew them up upon the beach with intent to conduct Captain Cheap on board; but he was at length persuaded to desist from this resolution by Mr Bulkely. The men too, finding they were straitened for room, and that their stock of provision would not admit of taking supernumeraries aboard, were now no less strenuous for his enlargement, and being left to his option of staying behind. Therefore, after having distributed their share in the reserved stock of provision, which was very small, we departed, leaving Captain Cheap, Mr Hamilton of the marines, and the surgeon upon the island. I had all along been in the dark as to the turn this matter would take; and not in the least suspecting but that it was determined Captain Cheap should be taken with us, readily imbarked under that persuasion; but when I found that this design, which was so seriously carried on to the last, was suddenly dropped, I was determined, upon the first opportunity, to leave them, which was at that instant impossible for me to do, the long-boat lying some distance offshore, at anchor. We were in all eighty-one, when we left the island, distributed into the long-boat, cutter, and barge; fifty-nine on board the first; twelve in the second; in the last, ten. It was our purpose to put into some harbour, if possible, every evening, as we were in no condition to keep those terrible seas long; for without other assistance our stock of provisions was no more than might have been consumed in a few days; our water was chiefly contained in a few powder-barrels; our flour was to be lengthened out by a mixture of seaweed; and our other supplies depended upon the success of our guns, and industry among the rocks. Captain Pemberton having brought on board his men, we weighed; but by a sudden squall of wind having split our foresail, we with difficulty cleared the rocks, by means of our boats, bore away for a sandy bay, on the south side of the lagoon, and anchored in ten fathom. The next morning we got under weigh; but it blowing hard at W by N with a great swell, put into a small bay again, well sheltered by a ledge of rocks without us. At this time, it was thought necessary to send the barge away back to Cheap's Bay, for some spare canvas, which was imagined would be soon wanted. I thought this a good opportunity of returning, and therefore made one with those who went upon this business in the barge. We were no sooner clear of the longboat, than all those in the barge with me declared they had the same intention. When we arrived at the island, we were extremely welcome to Captain Cheap. The next day, I asked him leave to try if I could prevail upon those in the long-boat to give us our share of provision: this he granted; but said, if we went in the barge, they would certainly take her from us. I told him my design was to walk it, and only desired the barge might land me upon the main, and wait for me till I came back. I had the most dreadful journey of it imaginable, through thick woods and swamps all the way; but I might as well have spared myself that trouble, as it was to no manner of purpose; for they would not give me, nor any one of us that left them, a single ounce of provisions of any kind. I therefore returned, and after that made a second attempt; but all in vain. They even threatened, if we did not return with the barge, they would fetch her by force. It is impossible to conceive the distressed situation we were now in, at the time of the long-boat's departure. I don't mention this event as the occasion of it; by which, if we who were left on the island experienced any alteration at all, it was for the better; and which, in all probability, had it been deferred, might have been fatal to the greatest part of us; but, at this time, the subsistence on which we had hitherto depended chiefly, which was the shellfish, were every where, along shore, eat up; and as to stock saved from the wreck, it may be guessed what the amount of that might be, when the share allotted to the captain, Lieutenant Hamilton, and the surgeon, was no more than six pieces of beef, as many of pork, and ninety pounds of flour. As to myself, and those that left the long-boat, it was the least revenge they thought they could take of us to withhold our provision from us, though, at the same time, it was hard and unjust. For a day or two after our return, there was some little pittance dealt out to us, yet it was upon the foot of favour; and we were soon left to our usual industry for a farther supply. This was now exerted to very little purpose, for the reason before assigned: to which may be added, the wreck was now blown up, all her upper works gone, and no hopes of any valuable driftage from her for the future. A weed, called slaugh, fried in the tallow of some candles we had saved, and wild sellery, were our only fare; by which our strength was so much impaired, that we could scarcely crawl. It was my misfortune too to labour under a severe flux, by which I was reduced to a very feeble state; so that in attempting to traverse the rocks in search of shellfish, I fell from one into very deep water, and with difficulty saved my life by swimming. As the captain was now freed, by the departure of the long boat, from the riotous applications, menaces, and disturbance of an unruly crew, and left at liberty to follow the plan he had resolved upon, of going northward, he began to think seriously of putting it in execution; in order to which, a message was sent to the deserters, who had seated themselves on the other side of the neighbouring lagoon, to sound them, whether they were inclined to join the captain in his undertaking; and if they were, to bring them over to him. For this sett, the party gone off in the long-boat, had left an half allowance proportion of the common stock of provision. These men, upon the proposal, readily agreed to join their commander; and being conducted to him, increased our number to twenty. The boats which remained in our possession to carry off all these people were only the barge and yawl, two very creazy bottoms; the broadside of the last was entirely out, and the first had suffered much in a variety of bad weather she had gone through, and was much out of repair. And now as our carpenter was gone from us, we had no remedy for these misfortunes, but the little skill we had gained from him. However, we made tolerable shifts to patch up the boats for our purpose. In the height of our distresses, when hunger, which seems to include and absorb all others, was most prevailing, we were cheared with the appearance, once more, of our friendly Indians, as we thought, from whom we hoped for some relief; but as the consideration was wanting, for which alone they would part with their commodities, we were not at all benefited by their stay, which was very short. The little reserve too of flour made by the captain for our sea-stock when we should leave the island, was now diminished by theft: the thieves, who were three of our men, were however soon discovered, and two of them apprehended; but the third made his escape to the woods. Considering the pressing state of our necessities, this theft was looked upon as a most heinous crime, and therefore required an extraordinary punishment: accordingly the captain ordered these delinquents to be severely whipped, and then to be banished to an island at some distance from us; but before this latter part of the sentence could be put in execution, one of them fled; but the other was put alone upon a barren island, which afforded not the least shelter; however, we, in compassion, and contrary to order, patched him up a bit of a hut, and kindled him a fire, and then left the poor wretch to shift for himself. In two or three days after, going to the island in our boat with some little refreshment, such as our miserable circumstances would admit of, and with an intent of bringing him back, we found him dead and stiff. I was now reduced to the lowest condition by my illness, which was increased by the vile stuff I eat. When we were favoured by a fair day, a thing very extraordinary in this climate, we instantly took the advantage of it, and once more visited the last remains of the wreck, her bottom. Here our pains were repaid with the great good fortune of hooking up three casks of beef, which were brought safe to shore. This providential supply could not have happened at a more seasonable time than now, when we were afflicted with the greatest dearth we had ever experienced, and the little strength we had remaining was to be exerted in our endeavours to leave the island. Accordingly we soon found a remedy for our sickness, which was nothing but the effects of famine, and were greatly restored by food. The provision was equally distributed among us all, and served us for the remainder of our stay here.

We began to grow extremely impatient to leave the island, as the days were now nearly at their longest, and about mid-summer in these parts; but as to the weather, there seems to be little difference of seasons. Accordingly, on the 15th of December, the day being tolerable, we told Captain Cheap, we thought it a fine opportunity to run across the bay. But he most desired two or three of us to accompany him to our place of observation, the top of Mount Misery; when looking through his perspective, he observed to us that the sea ran very high without. However, this had no weight with the people, who were desirous, at all events, to be gone. I should here observe, that Captain Cheap's plan was, if possible, to get to the island of Chiloe; and if we found any vessel there, to board her immediately, and cut her out. This he certainly might have done with ease, had it been his good fortune to get round with the boats. We now launched both boats, and got every thing on board of them as quick as possible. Captain Cheap, the surgeon, and myself, were in the barge with nine men; and Lieutenant Hamilton and Mr Campbell in the yawl with six. I steered the barge, and Mr Campbell the yawl; but we had not been two hours at sea before the wind shifted more to the westward, and began to blow very hard, and the sea ran extremely high; so that we could no longer keep our heads towards the cape, or headland we had designed for. This cape we had had a view of in one of the intervals of fair weather, during our abode on the island, from Mount Misery; and it seemed to be distant between twenty and thirty leagues from us. We were now obliged to bear away right before the wind. Though the yawl was not far from us, we could see nothing of her, except now and then, upon the top of a mountaneous sea. In both the boats, the men were obliged to sit as close as possible, to receive the seas on their backs, to prevent their filling us, which was what we every moment expected. We were obliged to throw every thing over board to lighten the boats, all our beef, and even the grapnel, to prevent sinking. Night was coming on, and we were running on a lee-shore fast, where the sea broke in a frightful manner. Not one amongst us imagined it possible for boats to live in such a sea. In this situation, as we neared the shore, expecting to be beat to pieces by the first breaker, we perceived a small opening between the rocks, which we stood for, and found a very narrow passage between them, which brought us into a harbour for the boats as calm and smooth as a millpond. The yawl had got in before us, and our joy was great at meeting again after so unexpected a deliverance. Here we secured the boats, and ascended a rock. It rained excessively hard all the first part of the night, and was extremely cold; and though we had not a dry thread about us, and no wood could be found for firing, we were obliged to pass the night in that incomfortable situation, without any covering, shivering in our wet cloaths. The frost coming on with the morning, it was impossible for any of us to get a moment's sleep; and having flung overboard our provision the day before, there being no prospect of finding any thing to eat on this coast, in the morning we pulled out of the cove; but found so great a sea without, that we could make but little of it. After tugging all day, towards night we put in among some small islands, landed upon one of them, and found it a mere swamp. As the weather was the same, we passed this night much as we had done the preceding; seatangle was all we could get to eat at first, but the next day we had better luck; the surgeon got a goose, and we found materials for a good fire. We were confined here three or four days, the weather all that time proving so bad, that we could not put out. As soon as it grew moderate, we left this place, and shaped our course to the northward; and perceiving a large opening between very high land and a low point, we steered for it; and when got that length, found a large bay, down which we rowed, flattering ourselves there might be a passage that way; but towards night we came to the bottom of the bay, and finding no outlet, we were obliged to return the same way we came, having found nothing the whole day to alleviate our hunger.

Next night we put into a little cove, which, from the great quantity of red wood found there, we called Redwood Cove.

Leaving this place in the morning, we had the wind southerly, blowing fresh, by which we made much way that day, to the northward. Towards evening we were in with a pretty large island. Putting ashore on it, we found it cloathed with the finest trees we had ever seen, their stems running up to a prodigious height, without knot or branch, and as streight as cedars: the leaf of these trees resembled the myrtle leaf, only somewhat larger. I have seen trees larger than these in circumference, on the coast of Guinea, and there only; but for length of stem, which gradually tapered, I have no where met with any to compare to them. The wood was of a hard substance, and if not too heavy, would have made good masts; the dimension of some of these trees being equal to a main-mast of a first-rate man of war. The shore was covered with drift wood of a very large size; most of it cedar, which makes a brisk fire; but is so subject to snap and fly, that when we waked in the morning after a sound sleep, we found our cloaths singed in many places with the sparks, and covered with splinters.

The next morning being calm, we rowed out; but as soon as clear of the island, we found a great swell from the westward; we rowed to the bottom of a very large bay, which was to the northward of us, the land very low, and we were in hopes of finding some inlet through, but did not; so kept along shore to the westward. This part, which I take to be above fifty leagues from Wager's Island, is the very bottom of the large bay it lies in. Here was the only passage to be found, which (if we could by any means have got information of it) would have saved us much fruitless labour. Of this passage I shall have occasion to say more hereafter.

Having at this time an offshore wind, we kept the land close on board, till we came to a headland: it was near night before we got ahead of the breast-land, and opening it, discovered a very large bay to the northward, and another headland to the westward, at a great distance. We endeavoured to cut short our passage to it by crossing, which is very seldom to be effected, in these over-grown seas, by boats: and this we experienced now; for the wind springing up, and beginning to blow fresh, we were obliged to put back towards the first headland, into a small cove just big enough to shelter the two boats. Here an accident happened that alarmed us much. After securing our boats, we climbed up a rock scarcely large enough to contain our numbers: having nothing to eat, we betook ourselves to our usual receipt for hunger, which was going to sleep. We accordingly made a fire, and stowed ourselves round it as well as we could, but two of our men being incommoded for want of room, went a little way from us, into a small nook, over which a great cliff hung, and served them for a canopy. In the middle of the night we were awakened with a terrible rumbling, which we apprehended to be nothing less than the shock of an earthquake, which we had before experienced in these parts: and this conjecture we had reason to think not ill-founded, upon hearing hollow groans and cries as of men half swallowed up. We immediately got up, and ran to the place from whence the cries came, and then we were put out of all doubt as to the opinion we had formed of this accident; for here we found the two men almost buried under loose stones and earth: but upon a little farther inquiry, we were undeceived as to the cause we had imputed this noise to, which we found to be occasioned by the sudden giving way of the impending cliff, which fell a little beyond our people, carrying trees and rocks with it, and loose earth; the latter of which fell in part on our men, whom we with some pains rescued from their uneasy situation, from which they escaped with some bruises. The next morning we got out early, and the wind being westerly, rowed the whole day for the headland we had seen the night before; but when we had got that length could find no harbour, but were obliged to go into a sandy bay, and lay the whole night upon our oars; and a most dreadful one it proved, blowing and raining very hard. Here we were so pinched with hunger, that we eat the shoes off our feet, which consisted of raw seal skin. In the morning we got out of the bay; but the incessant foul weather had overcome us, and we began to be indifferent as to what befel us; and the boats, in the night, making into a bay, we nearly lost the yawl, a breaker having filled her, and driven her ashore upon the beach. This, by some of our accounts, was Christmas Day; but our accounts had so often been interrupted by our distresses, that there was no depending upon them. Upon seeing the yawl in this imminent danger, the barge stood off, and went into another bay to the northward of it, where it was smoother lying; but there was no possibility of getting on shore. In the night the yawl joined us again. The next day was so bad, that we despaired reaching the headland, so rowed down the bay in hopes of getting some seal, as that animal had been seen the day before, but met with no success; so returned to the same bay we had been in the night before, where the surf having abated some-what, we went ashore, and picked up a few shellfish. In the morning, we got on board early, and ran along shore to the westward, for about three leagues, in order to get round a cape, which was the westernmost land we could see. It blew very hard, and there ran such a sea, that we heartily wished ourselves back again, and accordingly made the best of our way for that bay which we had left in the morning; but before we could reach it night came on, and we passed a most dismal one, lying upon our oars.

The weather continuing very bad, we put in for the shore in the morning, where we found nothing but tangle and seaweed. We now passed some days roving about for provisions, as the weather was too bad to make another attempt to get round the cape as yet. We found some fine lagoons towards the head of the bay; and in them killed some seal, and got a good quantity of shellfish, which was a great relief to us. We now made a second attempt to double the cape; but when we got the length of it, and passed the first headland, for it consists of three of an equal height, we got into a sea that was horrid; for it ran all in heaps, like the Race of Portland, but much worse. We were happy to put back to the old place, with little hopes of ever getting round this cape.

Next day, the weather proving very bad, all hands went ashore to procure some sustenance, except two in each boat, which were left as boat-keepers: this office we took by turns, and it was now my lot to be upon this duty with another man. The yawl lay within us at a grapnel; in the night it blew very hard, and a great sea tumbled in upon the shore; but being extremely fatigued, we in the boats went to sleep: notwithstanding, however, I was at last awakened by the uncommon motion of the boat, and the roaring of the breakers everywhere about us. At the same time I heard a shrieking, like to that of persons in distress; I looked out, and saw the yawl canted bottom upwards by a sea, and soon afterwards disappeared. One of our men, whose name was William Rose, a quartermaster, was drowned; the other was thrown ashore by the surf, with his head buried in the sand; but by the immediate assistance of the people on shore, was saved. As for us in the barge, we expected the same fate every moment; for the sea broke a long way without us. However, we got her head to it, and hove up our grapnel, or should rather say kellick, which we had made to serve in the room of our grapnel, hove overboard some time before, to lighten the boat. By this means we used our utmost efforts to pull her without the breakers some way, and then let go our kellick again. Here we lay all the next day, in a great sea, not knowing what would be our fate. To add to our mortification, we could see our companions in tolerable plight ashore eating seal, while we were starving with hunger and cold. For this month past, we had not known what it was to have a dry thread about us.

The next day being something more moderate, we ventured in with the barge as near as we could, in safety, to the shore, and our companions threw us some seals liver; which, having eat greedily, we were seized with excessive sickness, which affected us so much that our skin peeled off from head to foot.

Whilst the people were on shore here, Mr Hamilton met with a large seal, or sea-lion, and fired a brace of balls into him, upon which the animal turned upon him open-mouthed; but presently fixing his bayonet, he thrust it down its throat, with a good part of the barrel of the gun, which the creature bit in two seemingly with as much ease as if it had been a twig. Notwithstanding the wounds it received, it eluded all farther efforts to kill it, and got clear off.

I call this animal a large seal, or sea-lion, because it resembles a seal in many particulars; but then it exceeds it so much in size, as to be sufficiently determined by that distinction only, to be of another species. Mr Walter, in Lord Anson's *Voyage*, has given a particular description of those which are seen about Juan Fernandes; but they have in other climates, different appearances as well as different qualities, as we had occasion to observe in this, and a late voyage I made. However, as so much already has been said of the sea-lion, I shall only mention two peculiarities; the one relative to its appearance, and the other to its properties of action, which distinguish it from those described by him. Those I saw were, without that snout, or trunk, hanging below the end of the upper jaw; but then the males were furnished with a large shaggy mane, which gave them a most formidable appearance. And, whereas, he says those he saw were unwieldy, and easily destroyed, we found some, on the contrary, that lay at a mile's distance from the water, which came down upon us when disturbed, with such impetuosity, that it was as much as we could do to get out of their way; and when attacked, would turn upon us with great agility.

Having lost the yawl, and being too many for the barge to carry off, we were compelled to leave four of our men behind. They were all marines, who seemed to have no great objection to the determination made with regard to them, so exceedingly disheartened and worn out were they with the distresses and dangers they had already gone through. And, indeed, I believe it would have been a matter of indifference to the greatest part of the rest, whether they should embark, or take their chance. The captain distributed to these poor fellows arms and ammunition, and some other necessaries. When we parted, they stood upon the beach, giving us three chears, and called out, God bless the King. We saw them a little after, setting out upon their forlorn hope, and helping one another over a hideous track of rocks; but considering the difficulties attending this only way of travelling left them; for the woods are impracticable, from their thickness, and the deep swamps to be met every where in them; considering too, that the coast here is rendered so inhospitable, by the heavy seas that are constantly tumbling upon it, as not to afford even a little shellfish, it is probable that all met with a miserable end.

We rowed along shore to the westward, in order to make one more attempt to double the cape: when a breast of the first headland, there ran such a sea, that we expected every instant the boat would go down. But as the preservation of life had now, in a great measure, lost its actuating principle upon us, we still kept pushing through it, till we opened a bay to the northward. In all my life, I never saw so dreadful a sea as drove in here; it began to break at more than half-a-mile from the shore. Perceiving now that it was impossible for any boat to get round, the men lay upon their oars till the boat was very near the breakers, the mountainous swell that then ran, heaving her in at a great rate. I thought it was their intention to put an end to their lives and misery at once; but nobody spoke for some time. At last, Captain Cheap told them, they must either perish immediately, or pull stoutly for it to get off the shore; but they might do as they pleased. They chose, however, to exert themselves a little, and after infinite difficulty, got round the headland again, giving up all thoughts of making any further attempts to double the cape. It was night before we could get back to the bay, where we were compelled to leave four of our men, in order to save, if possible, the remainder; for we must all have certainly perished, if more than sixteen had been crouded into so small a boat. This bay we named Marine Bay. When we had returned to this bay, we found the surf ran so high, that we were obliged to lay upon our oars all night; and it was now resolved to go back to Wager's Island, there to linger out a miserable life, as we had not the least prospect of returning home.

But before we set out, in consequence of this resolution, it was necessary, if possible, to get some little stock of seal to support us in a passage, upon which, wherever we might put in, we were not likely to meet with any supply. Accordingly, it was determined to go up that lagoon in which we had before got some seal, to provide ourselves with some more; but we did not leave the bay till we had made some search after the unhappy marines we had left on shore. Could we have found them, we had now agreed to take them on board again, though it would have been the certain destruction of us all. This, at another time, would have been mere madness; but we were now resigned to our fate, which we none of us thought far off; however, there was nothing to be seen of them, and no traces but a musket on the beach.

Upon returning up the lagoon, we were so fortunate as to kill some seal, which we boiled, and laid in the boat for seastock. While we were ranging along shore in detached parties in quest of this, and whatever other eatables might come in our way, our surgeon, who was then by himself, discovered a pretty large hole, which seemed to lead to some den, or repository, within the rock. It was not so rude or natural, but that there were some signs of it having been cleared, and made more accessible by industry. The surgeon for some time hesitated whether he should venture in, from his uncertainty as to the reception he might meet with from any inhabitant; but his curiosity getting the better of his fears, he determined to go in; which he did upon his hands and knees, as the passage was too low for him to enter otherwise. After having proceeded a considerable way thus, he arrived at a spacious chamber; but whether hollowed out by hands or natural, he could not be positive. The light into this chamber was conveyed thro' a hole at the top; in the midst was a kind of bier, made of sticks laid crossways, supported by props of about five foot in height. Upon this bier, five or six bodies were extended; which, in appearance, had been deposited there a long time; but had suffered no decay or diminution. They were without covering, and the flesh of their bodies was become perfectly dry and hard; which, whether done by any art, or secret, the savages may be possessed of, or occasioned by any drying virtue in the air of the cave, could not be guessed. Indeed, the surgeon, finding nothing there to eat, which was the chief inducement for his creeping into this hole, did not amuse himself with long disquisitions, or make that accurate examination which he would have done at another time; but crawling out as he came in, he went and told the first he met of what he had seen. Some had the curiosity to go in likewise. I had forgot to mention that there was another range of bodies deposited in the same manner, upon another platform under the bier. Probably this was the burial-place of their great men, called Caciques; but from whence they could be brought we were utterly at a loss to conceive, there being no traces of any Indian settlement hereabout. We had seen no savage since we left the island, or observed any marks in the coves, or bays to the northward, where we had touched, such as of fireplaces, or old wigwams, which they never fail of leaving behind them; and it is very probable, from the violent seas that are always beating upon this coast, its deformed aspect, and the very swampy soil that every where borders upon it, that it is little frequented.

We now crossed the first bay for the headland we left on Christmas Day, much dejected; for under our former sufferings, we were in some measure supported with the hopes that, as we advanced, however little, they were so much nearer their termination; but now our prospects was dismal and dispiriting indeed, as we had the same difficulties and dangers to encounter, not only without any flattering views to lessen them, but under the aggravating circumstance of their leading to an inevitable and miserable death; for we could not possibly conceive that the fate of starving could be avoided by any human means, upon that desolate island we were returning to. The shellfish, which was the only subsistence that island had hitherto afforded in any measure, was exhausted; and the Indians had shewn themselves so little affected by the common incitements of compassion, that we had no hopes to build upon any impressions of that sort in them. They had already refused to barter their dogs with us, for want of a valuable commodity on our side; so that it is wonderful we did not give ourselves up to dispondency, and lay aside all farther attempts; but we were supported by that invisible Power, who can make the most untoward circumstances subservient to his gracious purposes.

At this time, our usual bad weather attended us; the night too set in long before we could reach the cove we before had taken shelter in: so that we were obliged to keep the boat's head to the sea all night, the sea every where astern of us, running over hideous breakers. In the morning, we designed standing over for that island in which we had observed those streight and lofty trees before mentioned, and which Captain Cheap named Montrose Island; but as soon as we opened the headland to the westward of us, a sudden squall took the boat, and very near overset her. We were instantly full of water; but by baling with our hats and hands, and any thing that would hold water, we with difficulty freed her. Under this alarming circumstance, we found it advisable to return back, and put into the cove, which the night before we were prevented getting into. We were detained here two or three days, by exceeding bad weather; so that, had we not fortunately provided ourselves with some seal, we must have starved, for this place afforded us nothing.

At length we reached Montrose Island. This is by much the best and pleasantest spot we had seen in this part of the world; tho' it has nothing on it eatable but some berries, which resembled gooseberries in flavour: they are of a black hue, and grow in a swampy ground; and the bush or tree, that bears them, is much taller than that of our gooseberries. We remained here some time, living upon these berries, and the remainder of our seal, which was now grown quite rotten. Our two or three first attempts to put out from this island were without success, the tempestuous weather obliging us to put back again. One of our people was much inclined to remain here, thinking it at least as good a place as Wager's Island to end his days upon; but he was obliged by the rest to go off with them. We had not been long out before it began to blow a storm of wind; and the mist came on so thick, that we could not see the land, and were at a loss which way to steer; but we heard the sea, which ran exceedingly high, breaking near us; upon which we immediately hauled aft the sheet, and hardly weathered the breakers by a boat's length. At the same time we shipped a sea that nearly filled us: it struck us with that violence as to throw me, and one or two more, down into the bottom of the boat, where we were half drowned before we could get up again. This was one of the most extraordinary escapes we had in the course of this expedition; for Captain Cheap, and every one else, had entirely given themselves up for lost. However, it pleased God that we got that evening into Redwood Cove, where the weather continued so bad all night, we could keep no fire in to dry ourselves with; but there being no other alternative for us, but to stay here and starve, or put to sea again, we chose the latter, and put out in the morning again, though the weather was very little mended. In three or four days after, we arrived at our old station, Wager's Island; but in such a miserable plight, that though we thought our condition upon setting out would not admit of any additional circumstance of misery, yet it was to be envied in comparison of what we now suffered, so worn and reduced were we by fatigue and hunger; having eat nothing for some days but seaweed and tangle. Upon this expedition, we had been out, by our account, just two months; in which we had rounded, backwards and forwards, the great bay formed to the northward by that high land we had observed from Mount Misery.

The first thing we did upon our arrival, was to secure the barge, as this was our sole dependence for any relief that might offer by sea; which done, we repaired to our huts, which formed a kind of village or street, consisting of several irregular habitations; some of which being covered by a kind of brushwood thatch, afforded tolerable shelter against the inclemency of the weather. Among these, there was one which we observed with some surprise to be nailed up. We broke it open, and found some iron-work, picked out with much pains from those pieces of the wreck, which were driven ashore. We concluded from hence, that the Indians who had been here in our absence, were not of that tribe with which we had some commerce before, who seemed to set no value upon iron, but from some other quarter; and must have had communication with the Spaniards, from whom they had learned the value and use of that commodity. Thieving from strangers is a commendable talent among savages in general, and bespeaks an address which they much admire; though the strictest honesty, with regard to the property of each other, is observed among them. There is no doubt but they ransacked all our houses; but the men had taken care, before they went off in the long-boat, to strip them of their most valuable furniture; that is, the bales of cloth used for lining, and coverted them into trowsers and watch-coats. Upon farther search, we found, thrown aside in the bushes, at the back of one of the huts, some pieces of seal, in a very putrid condition; which, however, our stomachs were far from loathing. The next business, which the people set about very seriously, was to proceed to Mount Misery, and bury the corpse of the murdered person, mentioned to have been discovered there some little time after our being cast away; for to the neglect of this necessary tribute to that unfortunate person, the men assigned all their ill success upon the late expedition.

That common people in general are addicted to superstitious

conceits, is an observation founded on experience; and the reason is evident: but I cannot allow that common seamen are more so than others of the lower class. In the most enlightened ages of antiquity, we find it to have been the popular opinion, that the spirits of the dead were not at rest till their bodies were interred; and that they did not cease to haunt and trouble those who had neglected this duty to the departed. This is still believed by the vulgar, in most countries; and in our men this persuasion was much heightened by the melancholy condition they were reduced to; and was farther confirmed by an occurrence which happened some little time before we went upon our last expedition. One night we were alarmed with a strange cry, which resembled that of a man drowning. Many of us ran out of our huts towards the place from whence the noise proceeded, which was not far off shore; where we could perceive, but not distinctly (for it was then moonlight) an appearance like that of a man swimming half out of water. The noise that this creature uttered was so unlike that of any animal they had heard before, that it made a great impression upon the men; and they frequently recalled this apparition at the time of their distresses, with reflections on the neglect of the office they were now fulfilling.

We were soon driven again to the greatest straits for want of something to subsist upon, by the extreme bad weather that now set in upon us. Wild sellery was all we could procure, which racked our stomachs instead of assuaging our hunger. That dreadful and last resource of men, in not much worse circumstances than ours, of consigning one man to death for the support of the rest, began to be mentioned in whispers; and indeed there was some among us who, by eating what they found raw, were become little better than canibals. But fortunately for us, and opportunely to prevent this horrid proceeding, Mr Hamilton, at this time, found some rotten pieces of beef, cast up by the sea at some miles distance from the huts, which he, though a temptation which few would have resisted in parallel circumstances, scorned to conceal from the rest; but generously distributed among us.

A few days after, the mystery of the nailing up of the hut, and what had been doing by the Indians upon the island in our absence, was partly explained to us; for about the 15th day after our return, there came a party of Indians to the island in two canoes, who were not a little surprised to find us here again. Among these, was an Indian of the tribe of the Chonos, who live in the neighbourhood of Chiloe.* He talked the Spanish language; but with that savage accent which renders it almost unintelligible to any but those who are adepts in that language. He was likewise a cacique, or leading man of his tribe; which authority was confirmed to him by the Spaniards; for he carried the usual badge and mark of distinction, by which the Spaniards, and their dependents, hold their military and civil employments; which is a stick with a silver head. These badges, of which the Indians are very vain, at once serve to retain the cacique in the strongest attachment to the Spanish government, and give him greater weight with his own dependents: yet, withal, he is the merest slave, and has not one thing he can call his own. This report of our shipwreck (as we supposed) having reached the Chonos, by means of the intermediate tribes, which handed it to one another, from those Indians who first visited us; this cacique was either sent to learn the truth of the rumour, or having first got the intelligence, set out with a view of making some advantage of the wreck, appropriating such iron-work as he could gather from it to his own use: for that metal is become very useful to those savages, since their commerce with the Spaniards has taught them to apply it to several purposes. But as the secreting any thing from a rapacious Spanish rey, or governor (even an old rusty nail) by any of their Indian dependents, is a very dangerous offence, he was careful to conceal the

---

* Chiloe is an island on the western coast of America, situated in 42° 40 of S. latitude; and the southernmost settlement under the Spanish jurisdiction on that coast.

little prize he had made, till he could conveniently carry it away; for in order to make friends of these savages, we had left their hoard untouched.

Our surgeon, Mr Elliot, being master of a few Spanish words, made himself so far understood by the cacique, as to let him know, that our intention was to reach some of the Spanish settlements, if we could; that we were unacquainted with the best and safest way, and what track was most likely to afford us subsistence in our journey; promising, if he would undertake to conduct us in the barge, he should have it, and every thing in it for his trouble, as soon as it had served our present occasions. To these conditions, the cacique, after much persuasion, at length agreed. Accordingly, having made the best preparation we could, we embarked on board the barge to the number of fifteen, including the cacique, whose name was Martin, and his servant Emanuel. We were, indeed, sixteen, when we returned from our last fruitless attempt to get off the island; but we had buried two since, who perished with hunger; and a marine, having committed theft, run away to avoid the punishment his crime deserved, and hid himself in the woods; since which he was never heard of. We now put off, accompanied with the two Indian canoes; in one of which was a savage, with his two wives, who had an air of dignity superior to the rest, and was handsome in his person. He had his hut, during his stay with us, separate from the other Indians, who seemed to pay him extraordinary respect; but in two or three nights, these Indians, being independent of the Spaniards, and living somewhere to the southward of our Chono guide, left us to proceed on our journey by ourselves.

The first night we lay at an island destitute of all refreshment; where having found some shelter for our boat, and made ourselves a fire, we slept by it. The next night we were more unfortunate, though our wants were increasing; for having run to the westward of Montrose island, we found no shelter for the barge, but were under the necessity of lying upon our oars, suffering the most extreme pangs of hunger. The next day brought us to the bottom of a great bay, where the Indian guide had left his family, a wife and two children, in a hut. Here we staid two or three days, during which we were constantly employed in ranging along shore in quest of shellfish.

We now again proceeded on our voyage, having received on board the family of our guide, who conducted us to a river, the stream of which was so rapid, that after our utmost efforts from morning to evening, we gained little upon the current; and at last were obliged to desist from our attempt and return. I had hitherto steered the boat; but one of our men sinking under the fatigue, expired soon after, which obliged me to take the oar in his room, and rowed against this heart-breaking stream. Whilst I was thus employed, one of our men, whose name was John Bosman, though hitherto the stoutest man among us, fell from his seat under the thwarts; complaining that his strength was quite exhausted for want of food, and that he should die very shortly. As he lay in this condition, he would every now and then break out in the most pathetic wishes for some little sustenance; that two or three mouthfuls might be the means of saving his life. The captain at this time had a large piece of boiled seal by him, and was the only one that was provided with any thing like a meal: but we were become so hardened against the impressions of others sufferings by our own; so familiarised to scenes of this and every other kind of misery, that the poor man's dying intreaties were vain. I sat next to him when he dropped, and having a few dried shellfish (about five or six) in my pocket, from time to time put one in his mouth, which served only to prolong his pains; from which, however, soon after my little supply failed, he was released by death. For this, and another man I mentioned a little before to have expired under the like circumstances, when we returned from this unsuccessful enterprise, we made a grave in the sands.

It would have redounded greatly to the tenderness and humanity of Captain Cheap, if, at this time, he had remitted somewhat of that attention he shewed to self-preservation, which is hardly allowable but where the consequence of relieving others must be immediately and manifestly fatal to ourselves; but I would venture to affirm, that in these last affecting exigencies, as well as some others, a sparing perhaps adequate to the emergency, might have been admitted consistently with a due regard to his own necessities. The captain had better opportunities of recruiting his stock than any of us; for his rank was considered by the Indian as a reason for supplying him when he would not find a bit for us. Upon the evening of the day in which these disasters happened, the captain producing a large piece of boiled seal, suffered no one to partake with him but the surgeon, who was the only man in favour at this time. We did not expect, indeed, any relief from him in our present condition; for we had a few small mussles and herbs to eat; but the men could not help expressing the greatest indignation at this neglect of the deceased; saying that he deserved to be deserted by the rest for his savage behaviour.

The endeavouring to pass up this river was for us, who had so long struggled with hunger, a most unseasonable attempt; by which we were harrassed to a degree that threatened to be fatal to more of us: but our guide, without any respect to the condition our hardships had reduced us to, was very sollicitous for us to go that way, which possibly he had gone before in light canoes; but for such a boat as ours, was impracticable. We conceived, therefore, at that time, that this was some short cut, which was to bring us forward in our voyage; but we had reason to think afterwards, that the greater probability there was of his getting the barge, which was the wages of his undertaking, safe to his settlement by this, rather than another course, was his motive for preferring it to the way we took afterwards, where there was a carrying place of considerable length, over which it would have been impossible to have carried our boat.

The country hereabouts wears the most uncouth, desolate, and rugged aspect imaginable; it is so circumstanced as to discourage the most sanguine adventurers from attempts to settle in it: were it for no other reason than the constant heavy rains, or rather torrents, which pour down here, and the vast sea and surf which the prevailing westerly winds impel upon this coast, it must be rendered inhospitable. All entrance into the woods is not only extremely difficult, but hazardous; not from any assaults you are likely to meet with from wild beasts; for even these could hardly find convenient harbour here; but from the deep swamp, which is the reigning soil of this country, and in which the woods may be said rather to float than grow; so that, except upon a range of deformed broken rocks, which form the sea-coast, the traveller cannot find sound footing any where. With this unpromising scene before us, we were now setting out in search of food, which nothing but the most pressing instances of hunger could induce us to do: we had, indeed, the young Indian servant to our cacique for our conductor, who was left by him to shew us where the shellfish was most plenty. The cacique was gone with the rest of his family, in the canoe, with a view of getting some seal, upon a trip which would detain him from us three or four days.

After searching the coast some time with very little success, we began to think of returning to the barge; but six of the men, with the Indian, having advanced some few paces before the officers, got into the boat first; which they had no sooner done than they put off, and left us, to return no more. And now all the difficulties we had hitherto endured, seemed light in comparison of what we expected to suffer from this treachery of our men, who, with the boat, had taken away every thing that might be the means of preserving our lives. The little cloaths we had saved from the wreck, our muskets and ammunition, were gone, except a little powder, which must be preserved for kindling fires, and one gun, which I had, and was now become useless for want of ammunition; and all these wants were now come upon us at a time when we could not be worse situated for supplying them. Yet, under these dismal and forlorn appearances, was our delivery now preparing; and from these hopeless circumstances, were we to draw hereafter an instance, scarce to be paralleled, of the unsearchable ways of Providence. It was at that time little suspected by us, that the barge, in which we founded all our hopes of escaping from this savage coast, would certainly have proved the fatal cause of detaining us till we were consumed by the labour and hardships requisite to row her round the capes and great headlands; for it was impossible to carry her by land, as we did the boats of the Indians. At present, no condition could be worse than we thought ours to be: there ran at this time a very high sea, which breaking with great fury upon this coast, made it very improbable that sustenance in any proportion to our wants could be found upon it; yet, unpromising as this prospect was, and though little succour could be expected from this quarter, I could not help, as I strolled along shore from the rest, casting my eyes towards the sea. Continuing thus to look out, I thought I saw something now and then upon the top of a sea that looked black, which, upon observing still more intently, I imagined at last to be a canoe; but reflecting afterwards how unusual it was for Indians to venture out in so mountainous a sea, and at such a distance from the land, I concluded myself to be deceived. However, its nearer approach convinced me, beyond all doubt, of its being a canoe; but that it could not put in any where hereabouts, but intended for some other part of the coast. I ran back as fast as I could to my companions, and acquainted them with what I had seen. The despondency they were in would not allow them to give credit to it at first; but afterwards, being convinced that it was as I reported it, we were all in the greatest hurry to strip off some of our rags to make a signal withal, which we fixed upon a long pole. This had the desired effect: the people in the canoe seeing the signal, made towards the land at about two miles distance from us; for no boat could approach the land where we were: there they put into a small cove, sheltered by a large ledge of rocks without, which broke the violence of the sea. Captain

Cheap and I walked along shore, and got to the cove about the time they landed. Here we found the persons arrived in this canoe, to be our Indian guide and his wife, who had left us some days before. He would have asked us many questions, but neither Captain Cheap nor I understanding Spanish at that time; we took him along with us to the surgeon, whom we had left so ill that he could hardly raise himself from the ground. When the Indian began to confer with the surgeon, the first question was, what was become of the barge and his companion? And as he could give him no satisfactory answer to this question, the Indian took it for granted that Emanuel was murdered by us, and that he and his family ran the same risk; upon which he was preparing to provide for his security, by leaving us directly. The surgeon seeing this, did all in his power to pacify him, and convince him of the unreasonableness of his apprehensions; which he at length found means to do, by assuring him that the Indian would come to no harm, but that he would soon see him return safe; which providentially, and beyond our expectation, happened accordingly; for in a few days after, Emanuel having contrived to make his escape from the people in the barge, returned by ways that were impassible to any creature but an Indian. All that we could learn from Emanuel relative to his escape, was, that he took the first opportunity of leaving them; which was upon their putting into a bay somewhere to the westward.

We had but one gun among us, and that was a small fowlingpiece of mine; no ammunition but a few charges of powder I had about me; and as the Indian was very desirous of returning to the place where he had left his wife and canoe, Captain Cheap desired I would go with him, and watch over him all night, to prevent his getting away. Accordingly I set out with him; and when he and his family betook themselves to rest in the little wigwam they had made for that purpose, I kept my station as centinel over them all night.

The next morning, Captain Cheap, Mr Hamilton, and the

surgeon, joined us: the latter, by illness, being reduced to the most feeble condition, was supported by Mr Hamilton and Mr Campbell. After holding some little consultation together, as to the best manner of proceeding in our journey, it was agreed, that the Indian should haul his canoe, with our assistance, over land, quite across the island we were then upon, and put her into a bay on the other side, from whence he was to go in quest of some other Indians, by whom he expected to be joined: but as his canoe was too small to carry more than three or four persons, he thought it advisable to take only Captain Cheap and myself with him, and to leave his wife and children as pledges with our companions till his return.

As it was matter of uncertainty whether we should ever recover the barge or not, which was stipulated, on our side, to become the property of the cacique, upon his fulfilling his engagements with us; the inducements we now made use of to prevail upon him to proceed with us in our journey were, that he should have my fowling-piece, some little matters in the possession of Captain Cheap, and that we would use our interest to procure him some small pecuniary reward.

We were now to set off in the canoe, in which I was to assist him in rowing. Accordingly, putting from this island, we rowed hard all this day and the next, without any thing to eat but a scrap of seal, a very small portion of which fell to my share. About two hours after the close of the day, we put ashore, where we discovered six or seven wigwams. For my part, my strength was so exhausted with fatigue and hunger, that it would have been impossible for me to have held out another day at this toilsome work. As soon as we landed, the Indian conducted Captain Cheap with him into a wigwam; but I was left to shift for myself.

Thus left, I was for some time at a loss what I had best do; for knowing that in the variety of dispositions observable among the Indians, the surly and savage temper is the most prevalent, I had good reason to conclude, that if I obtruded myself upon them, my reception would be but indifferent. Necessity, however, put me upon the risk; I accordingly pushed into the next wigwam upon my hands and knees; for the entrance into these kind of buildings is too low to admit of any other manner of getting into them. To give a short description of these temporary houses, called wigwams, may not be improper here, for the satisfaction of those who never saw any; especially as they differ somewhat from those of North America, which are more generally known from the numerous accounts of that country.

When the Indians of this part of the world have occasion to stop any where in their rambles, if it be only for a night or two, the men, who take this business upon them, while the women are employed in much more laborious offices, such as diving in the sea for sea-eggs, and searching the rocks for shellfish, getting feuel, &c. repair to the woods, and cutting a sufficient number of tall, straight branches, fix them in an irregular kind of circle of uncertain demensions; which having done, they bend the extremities of these branches so as to meet in a centre at top, where they bind them by a kind of woodbine, called Supple-Jack, which they split by holding it in their teeth. This frame, or skeleton of a hut, is made tight against the weather with a covering of boughs and bark; but as the bark is not got without some trouble, they generally take it with them when they remove, putting it at the bottom of their canoes: the rest of the wigwam they leave standing. The fire is made in the middle of the wigwam, round which they sit upon boughs; and as there is no vent for the smoke, besides the doorway, which is very low, except through some crevices, which cannot easily be stopped, they are not a little incommoded on that account; and the eyes of some of them are much affected by it.

But to return: in this wigwam, into which I took the liberty to introduce myself, I found out two women, who, upon first seeing a figure they were not accustomed to, and such a figure too as I then made, were struck with astonishment. They were sitting by a fire, to which I approached without any apology. However inclined I might have been to make one, my ignorance of their language made it impossible to attempt it. One of these women appeared to be young, and very handsome for an Indian; the other old, and as frightful as it is possible to conceive any thing in human shape to be. Having stared at me some little time, they both went out; and I, without farther ceremony, sat me down by the fire to warm myself, and dry the rags I wore. Yet I cannot say my situation was very easy, as I expected every instant to see two or three men come in and thrust me out, if they did not deal with me in a rougher manner.

Soon after the two women came in again, having, as I supposed, conferred with the Indian our conductor; and appearing to be in great good humour, began to chatter and laugh immoderately. Perceiving the wet and cold condition I was in, they seemed to have compassion on me, and the old woman went out and brought some wood, with which she made a good fire; but my hunger being impatient, I could not forbear expressing my desire that they would extend their hospitality a little further, and bring me something to eat. They soon comprehended my meaning, and the younger beginning to rummage under some pieces of bark that lay in the corner of the wigwam, produced a fine large fish; this they presently put upon the fire to broil; and when it was just warm through, they made a sign for me to eat. They had no need to repeat the invitation; I fell to, and dispatched it in so short a time, that I was in hopes they would comprehend, without further tokens, that I was ready for another; but it was of no consequence, for their stock of eatables was entirely exhausted.

After sitting some time in conference together, in which conversation I could bear no part, the women made some signs to me to lay down and go to sleep, first having strewed some dry boughs upon the ground. I laid myself down, and soon fell fast asleep; and about three or four hours after awaking, I found myself covered with a bit of blanket, made of the down of birds, which the women usually wear about their waist. The young woman, who had carefully covered me, whilst sleeping, with her own blanket, was lying close by me: the old woman on the other side of her. The fire was low, and almost burnt out; but as soon as they found me awake, they renewed it, by putting on more fuel. What I had hitherto eat served only to sharpen my appetite; I could not help, therefore, being earnest with them to get me some more victuals. Having understood my necessities, they talked together some little time; after which getting up, they both went out, taking with them a couple of dogs, which they train to assist them in fishing. After an hour's absence, they came in trembling with cold, and their hair streaming with water, and brought two fish; which, having broiled, they gave me the largest share; and then we all laid down as before to rest.

In the morning, my curiosity led me to visit the neighbouring wigwams, in which were only one or two men; the rest of the inhabitants were all women and children. I then proceeded to enquire after Captain Cheap and our Indian guide, whom I found in the wigwam they had first occupied: the authority of the cacique had procured the captain no despicable entertainment. We could not learn what business the men, whose wives and children were here left behind, were gone out upon; but as they seldom or never go upon fishing parties (for they have no hunting here) without their wives, who take the most laborious part of this pursuit upon themselves, it is probable they were gone upon some warlike expedition, in which they use bows and arrows sometimes, but always the lance. This weapon they throw with great dexterity and force, and never stir abroad without it. About this time their return was looked for; a hearing by no means pleasant to me; I was therefore determined to enjoy myself as long as they were absent, and make the most of the good fare I was possessed of; to the pleasure of which I thought a little cleanliness might in some measure contribute; I therefore went to a brook, and taking off my shirt, which might be said to be alive with vermin, set myself about to wash it; which having done as well as I could, and hung on a bush to dry, I heard a bustle about the wigwams; and soon perceived that the women were preparing to depart, having stripped their wigwams of their bark covering, and carried it into their canoes. Putting on, therefore, my shirt, just as it was, I hastened to join them, having a great desire of being present at one of their fishing parties.

It was my lot to be put into the canoe with my two patronesses, and some others who assisted in rowing: we were in all four canoes. After rowing some time, they gained such an offing as they required, where the water here was about eight or ten fathom deep, and there lay upon their oars. And now the youngest of the two women, taking a basket in her mouth, jumped over board, and diving to the bottom, continued under water an amazing time: when she had filled the basket with sea-eggs, she came up to the boatside; and delivering it so filled to the other women in the boat, they took out the contents, and returned it to her. The diver then, after having taken a short time to breathe, went down and up again with the same success; and so several times for the space of half an hour. It seems as if Providence had endued this people with a kind of amphibious nature, as the sea is the only source from whence almost all their subsistence is derived. This element too, being here very boisterous, and falling with a most heavy surf upon a rugged coast, very little, except some seal, is not to be got any where but in the quiet bosom of the deep. What occasions this reflection is the early propensity I had so frequently observed in the children of these savages to this occupation; who, even at the age of three years, might be seen crawling upon their hands and knees among the rocks and breakers; from which they would tumble themselves into the sea without regard to the cold, which is here often intense; and shewing no fear of the noise and roaring of the surf.

This sea-egg is a shellfish, from which several prickles project in all directions, by means whereof it removes itself from place to place. In it are found four or five yolks, resembling the inner divisions of an orange, which are of a very nutritive quality, and excellent flavour.

The water was at this time extremely cold; and when the divers got into the boats, they seemed greatly benumbed; and it is usual with them after this exercise, if they are near enough their wigwams, to run to the fire; to which presenting one side, they rub and chafe it for some time: then turning the other, use it in the same manner, till the circulation of the blood is restored. This practice, if it has no worse effect, must occasion their being more susceptible of the impressions of cold, than if they waited the gradual advances of their natural warmth in the open air. I leave it to the decision of the gentlemen of the faculty, whether this too hasty approach to the fire may not subject them to a disorder I observed among them, called the elephantiasis, or swelling of the legs.*

The divers having returned to their boats, we continued to row till towards evening, when we landed upon a low point. As soon as the canoes were hauled up, they employed themselves in erecting their wigwams, which they dispatch with great address and quickness. I still enjoyed the protection of my two good Indian women, who made me their guest here as before; they first regaled me with sea-eggs, and then went out upon another kind of fishery by the means of dogs and nets. These dogs are a cur-like looking animal; but very sagacious, and easily trained to this business. Though, to appearance, an

---

* There are two very different disorders incident to the human body, which bear the same name, derived from some resemblance they hold with different parts of the animal, so well known in the countries to which these disorders are peculiar. That which was first so named is the leprosy, which brings a scurf on the skin not unlike the hide of an elephant. The other affects the patient with such enormous swellings of the legs and feet, that they give the idea of those shapeless pillars which support that creature; and therefore this disease has also been called elephantiasis by the Arabian physicians; who, together with the Malabrians, among whom it is endemial, attribute it to the drinking of bad waters, and the too sudden transitions from heat to cold.

uncomfortable kind of sport; yet they engage in it readily, seem to enjoy it much, and express their eagerness, by barking every time they raise their heads above the water to breathe. The net is held by two Indians, who get into the water; then the dogs taking a large compass, dive after the fish, and drive them into the net; but it is only in particular places that the fish are taken in this manner. At the close of the evening, the women brought in two fish, which served us for supper; and then we reposed ourselves as before. Here we remained all the next day; and the morning after embarked again, and rowed till noon; then landing, we descried the canoes of the Indian men, who had been some time expected from an expedition they had been upon. This was soon to make a great alteration in the situation of affairs, a presage of which I could read in the melancholy countenance of my young hostess. She endeavoured to express herself in very earnest terms to me; but I had not yet acquired a competent knowledge of the Indian language to understand her.

As soon as the men were landed, she and the old Indian woman went up, not without some marks of dread upon them, to an elderly Indian man, whose remarkable surly and stern countenance was well calculated to raise such sensations in his dependents. He seemed to be a cacique, or chief man among them, by the airs of importance he assumed to himself, and the deference paid him by the rest. After some little conference passed between these Indians, and our cacique conductor, of which, most probably, the circumstances of our history, and the occasion of our coming here, might be the chief subject; for they fixed their eyes constantly upon us; they applied themselves to building their wigwams. I now understood that the two Indian women with whom I had sojourned, were wives to this chieftain, though one was young enough to be his daughter; and as far as I could learn, did really stand in the different relations to him both of daughter and wife. It was easy to be perceived, that all did not go well between them at this time;

either that he was not satisfied with the answers that they returned him to his questions, or that he suspected some misconduct on their side; for presently after, breaking out into savage fury, he took the young one into his arms, and threw her with violence against the stones; but his brutal resentment did not stop here, he beat her afterwards in a cruel manner. I could not see this treatment of my benefactress without the highest concern for her, and rage against the author of it; especially as the natural jealousy of these people gave occasion to think that it was on my account she suffered. I could hardly suppress the first emotions of my resentment, which prompted me to return him his barbarity in his own kind; but besides that this might have drawn upon her fresh marks of his severity, it was neither politic, nor indeed in my power, to have done it to any good purpose at this time.

Our cacique now made us understand that we must embark directly in the same canoe which brought us, and return to our companions; and that the Indians we were about to leave, would join us in a few days, when we should all set out in a body, in order to proceed to the northward. In our way back, nothing very material happened; but upon our arrival, which was the next day, we found Mr Elliot, the surgeon, in a very bad way; his illness had been continually increasing since we left him. Mr Hamilton and Mr Campbell were almost starved, having fared very ill since we left them; a few sea-eggs were all the subsistence they had lived upon; and these procured by the cacique's wife, in the manner I mentioned before. This woman was the very reverse of my hostess; and as she found her husband was of so much consequence to us, took upon her with much haughtiness, and treated us as dependents and slaves. He was not more engaging in his carriage towards us; he would give no part of what he had to spare to any but Captain Cheap, whom his interest led him to prefer to the rest, though our wants were often greater. The captain, on his part, contributed to keep us in this abject situation, by approving this distinction the cacique shewed to him. Had he treated us with not quite so much distance, the cacique might have been more regardful of our wants. The little regard and attention which our necessitous condition drew from Captain Cheap, may be imputed likewise, in some measure, to the effects of a mind soured by a series of crosses and disappointments; which, indeed, had operated on us all to a great neglect of each other, and sometimes of ourselves.

We were not suffered to be in the same wigwam with the cacique and his wife; which, if we had had any countenance from Captain Cheap, would not have been refused. What we had made for ourselves was in such a bungling manner, that it scarce deserved the name even of this wretched sort of habitation. But our untoward circumstances now found some relief in the arrival of the Indians we waited for; who brought with them some seal, a small portion of which fell to our share. A night or two after, they sent out some of their young men, who procured us a quantity of a very delicate kind of birds, called shags and cormorants. Their manner of taking these birds resembles something of a sport called bat-fowling. They find out their haunts among the rocks and cliffs in the night, when taking with them torches made of the bark of the birch tree, which is common here, and grows to a very large size (this bark has a very unctuous quality, and emits a bright and clear light; and in the northern parts of America is used frequently instead of candle) they bring the boat's side as near as possible to the rocks, under the roosting-places of these birds; then waving their lights backwards and forwards, the birds are dazzled and confounded so as to fall into the canoe, where they are instantly knocked on the head with a short stick the Indians take with them for that purpose.

Seal are taken in some less frequented parts of these coasts, with great ease; but when their haunts have been two or three times disturbed, they soon learn to provide for their safety, by repairing to the water upon the first alarm. This is the case with them hereabouts; but as they frequently raise their heads above water, either to breathe or look about them, I have seen an Indian at this interval, throw his lance with such dexterity as to strike the animal through both its eyes, at a great distance; and it is very seldom that they miss their aim.

As we were wholly unacquainted with these methods of providing food for ourselves, and were without arms and amunition, we were drove to the utmost straits; and found ourselves rather in worse condition than we had been at any time before. For the Indians, having now nothing to fear from us, we found we had nothing to expect from them upon any other motive. Accordingly, if they ever did relieve us, it was through caprice; for at most times they would shew themselves unconcerned at our greatest distresses. But the good Indian women, whose friendship I had experienced before, continued, from time to time, their good offices to me. Tho' I was not suffered to enter their wigwams, they would find opportunities of throwing in my way such scraps as they could secrete from their husbands. The obligation I was under to them on this account is great, as the hazard they ran in conferring these favours was little less than death. The men, unrestrained by any laws or ties of conscience, in the management of their own families, exercise a most despotic authority over their wives, whom they consider in the same view they do any other part of their property, and dispose of them accordingly: even their common treatment of them is cruel; for though the toil and hazard of procuring food lies entirely upon the women, yet they are not suffered to touch any thing of it till the husband is satisfied; and then he assigns them their portion, which is generally very scanty, and such as he has not a stomach for himself. This arbitrary proceeding, with respect to their own families, is not peculiar to this people only. I have had occasion to observe it in more instances than this I have mentioned, among many other nations of savages I have seen.

These Indians are of a middling stature, well set, and very active; and make their way among the rocks with an amazing agility. Their feet by this kind of exercise, contract a callosity which renders the use of shoes quite unnecessary to them. But before I conclude the few observations I have to make on a people so confined in all their notions and practice, it may be expected I would say something of their religion; but as their gross ignorance is in nothing more conspicuous, and as we found it adviseable to keep out of their way when the fits of devotion came upon them, which is rather frantic than religious, the reader can expect very little satisfaction on this head. Accident has sometimes made me unavoidably a spectator of scenes I should chosen to have withdrawn myself from; and so far I am instructed. As there are no fixed seasons for their religious exercises, the younger people wait till the elders find themselves devotely disposed; who begin the ceremony by several deep and dismal groans, which rise gradually to a hideous kind of singing, from which they proceed to enthusiasm, and work themselves into a disposition that borders on madness; for suddenly jumping up, they snatch fire-brands from the fire, put them in their mouths, and run about burning every body they come near: at other times, it is a custom with them to wound one another with sharp mussel-shells till they are besmeared with blood. These orgies continue till those who preside in them foam at the mouth, grow faint, are exhausted with fatigue, and dissolve in a profusion of sweat. When the men drop their part in this frenzy, the women take it up, acting over again much the same kind of wild scene, except that they rather outdo the men in shrieks and noise. Our cacique, who had been reclaimed from these abominations by the Spaniards, and just knew the exterior form of crossing himself, pretended to be much offended at these profane ceremonies, and that he would have died sooner than have partaken of them. Among other expressions of his disapprobation, he declared, that whilst the savages solemnised these horrid rites, he never failed to hear strange and uncommon noises in the woods, and to see frightful visions; and assured us that the devil was the chief actor among them upon these occasions.

It might be about the middle of March, that we embarked with these Indians. They separated our little company entirely, not putting any two of us together in the same canoe. The oar was my lot, as usual, as also Mr Campbell's; Mr Hamilton could not row, and Captain Cheap was out of the question; our surgeon was more dead than alive at the time, and lay at the bottom of the canoe he was in. The weather coming on too bad for their canoes to keep the sea, we landed again, without making great progress that day. Here Mr Elliot, our surgeon, died. At our first setting out, he promised the fairest for holding out, being a very strong, active young man: he had gone through an infinite deal of fatigue, as Mr Hamilton and he were the best shots amongst us, and, whilst our ammunition lasted, never spared themselves, and in a great measure provided for the rest; but he died the death many others had done before him, being quite starved. We scraped a hole for him in the sand, and buried him in the best manner we could.

Here I must relate a little anecdote of our Christian cacique. He and his wife had gone off, at some distance from the shore, in their canoe, when she dived for sea-eggs; but not meeting with great success, they returned a good deal out of humour. A little boy of theirs, about three years old, whom they appeared to be doatingly fond of, watching for his father and mother's return, ran into the surf to meet them: the father handed a basket of sea-eggs to the child, which being too heavy for him to carry, he let it fall; upon which the father jumped out of the canoe, and catching the boy up in his arms, dashed him with the utmost violence against the stones. The poor little creature lay motionless and bleeding, and in that condition was taken up by the mother: but died soon after. She appeared inconsolable for some time; but the brute his father shewed little concern about it. A day or two after we put to sea again, and crossed the great bay I mentioned we had been to the bottom of, when we first hauled away to the westward. The land here was very low and sandy, with something like the mouth of a river which discharged itself into the sea; and which had been taken no notice of by us before, as it was so shallow that the Indians were obliged to take every thing out of their canoes, and carry it over the neck of land, and then haul the boats over into a river, which, at this part of it, was very broad, more resembling a lake than a river. We rowed up it four or five leagues, and then took into a branch of it, that ran first to the eastward, and then to the northward: here it became much narrower, and the stream excessively rapid, so that we made but little way, though we worked very hard. At night we landed upon its banks, and had a most uncomfortable lodging, it being a perfect swamp; and we had nothing to cover us, tho' it rained very hard. The Indians were little better off than we, as there was no wood here to make their wigwams; so that all they could do was to prop up the bark they carry in the bottom of their canoes with their oars, and shelter themselves as well as they could to leeward of it. They, knowing the difficulties that were to be encountered here, had provided themselves with some seal; but we had not the least morsel to eat, after the heavy fatigues of the day, excepting a sort of root we saw some of the Indians make use of, which was very disagreeable to the taste. We laboured all next day against the stream, and fared as we had done the day before. The next day brought us to the carrying place. Here was plenty of wood; but nothing to be got for sustenance. The first thing the Indians did was to take every thing out of their canoes; and after hauling them ashore, they made their wigwams. We passed this night, as generally we had done, under a tree; but what we suffered at this time is not easily to be expressed. I had been three days at the oar without any kind of nourishment, but the wretched root I mentioned before. I had no shirt, as mine was rotted off by bits; and we were devoured by vermin. All my cloaths consisted of an old short grieko, which is something like a bear-skin, with a piece of a waistcoat under it, which once had been of red cloth, both which I had on when I was cast away; I had a ragged pair of trowsers, without either shoe or stocking. The first thing the Indians did in the morning was to take their canoes to pieces and here, for the information of the reader, it will be necessary to describe the structure of these boats, which are extremely well calculated for the use of these Indians, as they are frequently obliged to carry them over land a long way together, through thick woods, to avoid doubling capes and headlands, in seas where no open boat could live. They generally consist of five pieces, or planks; one for the bottom, and two for each side; and as these people have no iron tools, the labour must be great in hacking a single plank out of a large tree with shells and flints, though with the help of fire. Along the edges of the plank, they make small holes, at about an inch from one to the other, and sew them together with the souple jack, or woodbine; but as these holes are not filled up by the substance of the woodbine, their boats would be immediately full of water, if they had not a method of preventing it. They do this very effectually by the bark of a tree, which they first steep in water for some time, and then beat it between two stones till it answers the use of oakum, and then chinse each hole so well that they do not admit of the least water coming through, and are easily taken asunder and put together again. When they have occasion to go over land, as at this time, each man or woman carries a plank; whereas it would be impossible for them to drag a heavy boat entire. Every body had something to carry excepting Captain Cheap; and he was obliged to be assisted, or never would have got over this march; for a worse than this, I believe, never was made. He, with the others, set out some time before me. I waited for two Indians, who belonged to the canoe I came in; and who remained to carry over the last of the things from the side we were on. I had a piece of wet heavy canvas, which belonged to Captain Cheap, with a bit of stinking seal wrapped in it (which had been given him that morning by some of the Indians) to carry upon my head, which was a sufficient weight for a strong man in health, through such roads, and a grievous burden to one in my condition. Our way was through a thick wood, the bottom of which was a mere quagmire, most part of it up to our knees, and often to our middle, and every now and then we had a large tree to get over; for they often lay directly in our road. Besides this, we were continually treading upon the stumps of trees, which were not to be avoided, as they were covered with water; and having neither shoe nor stocking, my feet and legs were frequently torn and wounded. Before I had got half a mile, the two Indians had left me ; and making the best of my way lest they should be all gone before I got to the other side, I fell off a tree that crossed the road, into a very deep swamp, where I very narrowly escaped drowning, by the weight of the burthen I had on my head. It was a long while before I could extricate myself from this difficulty; and when I did my strength was quite exhausted. I sat down under a tree, and there gave way to melancholy reflections. However, as I was sensible these reflections would answer no end, they did not last long. I got up, and marking a great tree, I then deposited my load, not being able to carry it any farther, and set out to join my company. It was some hours before I reached my companions. I found them sitting under a tree, and sat myself down by them without speaking a word nor did they speak to me as I remember, for some time; when Captain Cheap breaking silence, began to ask after the seal and piece of canvas. I told him the disaster I had met with, which he might have easily guessed by the condition the rags I had on were in, as well as having my feet and ancles cut to pieces; but instead of compassion for my sufferings, I heard nothing but grumbling from every one, for the irreparable loss they had sustained by me. I made no answer; but after resting myself a little, I got up and struck into the wood, and walked back at least five miles to the tree I had marked, and returned just time enough to deliver it before my companions embarked with the Indians upon a great lake, the opposite part of which seemed to wash the foot of the Cordilleras. I wanted to embark with them; but was given to understand I was to wait for some other Indians that were to follow them. I knew not where these Indians were to come from: I was left alone upon the beach, and night was at hand. They left me not even a morsel of the stinking seal that I had suffered so much about. I kept my eyes upon the boats as long as I could distinguish them; and then returned into the wood, and sat myself down upon the root of a tree, having eat nothing the whole day but the stem of a plant which resembles that of an artichoke, which is of a juicy consistence, and acid taste. Quite worn out with fatigue, I soon fell asleep; and awaking before day, I thought I heard some voices at no great distance from me. As the day appeared, looking farther into the wood, I perceived a wigwam, and immediately made towards it; but the reception I met with was not at all agreeable; for stooping to get into it, I presently received two or three kicks in my face, and at the same time heard the sound of voices, seemingly in anger; which made me retire, and wait at the foot of a tree, where I remained till an old woman peeped out, and made signs to me to draw near. I obeyed very readily, and went into the wigwam: in it were three men and two women; one young man seemed to have great respect shown to him by the rest, though he was the most miserable object I ever saw. He was a perfect skeleton, and covered with sores from head to foot. I was happy to sit a moment by their fire, as I was quite benumbed with cold. The old woman took out a piece of seal, holding one part of it between her feet, and the other end in her teeth, and then cut off some thin slices with a sharp shell, and distributed them about to the other Indians. She then put a bit on the fire, taking a piece of fat in her mouth, which she kept chewing, every now and then spirting some of it on the piece that was warming upon the fire; for they never do more with it than warm it through. When it was ready, she gave me a little bit, which I swallowed whole, being almost starved. As these Indians were all strangers to me, I did not know which way they were going;

and indeed it was now become quite indifferent to me which way I went, whether to the northward or southward, so that they would but take me with them, and give me something to eat. However, to make them comprehend me, I pointed first to the southward, and after to the lake, and I soon understood they were going to the northward. They all went out together, excepting the sick Indian, and took up the plank of the canoe, which lay near the wigwam, and carried it upon the beach, and presently put it together; and getting every thing into it, they put me to the oar. We rowed across the lake to the mouth of a very rapid river, where we put ashore for that night, not daring to get any way down in the dark; as it required the greatest skill, even in the day, to avoid running foul of the stumps and roots of trees, of which this river was full. I passed a melancholy night, as they would not suffer me to come near the wigwam they had made; nor did they give me the least bit of any one thing to eat since we embarked. In the morning we set off again. The weather proved extremely bad the whole day. We went down the river at an amazing rate; and just before night they put ashore upon a stony beach. They hauled the canoe up, and all disappeared in a moment, and I was left quite alone : it rained violently, and was very dark. I thought it was as well to lie down upon the beach, half side in water, as to get into a swamp under a dropping tree. In this dismal situation I fell asleep, and awaked three or four hours after in such agonies with the cramp, that I thought I must die upon the spot. I attempted several times to raise myself upon my legs, but could not. At last I made shift to get upon my knees, and looking towards the wood, I saw a great fire at some distance from me. I was a long time in crawling to it; and when I reached it, I threw myself almost into it, in hopes of finding some relief from the pain I suffered. This intrusion gave great offence to the Indians, who immediately got up, kicking and beating me till they drove me some distance from it; however, I contrived, a little after, to place myself so as to receive some warmth from it; by which I got rid of the cramp.

In the morning we left this place, and were soon after out of the river. Being now at sea again, the Indians intended putting ashore at the first convenient place, to look for shellfish, their stock of provisions having been quite exhausted for some time. At low water we landed upon a spot that seemed to promise well; and here we found plenty of limpets. Though at this time starving, I did not attempt to eat one, least I should lose a moment in gathering them; not knowing how soon the Indians might be going again. I had almost filled my hat when I saw them returning to the canoe. I made what haste I could to her; for I believe they would have made no conscience of leaving me behind. I sat down to my oar again, placing my hat close to me, every now and then eating a limpet. The Indians were employed the same way, when one of them seeing me throw the shells over-board, spoke to the rest in a violent passion; and, getting up, fell upon me, and seized me by an old ragged hand-kerchief I had about my neck, almost throttled me; whilst another took me by the legs, and was going to throw me over-board, if the old woman had not prevented them. I was all this time entirely ignorant by what means I had given offence, till I observed that the Indians, after eating the limpets, carefully put the shells in a heap at the bottom of the canoe. I then concluded there was some superstition about throwing these shells into the sea, my ignorance of which had very nearly cost me my life. I was resolved to eat no more limpets till we landed, which we did some time after, upon an island. I then took notice that the Indians brought all their shells ashore, and laid them above high water mark. Here, as I was going to eat a large bunch of berries I had gathered from a tree, for they looked very tempting, one of the Indians snatched them out of my hand, and threw them away, making me to understand that they were poisonous. Thus, in all probability, did these people now save my life, who, a few hours before, were going to take it from me, for throwing away a shell.

In two days after, I joined my companions again; but don't

remember that there was the least joy shewn on either side at meeting. At this place was a very large canoe belonging to our guide, which would have required at least six men to the oar to have made any kind of expedition: instead of that, there was only Campbell and myself, besides the Indian, his companion, or servant, to row, the cacique himself never touching an oar, but sitting with his wife all the time much at his ease. Mr Hamilton continued in the same canoe he had been in all along, and which, still was to keep us company some way further, though many of the others had left us. This was dreadful hard work to such poor starved wretches as we were, to be slaving at the oar all day long in such a heavy boat; and this inhuman fellow would never give us a scrap to eat, excepting when he took so much seal that he could not contrive to carry it all away with him, which happened very seldom. After working like galley-slaves all day, towards night, when we landed, instead of taking any rest, Mr Campbell and I were sometimes obliged to go miles along shore to get a few shellfish; and just as we have made a little fire in order to dress them, he has commanded us into the boat again, and kept us rowing the whole night without ever landing. It is impossible for me to describe the miserable state we were reduced to: our bodies were so emaciated, that we hardly appeared the figures of men. It has often happened to me in the coldest night, both in hail and snow, where we had nothing but an open beach to lay down upon, in order to procure a little rest, that I have been obliged to pull off the few rags I had on, as it was impossible to get a moment's sleep with them on for the vermin that swarmed about them; though I used, as often as I had time, to take my clothes off, and putting them upon a large stone, beat them with another, in hopes of killing hundreds at once ; for it was endless work to pick them off. What we suffered from this was ten times worse even than hunger. But we were clean in comparison to Captain Cheap; for I could compare his body to nothing but an ant-hill, with thousands of those insects crawling over it; for he was now past attempting to rid himself in the least from this torment, as he had quite lost himself, not recollecting our names that were about him, or even his own. His beard was as long as a hermit's: that and his face being covered with train oil and dirt, from having long accustomed himself to sleep upon a bag, by the way of pillow, in which he kept the pieces of stinking seal. This prudent method he took to prevent our getting at it whilst he slept. His legs were as big as mill-posts, though his body appeared to be nothing but skin and bone.

One day we fell in with about forty Indians, who came down to the beach we landed on, curiously painted. Our cacique seemed to understand but little of their language, and it sounded to us very different from what we had heard before. However, they made us comprehend that a ship had been upon the coast not far from where we then were, and that she had a red flag: this we understood some time after to have been the *Anne* pink, whose adventures are particularly related in Lord Anson's *Voyage;* and we passed through the very harbour she had lain in.

As there was but one small canoe that intended to accompany us any longer; and that in which Mr Hamilton had been to this time, intended to proceed no further to the northward; our cacique proposed to him to come into our canoe, which he refused, as the insolence of this fellow was to him insupportable; he therefore rather chose to remain where he was, till chance should throw in his way some other means of getting forward; so here we left him; and it was some months before we saw him again.

We now got on, by very slow degrees, to the northward; and as the difficulties and hardships we daily went through would only be a repetition of those already mentioned, I shall say no more, but that at last we reached an island about thirty leagues to the southward of Chiloe. Here we remained two days for a favourable opportunity to cross the bay, the very thoughts of which seemed to frighten our cacique out of his senses; and, indeed, there was great reason for his apprehensions; for there ran a most dreadful hollow sea, dangerous, indeed, for any open boat whatever, but a thousand times more for such a crazy vessel as we were in. He at last mustered up resolution enough to attempt it, first having crossed himself for an hour together, and made a kind of lugsail out of the bits of blankets they wore about them, sewed together with split Supple-Jacks. We then put off, and a terrible passage we had. The bottom plank of the canoe was split, which opened upon every sea; and the water continually rushing over the gunnel. I may say that we were in a manner full the whole way over, though all hands were employed in bailing without ceasing a moment. As we drew near the shore, the cacique was eager to land, having been terrified to that degree with this run, that if it had not been for us, every soul must have perished; for he had very near got in amongst the breakers, where the sea drove with such violence upon the rocks, that not even an Indian could have escaped, especially as it was in the night. We kept off till we got into smooth water, and landed upon the island of Chiloe; though in a part of it that was not inhabited. Here we staid all the next day, in a very heavy snow, to recover ourselves a little after our fatigue; but the cold was so excessive, having neither shoe nor stocking, we thought we should have lost our feet; and Captain Cheap was so ill, that if he had had but a few leagues further to have gone without relief, he could not have held out. It pleased God now that our sufferings, in a great measure, were drawing to an end.

What things our cacique had brought with him from the wreck, he here buried under ground, in order to conceal them from the Spaniards, who would not have left him a rusty nail, if they had known of it. Towards evening, we set off again; and about nine the same night, to our great joy, we observed something that had the appearance of a house. It belonged to an acquaintance of our cacique; and as he was possessed of my fowling-piece, and we had preserved about one charge of powder, he made us load it for him, and desired we would shew him how to discharge it; upon which, standing up, and holding his head from it as far as possible, he fired, and fell back into the bottom of the canoe. The Indians belonging to the house, not in the least used to fire arms, ran out and hid themselves in the woods. But after some time, one of them, bolder than the rest, got upon a hill, and hollowed to us, asking who and what we were. Our cacique now made himself known, and they presently came down to the boat, bringing with them some fish, and plenty of potatoes. This was the most comfortable meal we had made for many long months; and as soon as this was over, we rowed about two miles farther to a little village, where we landed. Here our cacique presently awaked all the inhabitants by the noise he made, and obliged one of them to open his door to us, and immediately to make a large fire; for the weather was very severe, this being the month of June, the depth of winter in this part of the world. The Indians now flocked thick about us, and seemed to have great compassion for us, as our cacique related to them what part he knew of our history. They knew not what countrymen we were, nor could our guide inform them; for he had often asked us if we were French, Dutch, or English, the only nations he had ever heard of besides the Spaniards. We always answered we were from Grande Bretagne, which he could make nothing of; for we were afraid, if he knew us to be English (as he had heard that nation was at war with the Spaniards), he never would have conducted us to Chiloe.

These good-natured compassionate creatures seemed to vie with each other who should take the most care of us. They made a bed of sheep-skins close to the fire, for Captain Cheap, and laid him upon it; and, indeed, had it not been for the kind assistance he now met with, he could not have survived three days longer. Though it was now about midnight, they went out and killed a sheep, of which they made broth, and baked a large cake of barley-meal. Any body may imagine what a treat this was to wretches who had not tasted a bit of bread, or any wholesome diet, for such a length of time. After we could eat no longer, we went to sleep about the fire, which the Indians took care to keep up. In the morning, the women came from far and near, each bringing with her something. Almost every one had a pipkin in her hand, containing either fowls, or mutton made into broth, potatoes, eggs, or other eatables. We fell to work as if we had eat nothing in the night, and employed ourselves so for the best part of the day. In the evening the men filled our house bringing with them some jars of a liquor they called chicha, made of barley-meal, and not very unlike our oatale in taste, which will intoxicate those who drink a sufficient quantity of it; for a little has no effect. As soon as the drink was out, a fresh supply of victuals was brought in; and in this manner we passed the whole time we remained with these hospitable Indians. They are a strong well-made people, extremely well featured, both men and women, and vastly neat in their persons. The mens dress is called by them a puncho, which is a square piece of cloth, generally in stripes of different colours, with a slit in the middle of it, wide enough to let their heads through, so that it hangs on their shoulders, half of it falling before, and the other behind them: under this they wear a short kind of flannel shirt without sleeves or neck. They have widekneed breeches, something like the Dutch seamen, and on their legs a sort of knit buskins without any feet to them; but never any shoes. Their hair is always combed very smooth, and tied very tight up in a great bunch close to the neck: some wear a very neat hat of their own making, and others go without. The women wear a shift like the mens shirts, without sleeves ; and over it a square piece of cloth, which they fasten before with a large silver pin, and a petticoat of different stripes: they take as much care of their hair as the men ; and both have always a kind of fillet bound very tight about the forehead, and made fast behind: in short these people are as cleanly as the several savage nations we had met with before, were beastly. Upon our first coming here, they had dispatched a messenger to the Spanish corregidore at

Castro, a town at a considerable distance from hence, to inform him of our arrival. At the end of three days, this man returned with an order to the chief caciques of these Indians we were amongst, to carry us directly to a certain place, where there would be a party of soldiers to receive us. These poor people now seemed to be under great concern for us, hearing by the messenger the preparations that were making to receive us; for they stand in vast dread of the Spanish soldiery. They were very desirous of knowing what countrymen we were. We told them we were English, and at that time at war with the Spaniards ; upon which they appeared fonder of us than ever; and I verily believe, if they durst, would have concealed us amongst them, least we should come to any harm. They are so far from being in the Spanish interest, that they detest the very name of a Spaniard. And, indeed, I am not surprised at it; for they are kept under such subjection, and such a laborious slavery, by mere dint of hard usage and punishments, that it appears to me the most absurd thing in the world, that the Spaniards should rely upon these people for assistance upon any emergency. We embarked in the evening, and it was night before we got to the place where we were to be delivered up to the Spanish guard. We were met by three or four officers, and a number of soldiers, all with their spados drawn, who surrounded us, as if they had the most formidable enemy to take charge of, instead of three poor helpless wretches, who, notwithstanding the good living we had met with amongst these kind Indians, could hardly support ourselves. They carried us to the top of a hill, and there put us under a shade; for it consisted of a thatched roof, without any sides or walls, being quite open; and here we were to lie upon the cold ground. All sorts of people now came to stare at us as a sight; but the Indian women never came empty handed; they always brought with them either fowls, mutton, or some kind of provision to us; so that we lived well enough. However, we found a very sensible difference between the treatment we had met with from the Indians, and what we now experienced from the Spaniards with the former we were quite at liberty to do as we pleased; but here, if we only went ten yards to attempt at getting rid of some of the vermin that devoured us, we had two soldiers with drawn spados, to attend us. About the third day, a Jesuit from Castro came to see us; not from a motive of compassion, but from a report spread by our Indian cacique, that we had some things of great value about us. Having by chance seen Captain Cheap pull out a gold repeating watch, the first thing the good father did was to lug out of his pocket a bottle of brandy, and give us a dram, in order to open our hearts. He then came roundly to the point, asking us if we had saved no watches or rings. Captain Cheap declared he had nothing, never suspecting that the Indian had seen his watch, having, as he thought, always taken great care to conceal it from him; but knowing that Campbell had a silver watch, which had been the property of our surgeon, he desired him to make it a present to the Jesuit, telling him, at the same time, that as these people had great power and authority, it might be of service to us hereafter. This Campbell very unwillingly did, and received from the father, not long after, a pitiful present, not a quarter part of the value of the rim of the watch. We understood afterwards, that this had come to the governor's ears, who was highly offended at it, as thinking that if any thing of that sort had been to be had, it was his due; and did not spare the Jesuits in the least upon the occasion. Soon after this, the officer of the guard informed us there was an order come to carry us to Castro. In the evening, we were conducted to the waterside, and put into a large *periago;* and there were several more to attend us, full of soldiers. About eight o'clock at night, we were off the town. Their boats all laid upon their oars, and there was a great deal of ceremony used in hailing and asking for the keys, as if it had been a regular fortification. After some time, we landed; but could see neither gates nor walls, nor anything that had the appearance of a garrison. As we walked up a steep hill into the town, the way was lined with men who had broomsticks upon their shoulders instead of muskets, and a lighted match in their hands. When we came to the corregidore's house, we found it full of people. He was an old man, very tall, with a long cloak on, a tye wig without any curel, and a spado of immense length by his side. He received us in great state and form; but as we had no interpreter, we understood little or nothing of the questions he asked us. He ordered a table to be spread for us with cold ham and fowls; which we three only sat down to, and in a short time dispatched more than ten men with common appetites would have done. It is amazing, that our eating to that excess we had done, from the time we first got amongst these kind Indians, had not killed us; we were never satisfied, and used to take all opportunities, for some months after, of filling our pockets when we were not seen, that we might get up two or three times in the night to cram ourselves. Captain Cheap used to declare, that he was quite ashamed of himself. After supper, the corregidore carried us to the Jesuits college, attended by the soldiers, and all the rabble of the town. This was intended, at present, for our prison, till orders were received from the governor, who resided at Chaco, above thirty leagues from this place. When we got to the college, the corregidore desired the father provincial, as they stiled him, or head of the Jesuits here, to find out what religion we were of, or whether we had any or not. He then retired, the gates were shut, and we were conducted to a cell. We found in it something like beds spread on the floor, and an old ragged shirt apiece but clean, which was of infinite service to us; nor did eating at first give me half the satisfaction this treasure of an old shirt did. Though this college was large, there were but four Jesuits in it, nor were there any more of that order upon the island. In the morning, Captain Cheap was sent for by the father provincial; their conversation was carried on in Latin, perhaps not the best on either side; however, they made shift to understand one another. When he returned, he told us the good fathers were still harping upon what things of value we might have saved and concealed about us; and that if we had any thing of that sort, we could not do better than to let them have it. Religion seemed to be quite out of the question at present; but a day or two after, the corregidore being informed that we were heretics, he desired these Jesuits would convert us; but one of them told him it was a mere joke to attempt it, as we could have no inducement upon that island to change our religion; but that when we got to Chili, in such a delightful country as that was, where there was nothing but diversions and amusements, we should be converted fast enough. We kept close to our cell till the bell rang for dinner, when we were conducted to a hall, where there was one table for the fathers, and another for us. After a very long Latin prayer, we sat down and eat what was put before us, without a single word passing at either table. As soon as we had finished, there was another long prayer, which, however, did not appear so tedious as the first; and then we retired to our cell again. In this manner we passed eight days without ever stirring out; all which time one might have imagined one's self out of the world; for excepting the bell for dinner, a silence reigned throughout the whole, as if the place had been uninhabited.

A little before dark, on the eighth evening, we heard a violent knocking at the gate, which was no sooner opened than there entered a young officer booted and spurred, who acquainted the fathers, that he was sent by the governor to conduct us to Chaco. This young man was the governor's son; by which means he obtained a commission next in authority, upon this island, to his father. He ought to have been kept at school; for he was a vain empty coxcomb, much disliked by the people of the island. After taking leave of the Jesuits, who I imagine were not sorry to be rid of us, after finding their expectations baulked, we set out, having about thirty soldiers on horseback to attend us. We rode about eight miles that night, when we came to an Estancia, or farm-house, belonging to an old lady, who had two handsome daughters. Here we were very well entertained; and the good old lady seemed to have great compassion for us. She asked the governor's son if he thought his father would have any objection to my passing a month with her at her farm. As she was a person of rank in this island, he said he would acquaint his father with her request, and made no doubt but he would grant it. I observed our soldiers, when they came into the house, had none of them any shoes on, but wore buskins, like the Indians, without any feet to them. They all had monstrous great spurs, some of silver and others of copper, which made a rattling when they walked, like chains. They were all stout, strong-looking men, as the Spaniards, natives of the island, in general are. After a good supper, we had sheepskins laid near the fire for us to sleep on. Early in the morning we mounted again; and after riding some miles across the country we came to the water-side, where we found several *periagoes* waiting for us, with some officers in them. Most of the soldiers dismounted and embarked with us, a few only being sent round with the horses. It was three days before we arrived at Chaco, as the tides between this island and the main are so rapid that no boat can stem them. The same precaution was taken here as at Castro; we passed through a whole lane of soldiers, armed as I mentioned those to have been before, excepting a few, who really had matchlocks, the only fire-arms they have here. The soldiers, upon our journey, had given a pompous account of el Palacio del Rey, or the king's palace, as they stiled the governor's house, and therefore we expected to see something very magnificent; but it was nothing better than a large thatched barn, partitioned off into several rooms. The governor was sitting at a large table covered with a piece of red serge, having all the principal officers about him. After some time, he made us sit down, attempting to converse with us by his linguist, who was a stupid old fellow, that could neither talk English nor Spanish, but said he was born in England, had resided above forty years in that country, and having formerly been a buccaneer, was taken by the Spaniards near Panama. The governor kept us to supper, and then we were conducted across the court to our apartment, which was a place that had served to keep the fire wood for the governor's kitchen; however, as it was dry over head, we thought ourselves extremely well lodged. There was a soldier placed at the door with a drawn spado in his hand, to prevent our stirring out; which was quite unnecessary, as we knew not where to go if we had been at liberty. One of these soldiers took a great fancy to my ragged grieko, which had still some thousands about it; and, in exchange, gave me an old puncho, the sort of garment with a hole in the middle to put one's head through; as above related to be worn by the Indians; and for the little bit of my waistcoat that remained, he gave me a pair of breeches. I now should have thought myself very handsomely equipped, if I had had but another shirt. The next day about noon, the governor sent for us, and we dined at his table; after which we returned to our lodging, where we were never alone; for every body was curious to see us. We passed about a week in this manner, when the centinel was taken off, and we were allowed to look about us a little, though not to go out of the palace, as they were pleased to call it. We dined every day with the governor; but were not very fond of his fast days, which succeeded each other too quickly. I contrived to make friends with his steward and cook; by which means I always carried my pockets full to my apartment, where I passed my time very agreeably. Soon after we had leave to walk about the town, or go wherever we pleased. Every house was open to us; and though it was but an hour after we had dined, they always spread a table, thinking we never could eat enough after what we had suffered; and we were much of the same opinion. They are, in general, a charitable, good sort of people; but very ignorant, and governed by their priests, who make them believe just what they please. The Indian language is chiefly spoken here, even by the Spaniards one amongst another; and they say they think it a finer language than their own. The women have fine complexions, and many of them are very handsome; they have good voices, and can strum a little upon the guittar; but they have an ugly custom of smoaking tobacco, which is a very scarce commodity here; and therefore is looked upon as a great treat when they meet at one another's houses. The lady of the house comes in with a large wooden pipe crammed with tobacco; and after taking two or three hearty whiffs, she holds her head under her cloak least any of the smoke should escape, and then swallows it; some time after you see it coming out of her nose and ears. She then hands the pipe to the next lady, who does the same, till it has gone through the whole company. Their houses are but very mean, as will be easily imagined by what I have said of the governor's. They make their fire in the middle of their rooms; but have no chimneys; there is a small hole at each end of the roof, to let the smoke out. It is only the better sort of people that eat bread made of wheat; as there grow but very little here, and they have no mills to grind it; but then they have great plenty of the finest potatoes in the world: these are always roasted in the ashes, then scraped, and served up at meals instead of bread. They breed abundance of swine, as they supply both Chili and Peru with hams. They are in no want of sheep, but are not overstocked with cows; owing, in a great measure, to their own indolence in not clearing away the woods; which, if they would be at the pains to do, they might have sufficient pasture. Their trade consists in hams, hogs-lard, which is used throughout all South America instead of butter, cedar-plank, which the Indians are continually employed in cutting quite to the foot of the Cordilleras, little carved boxes, which the Spanish ladies used to put their work in, carpets, quilts, and punchos neatly embroidered all round; for these, both in Chili and Peru, are used by the people of the first fashion, as well as the inferior sort, by way of riding-dress, and are esteemed to be much more convenient for a horseman than any kind of coat whatever.

They have what they call an annual ship from Lima, as they never expect more than one in the year; tho' sometimes it happens that two have come, and at other times they have been two or three years without any. When this happens, they are greatly distressed, as this ship brings them baize, cloth, linens, hats, ribbons, tobacco, sugar, brandy, and wine; but this latter article is chiefly for the use of the churches: matte, an herb from Paraguay, used all over South America instead of tea, is also a necessary article. This ship's cargo is chiefly consigned to the Jesuits, who have more Indians employed for them than all the rest of the inhabitants together, and of course engross almost the whole trade. There is no money current in this island. If any person wants a few yards of linen, a little sugar, tobacco, or any other thing brought from Peru, he gives so many cedar-planks, hams, or punchos, in exchange. Some time after we had been here, a [boat] arrived in the harbour from Lima, which occasioned great joy amongst the inhabitants, as they had no ship the year before, from the alarm Lord Anson had given upon the coast. This was not the annual vessel, but one of those that I mentioned before which came unexpectedly. The captain of her was an old man, well known upon the island, who had traded here once in two or three years, for more than thirty years past. He had a remarkable large head, and therefore was commonly known by a nick-name they had given him of Cabuco de Toro, or Bull's head. He had not been here a week before he came to the governor, and told him with a most melancholy countenance, that he had not slept a wink since he came into the harbour, as the governor was pleased to allow three English prisoners liberty to walk about instead of confining them; and that he expected every moment they would board his vessel, and carry her away: this he said when he had above thirty hands aboard. The governor assured him he would be answerable for us, and that he might sleep in quiet; though, at the same time, he could not help laughing at the man, as all the people in the town did. These assurances did not satisfy the captain: he used the utmost dispatch in disposing of his cargo, and put to sea again, not thinking himself safe till he had lost sight of the island. It was about three months after us, that Mr Hamilton was brought in, by a party that the governor had sent to the southward on purpose to fetch him. He was in a wretched condition upon his first arrival, but soon recovered with the good living he found here.

It is usual for the governor to make a tour every year through the several districts belonging to his government: on this occasion he took us with him. The first place he visited was Carelmapo, on the main; and from thence to Castro. At these places, he holds a kind of court; all the chief caciques meeting him, and informing him of what has passed since his last visit, and receiving fresh orders for the year to come. At Castro we had the same liberty we enjoyed at Chaco, and visited every body. It seemed they had forgot all the ceremony used upon our first landing here, which was with an intent to make us believe it was strongly fortified; for now they let us see plainly that they had neither fort nor gun. At Chaco they had a little earthen fort, with a small ditch palisadoed round it, and a few old honey-combed guns without carriages, and which does not defend the harbour in the least. Whilst we were at Castro, the old lady (at whose house we lay the first night upon leaving the Jesuits college) sent to the governor, and begged I might be allowed to come to her for a few weeks: this was granted; and accordingly I went and passed about three weeks with her very happily, as she seemed to be as fond of me as if I had been her own son. She was very unwilling to part with me again; but as the governor was soon to return to Chaco, he sent for me, and I left my bene-factress with regret.

Amongst the houses we visited at Castro, there was one belonging to an old priest, who was esteemed one of the richest persons upon the island. He had a niece, of whom he was extremely fond, and who was to inherit all he possessed. He had taken a great deal of pains with her education, and she was reckoned one of the most accomplished young ladies of Chiloe. Her person was good, tho' she could not be called a regular beauty. This young lady did me the honour to take more notice of me than I deserved, and proposed to her uncle to convert me, and afterwards begged his consent to marry me. As the old man doated upon her, he readily agreed to it; and accordingly on the next visit I made him, acquainted me with the young lady's proposal, and his approbation of it, taking me at the same time into a room where there were several chests and boxes, which he unlocked, first shewing me what a number of fine cloaths his niece had, and then his own wardrobe, which he said should be mine at his death. Amongst other things, he produced a piece of linen, which he said should immediately be made up into shirts for me. I own this last article was a great temptation to me; however, I had the resolution to withstand it, and made the best excuses I could for not excepting of the honour they intended me; for by this time I could speak Spanish well enough to make myself understood.

Amongst other Indians who had come to meet with the governor here, there were some caciques of those Indians who had treated us so kindly at our first landing upon Chiloe. One of these, a young man, had been guilty of some offence, and was put in irons, and threatened to be more severely punished. W e could not learn his crime, or whether the governor did not do it in a great measure to shew us his power over these Indian chiefs: however, we were under great concern for this young man, who had been extremely kind to us, and begged Captain Cheap to intercede with the governor for him. This he did, and the cacique was released; the governor acquainting him, at the same time, with great warmth, that it was to us only he owed it, or otherwise he would have made a severe example of him. The young man seemed to have been in no dread of farther punishment, as I believe he felt all a man could do from the indignity of being put in irons in the public square, before all his brother-caciques, and many hundreds of other Indians. I thought this was not a very politic step of the governor, as the cacique came after to Captain Cheap to thank him for his goodness, and in all probability would remember the English for some time after; and not only he, but all the other caciques who had been witnesses of it, and who seemed to feel, if possible, even more than the young man himself did. We now returned to Chaco, and the governor told us, when the annual ship came, which they expected in December, we should be sent in her to Chili. We felt several earthquakes while we were here. One day as I happened to be upon a visit, at a house where I was very well acquainted, an Indian came in, who lived at many leagues distance from this town, and who had made this journey, in order to purchase some little trifles he wanted; amongst other things, he had bought some prints of saints. Very proud of these, he produced them, and put them into the hands of the women, who very devoutly first crossed themselves with them, and afterwards kissed them; then gave them to me, saying, at the same time, they supposed such a heretic as I was would refuse to kiss them. They were right in their conjectures: I returned them to the Indian without going through that ceremony. At that very instant there happened a violent shock of an earthquake, which they imputed entirely to the anger of the saints; and all quitted the house as fast as they. could, least it should fall upon their heads. For my part, I made the best of my way home for fear of being knocked on the head, went out of the house, by the rabble, who looked on me as the cause of all this mischief, and did not return to that house again till I thought this affair was forgotten.

Here is a very good harbour; but the entrance is very dangerous for those who are unacquainted with it, as the tides are so extremely rapid, and there are sunken rocks in the midchannel. The island is above seventy leagues round; and the body of it lies in about 40 deg. 20 min. south, and is the most southern settlement the Spaniards have in these seas. Their summer is of no long duration, and most of the year round they have hard gales of wind and much rain. Opposite the island, upon the Cordilleras, there is a volcano, which, at times, burns with great fury, and is subject to violent eruptions. One of these alarmed the whole island, whilst we were here: it sounded in the night like great guns. In the morning, the governor mounted his horse, and rode backwards and forwards from his house to the earthen fort, saying, it was the English coming in, but that he would give them a warm reception ; meaning, I suppose, that he would have left them a good fire in his house; for I am certain he would have been soon in the woods, if he had seen any thing like an English ship coming in.

Women of the first fashion here seldom wears shoes or stockings in the house, but only keep them to wear upon particular occasions. I have often seen them coming to the church, which stood opposite to the governor's house, bare-legg'd, walking through mud and water; and at the church door put on their shoes and stockings, and pull them off again when they came out. Though they are in general handsome, and have good complexions, yet many of them paint in so ridiculous a manner, that it is impossible to help laughing in their faces when you see them.

The governor we found here was a native of Chili. The government, which is appointed by that presidency is for three years; which appears to be a long banishment to them, as their appointments are but small, though they make the most of it. The towns of Castro and Chaco consist only of scattered houses, without a regular street; though both have their places, or squares, as almost all Spanish towns have. Chaco is very thinly inhabited, excepting at the time the Lima ship arrives; then they flock thither from all parts of the island, to purchase what little matters they want; and as soon as that is done, retire to their estancias, or farms. It was about the middle of December this ship came in; and the second of January, 1742–3, we embarked on board of her. She was bound to Valparaiso. We got out to sea with some difficulty, having been driven by the strength of the tide very near those sunken rocks mentioned before. We found a great sea without; and as the ship was as deep as any laden collier, her decks were continually well washed. She was a fine vessel of about two hundred and fifty tons. The timber the ships of this country are built of is excellent, as they last a prodigious time: for they assured us that the vessel we were then in had been built above forty years. The captain was a Spaniard, and knew not the least of sea-affairs; the second captain, or master, the boatswain, and his mate, were all three Frenchmen, and very good seamen; the pilot was a Mulatto, and all the rest of the crew were Indians and Negroes. The latter were all slaves and stout fellows; but never suffered to go aloft, lest they should fall overboard, and the owners lose so much money by it. The Indians were active, brisk men, and very good seamen for that climate. We had on board the head of the Jesuits as passenger. He and Captain Cheap were admitted into the great cabin, and messed with the captain and his chaplain. As for us, we were obliged to ruff it the whole passage; that is, when we were tired, we lay down upon the quarter-deck, in the open air, and slept as well as we could; but that was nothing to us, who had been used to fare so much worse. We lived well, eating with the master and boatswain, who always had their meals upon the quarter-deck, and drank brandy at them as we do small-beer; and all the rest of the day were smoking segars.

The fifth day we made the land four or five leagues to the southward of Valparaiso; and soon after falling calm, a great western swell hurried us in very fast towards the shore. We dropped the lead several times, but had such deep water we could not anchor. They were all much alarmed when the Jesuit came out of the cabin for the first time, having been sea-sick the whole passage. As soon as he was informed of the danger, he went back into the cabin, and brought out the image of some saint, which he desired might be hung up in the mizenshrouds; which being done, he kept threatening it, that if we had not a breeze of wind soon, he would throw it overboard. Soon after, we had a little wind from off the land, when the Jesuit carried the image back with an air of triumph, saying, he was certain that we should not be without wind long, though he had given himself over for lost some time before it came. Next morning we anchored in the port of Valparaiso. In that part which is opposite to the fort, ships lay so near the land, that they have generally three anchors ashore, as there are eight or ten fathoms close to it; and the flaws come off the hills with such violence, that if it was not for this method of securing them, they would be blown out. This is only in summer-time, for in the winter months no ships ever attempt to come in here; the northerly winds then prevail, and drive in such a sea that they must soon be ashore.

The Spanish captain waited upon the governor of the fort, and informed him that he had four English prisoners on board. We were ordered ashore in the afternoon, and were received as we got upon the beach, by a file of soldiers, with their bayonets fixed, who surrounded us, and then marched up to the fort, attended by a numerous mob. We were carried before the governor, whose house was full of officers. He was blind, asked a few questions, and then spoke of nothing but the strength of the garrison he commanded, and desired to know if we had observed that all the lower battery was brass guns. We were immediately after, by his order, put into the condemned hole. There was nothing but four bare walls, excepting a heap of lime that filled one third of it, and made the place swarm with fleas in such a manner that we were presently covered with them. Some of Admiral Pizarro's soldiers were here in garrison that had been landed from his ships at Buenos Ayres, as he could not get round Cape Horn. A centinel's box was placed at our door, and we had always a soldier, with his bayonet fixed, to prevent our stirring out. The curiosity of the people was such, that our prison was continually full from morning till night, by which the soldiers made a pretty penny, as they took money from every person for the sight. In a few days, Captain Cheap and Mr Hamilton were ordered up to St Jago, as they were known to be officers by having saved their commissions; but Mr Campbell and I were to continue in prison. Captain Cheap expressed great concern when he left us; he told me it was what he had all along

214

dreaded, that they would separate us when we got into this country; but he assured me, if he was permitted to speak to the president, that he would never leave solliciting him till he obtained a grant for me to be sent up to him. No sooner were they gone than we fared very badly. A common soldier, who was ordered to provide for us by the governor, brought us each, once a day, a few potatoes mixed with hot water. The other soldiers of the garrison, as well as the people who flocked to see us, took notice of it, and told the soldier it was cruel to treat us in that manner. His answer was, 'the governor allows me but half a real a day for each of these men; what can I do? It is he that is to blame; I am shocked every time I bring them this scanty pittance, though even that could not be provided for the money he gives them.' We from this time lived much better, and the soldier brought us even wine and fruit. We took it for granted, that our case had been represented to the governor, and that he had increased our pay. As to the first, we were right in our conjectures; it had been mentioned to him, that it was impossible we could subsist on what he allowed; and his answer to it was, that we might starve; for we should have no more from him, and that he believed he should never be repaid even that. This charitable speech of the governor was made known every where, and now almost every one who came to see us, gave something; even the mule-drivers would take out their tobacco pouch, in which they kept their money, and gave us half a real. All this we would have given to our soldier, but he never would receive a farthing from us, telling us we might still want it; and the whole time we were there, which was some weeks, he laid aside half his daily pay to supply us, though he had a wife and six children, and never could have the least hope or expectation of any recompence. However, two years after this, I had the singular pleasure of making him some return, when my circumstances were much better than his. One night when we were locked up, there happened a dreadful shock of an earthquake. We expected, every moment, the roof and walls of our prison to fall in upon us, and crush us to pieces; and what added to the horror of it was, the noise of chains and imprecations in the next prison which joined to ours, where there were near seventy felons heavily loaded with chains, who are kept here to work upon the fortifications, as in other countries they are condemned to the gallies. A few days after this, we were told an order was come from the president to the governor to send us up to St Jago, which is ninety miles from Valparaiso, and is the capital of Chili. There were, at this time, several ships in the port from Lima delivering their cargoes; so that almost every day there were large droves of mules going up to St Jago with the goods. The governor sent for one of the master carriers, and ordered him to take us up with him. The man asked him how he was to be paid our expences, as he should be five days upon the road. The governor told him he might get that as he could, for he would not advance him a single farthing. After taking leave of our friendly soldier, who even now brought us some little matters to carry with us, we set out, and travelled about fourteen miles the first day, and lay at night in the open field, which is always the custom of these people, stopping where there is plenty of pasture and good water for the mules. The next morning we passed over a high mountain, called Zapata; and then crossing a large plain, we passed another mountain, very difficult for the mules, who each carried two heavy bales: there were above an hundred of them in this drove. The mules of Chili are the finest in the world; and though they are continually upon the road, and have nothing but what they pick up at nights, they are as fat and sleek as high-fed horses in England. The fourth night, we lay upon a plain in sight of St Jago, and not above four leagues from it. The next day as we moved towards the city, our master-carrier, who was naturally well-disposed, and had been very kind to us all the way upon the road, advised me, very seriously, not to think of remaining in St Jago, where he said there was nothing but extravagance, vice, and folly, but to proceed on with them as mule-driver, which, he said, I should soon be very expert at; and that they led an innocent and happy life, far preferable to any enjoyment such a great city as that before us could afford. I thanked him, and told hint I was very much obliged to him; but that I would try the city first, and if I did not like it, I would accept of the offer he was so good to make me. The thing that gave him this high opinion of me was, that as he had been so civil to us, I was very officious in assisting to drive in those mules that strayed from the rest upon those large plains we passed over; and this I thought was the least I could do towards making some returns for the obligations we were under to him.

When we got into St Jago, the carrier delivered us to the captain of the guard, at the palace gate; and he soon after introduced us to the president, don Joseph Manso, who received us very civilly, and then sent us to the house where Captain Cheap and Mr Hamilton were. We found them extremely well lodged at the house of a Scotch physician, whose name was don Patrico Gedd. This gentleman had been a long time in this city, and was greatly esteemed by the Spaniards, as well for his abilities in his profession, as his humane disposition. He no sooner heard that there were four English prisoners arrived in that country, than he waited upon the president, and begged they might be lodged at his house. This was granted; and had we been his own brothers, we could not have met with a more friendly reception; and during two years that we were with him, his constant study was to make every thing as agreeable to us as possible. We were greatly distressed to think of the expence he was at upon our account; but it was in vain for us to argue with him about it. In short, to sum up his character in a few words, there never was a man of more extensive humanity. Two or three days after our arrival, the president sent Mr Campbell and me an invitation to dine with him, where we were to meet Admiral Pizarro and all his officers. This was a cruel stroke upon us, as we had not any cloaths fit to appear in, and dared not refuse the invitation. The next day, a Spanish officer belonging to Admiral Pizarro's squadron, whose name was don Manuel de Guirro, came and made us an offer of two thousand dollars. This generous Spaniard made this offer without any view of ever being repaid, but purely out of a compassionate motive of relieving us in our present distress. We returned him all the acknowledgments his uncommon generous behaviour merited, and accepted of six hundred dollars only, upon his receiving our draught for that sum upon the English consul at Lisbon. We now got ourselves decently cloathed after the Spanish fashion; and as we were upon our parole, we went out where we pleased to divert ourselves.

This city is situated in about 33 degrees and 30 minutes, south latitude, at the west foot of the immense chain of mountains called the Cordilleras. It stands on a most beautiful plain of above thirty leagues extent. It was founded by don Pedro de Baldivia, the conqueror of Chili. The plan of it was marked out by him, in squares, like Lima; and almost every house belonging to people of any fashion, has a large court before it, with great gates, and a garden behind. There is a little rivulet, neatly faced with stones, runs through every street; by which they can cool the streets, or water their gardens, when they please. The whole town is extremely well paved. Their gardens are full of noble orange-trees and floripondies, with all sorts of flowers, which perfume the houses, and even the whole city. Much about the middle of it, is the great square, called the Placa Real, or the Royal Square; there are eight avenues leading into it. The west side contains the cathedral and the bishop's palace; the north side is the president's palace, the royal court, the council-house, and the prison; the south side is a row of piazzas, the whole length of which are shops, and over it a gallery to see the bull feasts; the east side has some large houses belonging to people of distinction; and in the middle is a large fountain, with a brass bason. The houses have, in general, only a ground floor, upon account of the frequent earthquakes; but they make a handsome appearance. The churches are rich in gilding, as well as in plate:

that of the Jesuits is reckoned an exceeding good piece of architecture; but it is much too high built for a country so subject to earthquakes, and where it has frequently happened that thousands of people have been swallowed up at once. There is a hill, or rather high rock, at the east end of the city, called St Lucia, from the top of which you have a view of all the city, and the country about for many leagues, affording a very delightful landscape. Their estancias, or country houses, are very pleasant, have generally a fine grove of olive trees, with large vineyards to them. The Chili wine, in my opinion, is full as good as Madeira, and made in such quantities that it is sold extremely cheap. The soil of this country is so fertile, that the husbandmen have very little trouble; for they do but in a manner scratch up the ground, and without any kind of manure it yields an hundred fold. Without doubt the wheat of Chili is the finest in the world, and the fruits are all excellent in their kinds. Beef and mutton are so cheap, that you may have a good cow for three dollars, and a fat sheep for two shillings. Their horses are extraordinary good; and though some of them go at a great price, you may have a very good one for four dollars, or about eighteen shillings of our money. It must be a very poor Indian who has not his four or five horses; and there are not better horsemen in the world than the Chileans; and that is not surprising, for they never chuse to go a hundred yards on foot. They have always their laco fixed to their saddle : the laco is a long thong of leather, at the end of which they make a sliding noose. It is of more general use to them than any weapon whatever; for with this they are sure of catching either horse or wild bull, upon full gallop, by any foot they please. Their horses are all trained to this, and the moment they find the thong straitened, as the other end if always made fast to the saddle, the horse immediately turns short, and throwing the beast thus caught, the huntsman wounds or secures him in what manner he thinks proper. These people are so dexterous, that they will take from the ground a glove or handkerchief, while their horse is upon full stretch; and I have seen them jump upon the back of the wildest bull, and all the efforts of the beast could not throw them. This country produces all sorts of metals; it is famous for gold, silver, iron, tin, lead, and quicksilver; but some of these they do not understand working, especially quicksilver. With copper they supply all Peru, and send, likewise, a great deal to Europe. The climate of Chili is, I believe, the finest in the world. What they call their winter does not last three months; and even that is very moderate, as may be imagined by their manner of building, for they have no chimneys in their houses. All the rest of the year is delightful; for though from ten or eleven in the morning, till five in the afternoon, it is very hot, yet the evenings and mornings are very cool and pleasant; and in the hottest time of the year, it is from six in the evening till two or three in the morning, that the people of this country meet to divert themselves with music, and other entertainments, at which there is plenty of cooling liquors, as they are well supplied with ice from the neighbouring Cordilleras. At these assemblies, many intrigues are carried on: for they think of nothing else throughout the year. Their fandangoes are very agreeable; the women dance inimitably well, and very gracefully. They are all born with an ear for music, and most of them have delightful voices; and all play upon the guittar and harp. The latter, at first appears a very aukward instrument for a woman; yet that prejudice is soon got over, and they far excel any other nation upon it. They are extremely complaisant and polite; and when asked either to play, dance, or sing, they do it without a moment's hesitation, and that with an exceeding good grace. They have many figure-dances; but what they take most delight in, are more like our hornpipes than any thing else I can compare them to; and, upon these occasions, they shew surprising activity. The women are remarkably handsome, and very extravagant in their dress. Their hair, which is as thick as is possible to be conceived, they wear of a vast length, without any other ornament upon the head than a few flowers; they plait it behind in four plaits, and twist them round a bodkin, at each end of which is a diamond rose. Their shifts are all over lace, as is a little tight waistcoat they wear over them. Their petticoats are open before, and lap over, and have commonly three rows of very rich lace of gold or silver. In winter, they have an upper waistcoat of cloth embroidered with gold or silver, and in summer, of the finest linen, covered all over with the finest Flanders lace. The sleeves of these are immensely wide. Over all this, when the air is cool, they have a mantle, which is only of bays, of the finest colours, round which there is abundance of lace. When they go abroad, they wear a vail, which is so contrived that one eye is only seen. Their feet are very small, and they value themselves as much upon it as the Chinese do. Their shoes are pinked and cut; their stockings silk, with gold and silver cloaks; and they love to have the end of an embroidered garter hang a little below the petticoat. Their breasts and shoulders are very naked; and, indeed, you may easily decern their whole shape by their manner of dress. They have fine sparkling eyes, ready wit, a great deal of good-nature, and a strong disposition to gallantry.

By the description of one house, you have an idea of all the rest. You first come into a large court, on one side of which is the stable: you then enter a hall; on one side of that is a large room, about twenty feet wide, and near forty feet long: that side next the window is the *estrado*, which runs the whole length of the room. The *estrado* is a platform, raised about five or six inches above the floor, and is covered with carpets and velvet cushions for the women to sit on, which they do, after the Moorish fashion, cross-legged. The chairs for the men are covered with printed leather. At the end of the *estrado*, there is an alcove, where the bed stands; and there is always a vast deal of sheets hanging out, with a profusion of lace to them, and the same on the pillows. They have a false door to the alcove, which sometimes is very convenient. Besides, there are generally two other rooms, one within another; and the kitchen and other offices are detached from the house, either at one side or the end of the garden.

The ladies are fond of having their Mulatto female slaves dressed almost as well as themselves in every respect, excepting jewels, in which they indulge themselves to the utmost extravagance. Paraguay tea, which they call matte, as I mentioned before, is always drunk twice a day: this is brought upon a large silver salver, with four legs raised upon it, to receive a little cup made out of a small calabash, or gourd, and tipped with silver. They put the herb first into this, and add what sugar they please, and a little orange juice; and then pour hot water on them, and drink it immediately through the conveyance of a long silver tube, at the end of which there is a round strainer, to prevent the herb getting through. And here it is reckoned a piece of politeness for the lady to suck the tube two or three times first, and then give it to the stranger to drink without wiping it.

They eat every thing so highly seasoned with red pepper, that those who are not used to it, upon the first mouthful, would imagine their throats on fire for an hour afterwards; and it is a common custom here, though you have the greatest plenty at your own table, to have two or three Mulatto girls come in at the time you dine, bringing, in a little silver plate, some of these high-seasoned ragouts with a compliment from Donna such-a-one, who desires you will eat a little bit of what she has sent you; which must be done before her Mulatto's face, or it would be deemed a great affront. Had this been the fashion at Chiloe, we should never have offended; but sometimes here we could have wished this ceremony omitted.

The president never asked any of us a second time to his table. He expected us once a fortnight to be at his levee, which we never failed; and he always received us very politely. He was a man of a very amiable character, and much respected by every body in Chili, and some time after we left that country, was appointed viceroy of Peru.

We had leave, whenever we asked it, to make an excursion into the country for ten or twelve days at a time; which we did sometimes to a very pleasant spot belonging to don Joseph Dunose, a Frenchman, and a very sensible, well-bred man, who had married a very agreeable lady at St Jago, with a very good fortune. We also sometimes had invitations from the Spaniards to their country-houses. We had a numerous acquaintance in the city, and in general received many civilities from the inhabitants. There are a great many people of fashion, and very good families from Old Spain settled here. A lady lived next door to us whose name was donna Francisca Giron: and my name sounded something like it, she would have it that we were Parientes. She had a daughter, a very fine young woman, who both played and sung remarkably well: she was reckoned the finest voice in St Jago. They saw a great deal of company, and we were welcome to her house whenever we pleased. We were a long time in this country, but we passed it very agreeably. The president alone goes with four horses to his coach; but the common vehicle here is a calash, or kind of vis-a-vis, drawn by one mule only. Bull-feasts are a common diversion here, and surpass any thing of that kind I ever saw at Lisbon, or any where else. Indeed, it is amazing to see the activity and dexterity of those who attack the bulls. It is always done here by those only who follow it as a trade, for it is too dangerous to be practised as a diversion; as a proof of which, it is found, that though some may hold out longer than others, there are few who constantly practise it that die a natural death. The bulls are always the wildest that can be brought in from the mountains or forests, and have nothing on their horns to prevent their piercing a man first stroke, as they have at Lisbon. I have seen a man, when the bull came at him with the utmost fury, spring directly over the beast's head, and perform this feat several times, at last jump on his back, and there sit a considerable time, the bull the whole time attempting every means to throw him. But though this practitioner was successful, several accidents happened while I was there. The ladies at these feasts, are always dressed as fine as possible; and, I imagine, go rather to be admired than to receive any amusement from a fight that one should think would give them pain. Another amusement for the ladies here, are the nights of their great processions, when they go out veiled; and as, in that dress, they amuse themselves in talking to people much in the manner that is done at our masquerades. One night in Lent, as I was standing close to the houses as the procession went by, and having nothing but a thin waistcoat on under my cloak, and happening to have my arm out, a lady came by, and gave me a pinch with so good a will, that I thought she had taken the piece out; and, indeed, I carried the marks for a long time after. I durst not take the least notice of this at the time; for, had I made any disturbance, I should have been knocked on the head. This kind lady immediately after mixed with the crowd, and I never could find out who had done me that favour. I have seen fifty or sixty penitents following these processions; they wear a long white garment with a long train to it, and high caps of the same, which fall down before, and cover all their faces, having only two small holes for their eyes: so that they are never known. Their backs are bare and they lash themselves with a cat-o-nine-tails till the long train behind is covered all over with blood. Others follow them with great heavy crosses upon their backs; so that they groan under the weight as they walk barefooted, and often faint away. The streets swarm with friers of all the different orders. The president has always a guard at his palace regularly cloathed. The rest of their forces consists of militia, who are numerous.

All European goods are very dear. English cloth of fourteen or fifteen shillings a yard, sells there for ten or eleven dollars; and every other article in proportion. We found many Spaniards here that had been taken by Commodore Anson, and had been for some time prisoners on board the *Centurion*. They all spoke in the highest terms of the kind treatment they had received; and, it is natural to imagine, that it was chiefly owing to that laudable example of humanity our reception here was so good. They had never had any thing but privateers and buccaneers amongst them before, who handled their prisoners very roughly; so that the Spaniards in general, both of Peru and Chili, had the greatest dread of being taken by the English; but some of them told us, that they were so happy on board the *Centurion,* that they should not have been sorry if the commodore had taken them with him to England.

After we had been here some time, Mr Campbell changed his religion, and of course left us.

At the end of two years, the president sent for us, and informed us a French ship from Lima bound to Spain, had put into Valparaiso, and that we should embark in her. After taking leave of our good friend Mr Gedd, and all our acquaintance at St Jago, we set out for Valparaiso, mules and a guide being provided for us. I had forgot to say before, that Captain Cheap had been allowed by the president six reals a day, and we had four for our maintenance the whole time we were at St Jago, which money we took up as we wanted. Our journey back was much pleasanter than we found it when we were first brought hither, as we had now no mules to drive. The first person I met, upon our entrance into Valparaiso, was the poor soldier whom I mentioned to have been so kind to us when we were imprisoned in the fort. I now made him a little present, which, as it came quite unexpected, made him very happy. We took lodgings till the ship was ready to sail, and diverted ourselves as we pleased, having the good fortune, at this time, to have nothing to do with the governor or his fort. The town is but a poor little place; there are, indeed, a good many store-houses built by the waterside for the reception of goods from the shipping.

About the 20th of December, 1744, we embarked on board the *Lys* frigate, belonging to St Malo. She was a ship of four hundred and twenty tons, sixteen guns, and sixty men. She had several passengers on board; and amongst the rest, don George

Juan, a man of very superior abilities (and since that time well known in England) who with don Antonio Ulloa had been several years in Peru, upon a design of measuring some degrees of the meridian near the equator. We were now bound to Conception, in order to join three other French ships that were likewise bound home. As this was a time of the year when the southerly winds prevail upon this coast, we stood off a long way to the westward, making the island of Juan Fernandez. We did not get into the bay of Conception till the sixth of January, 1745, where we anchored at Talcaguana, and their found the *Louis Erasme,* the *Marquis d'Antin,* and the *Deliverance,* the three French ships that we were to accompany. It is but sixty leagues from Valparaiso to Conception, though we had been so long in making this passage; but there is no beating up, near the shore, against the southerly wind, which is the trade, at this season, as you are sure to have a leecurrent; so that the quickest way of making a passage is to stand off a hundred and twenty or thirty leagues from the land.

The bay of Conception is a large fine bay; but there are several shoals in it, and only two good anchoring places, though a ship may anchor within a quarter of a league of the town; but this only in the very fine months, as you lay much exposed. The best anchoring place is Talcaguana, the southernmost neck of the bay, in five or six fathom water, good holding ground, and where you are sheltered from the northerly winds. The town has no other defence but a low battery, which only commands the anchoring place before it. The country is extremely pleasant, and affords the greatest plenty of provisions of all kinds. In some excursions we made daily from Talcaguana, we saw great numbers of very large snakes; but we were told they were quite harmless. I have read some former accounts of Chili, by the Jesuits, wherein they tell you, that no venomous creature is to be found in it, and that they even made the experiment of bringing bugs here, which died immediately, but I never was in any place that swarmed with them so much as St Jago; and they

226

have a large spider there, whose bite is so venomous, that I have seen from it some of the most shocking sights I ever saw in my life; and it certainly proves mortal, if proper remedies are not applied in time. I was once bit by one on the cheek, whilst asleep, and presently after, all that part of my face turned as black as ink. I was cured by the application of a bluish kind of stone (the same, perhaps, they call the serpentstone in the East Indies, and which is a composition). The stone stuck for some time of itself on my face, and dropping off, was put into milk till it had digested the poison it had extracted, and then applied again till the pain abated, and I was soon afterwards well. Whilst the ships remained at Conception, the people were employed in killing of cattle, and salting them for the voyage; and every ship took on board as many bullocks and sheep as their decks could well hold; and having compleated their business here, they sailed the 27th of January; but about eight days after, our ship sprung a very dangerous leak forward; but so low, that there was no possibility of stopping it, without returning into port, and lightening her till they could come at it. Accordingly we separated from the other ships, and made the best of our way for Valparaiso, keeping all hands at the pump night and day, passengers and all. However, as it happened, this proved a lucky circumstance for the *Lys,* as the three other ships were taken; and which certainly would have been her fate likewise, had she kept company with the rest. As soon as we got into port, they lightened the ship forwards, and brought her by the stern till they came to the leak, which was soon stopped. They made all the dispatch possible in compleating the water again. Whilst at Valparaiso, we had one of the most violent shocks of an earthquake that we had ever felt yet. On the first of March we put to sea again, the season being already far advanced, for passing Cape Horn. The next day we went to an allowance of a quart of water a day for each man, which continued the whole passage. We were obliged to stand a long way to the westward ; and went to the northward of Juan Fernandez above a degree, before we had a wind that we could make any soothing with. On the 25th, in the latitude of 46 degrees, we met with a hard gale at west, which obliged us to lie to under a reefed mainsail for some days; and before we got round the cape, we had many very hard gales, with a prodigious sea, and constant thick snow; and after being so long in so delightful a climate as Chili, the cold was also insupportable. After doubling the cape, we got but slowly to the northward; and, indeed, at the best of times, the ship never went above six knots; for she was a heavy going thing. On the 27th of May we crossed the line: when finding that our water was grown extremely short, and that it would be almost impossible to reach Europe without a supply, it was resolved to bearaway for Martinico. On the 29th of June, in the morning, we made the island of Tobago, and then shaped a course for Martinico; and on the first of July, by our reckonings, expected to see it, but were disappointed. This was imputed to the currents, which, whether they had set the ship to the eastward or westward, nobody could tell; but upon looking over the charts, it was imagined, if the current had driven her to the westward, it must have been among the Granadillos, which was thought impossible without seeing any of them, as they are so near together, and a most dangerous place for rocks. It was then concluded we were to the eastward, and accordingly we steered SW by W but having run this course for above thirty leagues, and no land appearing, it was resolved to stand to the northward till we should gain the latitude of Porto Rico, and on the 4th in the evening we made that island; so that it was now certain the ship had been hustled thro' the Granadillos in the night, which was, without doubt, as extraordinary a passage as ever ship made. It was now resolved to go between the islands of Porto Rico and St Domingo for Cape Francois, therefore we lay to that night. In the morning, we made sail along shore; and about ten o'clock, as I was walking the quarterdeck, Captain Cheap came out of the cabin, and told me he had just seen a beef-barrel go by the ship; that he was sure it had but lately been thrown overboard, and that he would venture any wager, we saw an English cruizer before long. In about half an hour after, we saw two sail to leeward, from off the quarterdeck; for they kept no look out from the mast-head, and we presently observed they were in chase of us. The French and Spaniards on board, now began to grow a good deal alarmed, when it fell stark calm; but not before the ships had neared us so much, that we plainly discerned them to be English men of war; the one a two-decker, the other a twenty-gun ship. The French had now thoughts, when a breeze should spring up, of running the ship on shore upon Porto Rico; but when they came to consider what a set of banditti inhabited that island, and that in all probability they would have their throats cut for the sake of plundering the wreck, they were resolved to take their chance, and stand to the northward between the two islands. In the evening a fresh breeze sprung up, and we shaped a course accordingly. The two ships had it presently afterwards, and neared us amazingly fast. Now every body on board gave themselves up; the officers were busy in their cabins, filling their pockets with what was most valuable; the men put on their best cloaths, and many of them came to me with little lumps of gold, desiring I would take them, as they said they had much rather I should benefit by them, whom they were acquainted with, than those that chaced them. I told them there was time enough, though I thought they were as surely taken as if the English had been already on board. A fine moonlight night came on, and we expected every moment to see the ships along-side of us; but we saw nothing of them in the night, and to our great astonishment in the morning, no ships were to be seen from the mast-head. Thus did these two cruizers lose one of the richest prizes, by not chasing an hour or two longer. There were near two millions of dollars on board, besides a valuable cargo. On the 8th, at six in the morning, we were off Cape La Grange; and, what is very remarkable, the French at Cape Francois told us afterwards that was the only day they ever remembered since the war, that the cape had been without one or two English privateers cruising off it; and, but the evening before, two of them had taken two outward bound St Domingo-men, and had gone with them for Jamaica; so that this ship might be justly esteemed a most lucky one. In the afternoon we came to an anchor in Cape Francois harbour.

In this long run we had not buried a single man; nor do I remember that there was one sick the whole passage: but at this place many were taken ill, and three or four died; for there is no part of the West Indies more unhealthy than this; yet the country is beautiful, and extremely well cultivated. After being here some time, the governor ordered us to wait upon him, which we did; when he took no more notice of us than if we had been his slaves, never asking us even to sit down.

Towards the end of August a French squadron of five men of war came in, commanded by Monsieur L'Etanducre, who were to convoy the trade to France. Neither he nor his officers ever took any kind of notice of Captain Cheap, though we met them every day ashore. One evening, as we were going aboard with the captain of our ship, a midshipman belonging to M. L'Etanducre jumped into our boat, and ordered the people to carry him on board the ship he belonged to, leaving us to wait upon the beach for two hours before the boat returned. On the sixth of September, we put to sea, in company with the five men of war, and about fifty sail of merchantmen. On the eight we made the Cayco Grande; and the next day a Jamaica priva-teer, a large fine sloop, hove in sight, keeping a little to wind-ward of the convoy, resolving to pick up one or two of them in the night, if possible. This obliged Monsieur L'Etanducre to send a frigate to speak to all the convoy, and order them to keep close to him in the night; which they did, and in such a manner, that sometimes seven or eight of them were on board one another together; by which they received much damage; and, to repair which, the whole squadron was obliged to lay to some-times for a whole day. The privateer kept her station, jogging on with the fleet. At last, the commodore ordered two of the best going ships to chace her. She appeared to take no notice of them till they were pretty near her, and then would make sail, and be out of sight presently. The chacing ships no sooner returned, than the privateer was in company again. As by this, every night some accident happened to some of the convoy by keeping so close together, a fine ship of thirty guns, belonging to Marseills, hauled out a little to windward of the rest of the fleet; which L'Etanducre perceiving in the morning, ordered the frigate to bring the captain of her on board of him; and then making a signal for all the convoy to close to him, he fired a gun, and hoisted a red flag at the ensign staff; and immediately after the captain of the merchantman was run up to the main yard-arm; and from thence ducked three times. He was then sent on board his ship again, with orders to keep his colours flying the whole day, in order to distinguish him from the rest. We were then told, that the person who was treated in this cruel manner, was a young man of an exceeding good family in the south of France, and likewise a man of great spirit; and that he would not fail to call Monsieur L'Etanducre to an account when an opportunity should offer; and the affair made much noise in France afterwards. One day, the ship we were in happened to be out of her station, by sailing so heavily, when the commodore made the signal to speak to our captain, who seemed frightened out of his wits. When we came near him, he began with the grossest abuse, threatening our captain, that if ever he was out of his station again, he would serve him as he had done the other. This rigid discipline, however, preserved the convoy; for though the privateer kept company a long time, she was not so fortunate as to meet with the reward of her perseverance.

On the 27th of October, in the evening, we made Cape Ortegal; and on the 31st, came to an anchor in Brest road. The *Lys* having so valuable a cargo on board, was towed into the harbour next morning, and lashed along-side one of their men of war. The money was soon landed; and the officers and men who had been so many years absent from their native country, were glad to get on shore. Nobody remained on board but a man or two to look after the ship, and we three English prisoners, who had no leave to go ashore. The weather was extremely cold, and felt particularly so to us, who had been so long used to hot climates; and what made it still worse, we were very thinly clad. We had neither. fire nor candle; for they were allowed on board of no ship in the harbour, for fear of accidents, being close to their magazines in the, dockyard. Some of the officers belonging to the ship were so good as to send us off victuals every day, or we might have starved; for Monsieur L'Intendant never sent us even a message; and tho' there was a very large squadron of men of war sitting out at that time, not one officer belonging to them ever came near Captain Cheap. From five in the evening we were obliged to sit in the dark; and if we chose to have any supper, it was necessary to place it very near us before that time, or we never could have found it. We had passed seven or eight days in this melancholy manner, when one morning a kind of row-gaily came alongside with a number of English prisoners, belonging to two large privateers the French had taken. We were ordered into the same boat with them, and were carried four leagues up the river to Landernaw. At this town we were upon our parole; so took the best lodgings we could get, and lived very well for three months, when an order came from the court of Spain to allow us to return home by the first ship that offered. Upon this, hearing there was a Dutch ship at Morlaix ready to sail, we took horses and travelled to that town, where we were obliged to remain six weeks, before we had an opportunity of getting away. At last we agreed with the master of a Dutch dogger to land us at Dover, and paid him beforehand. When we had got down the river into the road, a French privateer that was almost ready to sail upon a cruize, hailed the Dutchman, and told him to come to an anchor; and that if he offered to sail before him, he would sink him. This he was forced to comply with, and lay three days in the road, cursing the Frenchman, who at the end of that time put to sea, and then we were at liberty to do the same. We had a long uncomfortable passage. About the ninth day, before sunset, we saw Dover, and reminded the Dutchman of his agreement to land us there. He said he would; but instead of that, in the morning we were off the coast of France. We complained loudly of this piece of villany, and insisted upon his returning to land us, when an English man of war appeared to windward, and presently bore down to us. She sent her boat on board with an officer, who informed us the ship he came from was the *Squirrel*, commanded by Captain Masterson. We went on board of her, and Captain Masterson immediately sent one of the cutters he had with him, to land us at Dover, where we arrived that afternoon, and directly set out for Canterbury upon post-horses; but Captain Cheap was so tired by the time he got there, that he could proceed no further that night. The next morning he still found himself so much fatigued, that he could ride no longer; therefore it was agreed, that he and Mr Hamilton should take a post-chaise, and that I should ride: but here an unlucky difficulty was started; for, upon sharing the little money we had, it was found to be not sufficient to pay the charges to London; and my proportion fell so short, that it was, by calculation, barely enough to pay for horses, without a farthing for eating a bit upon the road, or even for the very turnpikes. Those I was obliged to defraud, by riding as hard as I could through them all, not paying the least regard to the men, who called out to stop me. The want of refreshment I bore as well as I could. When I got to the Borough, I took a coach, and drove to Marlborough Street, where my friends had lived when I left England; but when I came there, I found the house shut up. Having been absent so many years, and in all that time never having heard a word from home, I knew not who was dead, or who was living, or where to go next; or even how to pay the coachman. I recollected a linen-draper's shop, not far from thence, which our family had used. I therefore drove there next, and making myself known, they paid the coachman. I then inquired after our family, and was told my sister had married Lord Carlisle and was at that time in Soho Square. I immediately walked to the house, and knocked at the door; but the porter not liking my figure, which was half French, half Spanish, with the addition of a large pair of boots covered with dirt, he was going to shut the door in my face, but I prevailed with him to let me come in.

I need not acquaint my readers with what surprise and joy my sister received me. She immediately furnished me with money sufficient to appear like the rest of my countrymen; till that time I could not be properly said to have finished all the extraordinary scenes which a series of unfortunate adventures had kept me in for the space of five years and upwards.

FINIS

Epilogue

Bulkeley, in his Preface, shows a keen awareness that a charge of mutiny hung over him. The taking of the longboat, the arrest of Captain Cheap after the killing of Cozens, would not sit well with Cheap's fellow officers who would make up the court-martial. Highlighting this concern is Bulkeley's choice of an apt quotation from Edmund Waller on the title page of *A Voyage to the South-Seas*:

> Bold were the men who on the ocean first
> Spread the new sails, when ship-wreck was the worst:
> More dangers NOW from MAN alone we find,
> Than from the rocks, the billows, and the wind.

A Voyage had been published with the Admiralty's tacit permission. And from July 1743 to February 1744 lengthy extracts were published monthly in *The London Magazine*: making the gunner an honest-jack-tar celebrity and, no doubt, increasing the book's sales.

On 15 June 1744 Anson and the *Centurion*, having sailed in a thick fog through an enemy French squadron cruising in the Channel, came to anchor at Spithead.* She had circumnavigated the globe, harried the Spanish along the South American coast, and taken a Spanish treasure ship. Anson, an unknown captain when he had sailed from England, was now a national hero and

---

* The *Centurion* sailed in alone. The accounting for Anson's squadron is as follows: the *Industry* left the squadron on the Brazilian coast after transferring supplies; the *Severn* and *Pearl* turned north before the rounding of Cape Horn; the *Wager*, wrecked; the *Anna* and *Tryal*, scuttled; the *Gloucester*, fired and scuttled.

also, with his share of the prize money, a very wealthy man. On 4 July the treasure, estimated at more than £500,00, was paraded through the streets of London in thirty-two wagons guarded by the *Centurion*'s seamen and officers. Preceded by a kettle-drum, trumpets and French horns, the first wagon flew the English colours over the Spanish ensign. In these euphoric celebrations the grim accounting of those who had sailed and those who had returned was forgotten: 1,900 men had sailed and 1,400 had died; four from enemy action, a few from accidents and drowning, and the rest from disease, mainly scurvy.

Bulkeley had always treated the Admiralty with punctilious circumspection. In 1745 he wrote to the Board of Admiralty asking for consent ('lest your lordships should imagine I had flown from justice') to sail an old warship, at the request of some London merchants, from Plymouth to London for refitting. Consent was given, and with Bulkeley in command the old vessel sailed from Plymouth escorting three merchantships. During the passage up Channel the small convoy was sighted by two fast French privateers who bore down upon them. The merchantships uphelmed and made for the safety of the English coast; but Bulkeley hauled his wind and fired a warning shot at the privateers. Fearing this was but a taste of a broadside, the French altered course and sailed away. Bulkeley then gathered his scattered flock and completed a safe passage to London. He had again proved himself an able and resourceful seaman.

A few months later Bulkeley read in the newspapers of Cheap's arrival in England, and that all the returned officers and men of the *Wager* were to report to Spithead and give depositions and perhaps be witnesses at the inevitable court-martial. If Bulkeley had seen a letter from Cheap to Anson his peace of mind would have been seriously disturbed. In this self-serving letter Cheap warned Anson that those men who had returned 'probably have not told the truth, for what can be expected of such poltroons who, rather than do their duty by endeavouring to join you (which I might easily have done) and look the enemy in the face; chose to expose themselves to the fatigue of so long a navigation, and perishing of hunger; after most inhumanly abandoning us and destroying at their departure everything they thought could be of any use to us that they could not carry with them.' Cheap continued in the same fashion with an airy statement: 'I have very good grounds to believe that I should have brought the mutineers to reason ...'

The preliminaries to the court-martial, as with most of the *Wager's* story, reeks with melodrama. The fleet's chaplain, in his sermon to the Wagers, warned them with a certain amount of relish that 'Men should not feed themselves up in vain notions or expectations of a reprieve or pardon; for how often are men deceived even in their last moments.' Pen, ink, and paper were allowed them for their depositions, but they were warned darkly that 'no man after sentence of death shall be indulged with it on any account.'

The court-martial proved an anti-climax after these portentous opening chords: no charge of mutiny was brought as only the loss of the *Wager* was considered. Lieutenant Baynes was acquitted of blame, but reprimanded for omissions of duty. This decision to soft-pedal the proceedings was in the Admiralty's interest. Any charge of mutiny would have aired Cheap's curious conduct on the island and his shooting of Cozens: which in turn could be embarrassing for the Admiralty.

Cheap was soon given another command. And while sailing off Madeira he captured a Spanish ship which produced enough prize-money for him to retire from the Navy. One wonders if he ever remembered those days on the Chilean coast where he crouched over a bag of stinking seal meat, like a miser over a bag of gold, his body crawling with ants, his face and beard covered with dirt and train-oil, unable even to name his companions.

As to the party of eight men from the *Speedwell*, stranded on the shores of Freshwater Bay (close to today's fashionable Argentine resort town of Mar del Plata), only three returned to

England. Their story was told by Isaac Morris — who thought the stranding deliberate in order to save provisions — and is one of starvation, murder, and capture by Indians; followed by a thousand miles of wandering in Patagonia as slaves to the Indians, being bought and sold for trinkets; the only consolation during this period being some Spanish women, captured by the Indians, who served as their wives. The Indians eventually ransomed three of the captives to an English merchant living in Buenos Aires for thirty dollars each (the Indians kept John Duck, a mulatto). The three men then spent another year in a Spanish prison, this time without the consolation of wives, before being sent aboard the Spanish ship *Asia* lying at Montevideo, for transportation to a prison in Spain. As with anything connected with the *Wager*'s survivors the *Asia*'s passage to Spain was full of melodrama. Three days out from Montevideo eleven Indian prisoners, destined for the galleys, rose in revolt. They took the quarterdeck, killing a score of Spaniards. The Spaniards fought back, killing the Indian chief. At this all the remaining Indians jumped overboard, choosing drowning rather than death at the hands of the Spaniards. Isaac Morris and his companions spent more months in Spanish jails before being released and arriving in England in July 1746. They were the last of the *Wager*'s survivors to return home.

Bibliography

Bulkeley, John, and Cummins, John. *A Voyage to the South Seas, In the Years 1740–1.* London, 1743. Also second edition, with additions, London and Philadelphia, 1757.

Byron, John. *The Narrative of the Honourable John Byron Containing an Account of the Great Distresses suffered by himself and his Companions on the Coast of Patagonia.* London, 1768.

Charnock, John. *Biographia Navalis.* London, 1794–98.

Darwin, Charles. *The Voyage of the Beagle.* Edited by L. Engel, New York, 1962.

Gallagher, Robert E. (Editor). *Byron's Journal of his Circumnavigation 1764–1766.* Cambridge, 1964. Hakluyt Society Series 2/122.

Hydrographic Department. *South America Pilot.*vol II, 15th edition, Taunton, 1971.

Lind, James. *A Treatise of the Scurvy.* Edinburgh, 1753. Facsimile edition, edited by C. P. Stewart and D. Guthrie, Edinburgh, 1953.

Morris, Issac. *A Narrative of the Dangers and Distresses which Befel Issac Morris and Seven More of the Crew.* London, 1751.

Walter, Richard. *A Voyage Round the World in the Years 1740,1,2,3,4, by George Anson, Esq.* London, 1748.

Watt, Sir James. 'Some Consequences of Nutritional Disorders in Eighteenth-Century British Circumnavigations.' *Starving Sailors*, edited by J. Watt, E. J Freeman, and W. F. Bynum. National Maritime Museum, Greenwich, 1981.

Williams, Glyndwr. (Editor). *Documents relating to Anson's Voyage Round the World 1740–1744.* Naval Records Society, London, 1967.

Further Reading

Edwards, Philip. *The Story of the Voyage: Sea Narratives in Eighteenth Century England*. Cambridge, 1995.

O'Brian, Patrick. *The Golden Ocean*. London, 1956.

Pack, S. W. C. *The Wager Mutiny*. London, 1964.

Shankland, Peter. *Byron of the Wager*. London, 1975.

Williams, Glyndwr. *The Great South Sea: English Voyages and Encounters 1570–1750*. London, 1997.

———. *The Prize of All the Oceans*. New York, 2000.